MUSIC IN MY LIFE

NOTES FROM A LONGTIME FAN

Alec Wightman

SMALL BATCH BOOKS
AMHERST, MASSACHUSETTS

Library of Congress Control Number: 2020924586
Hardcover ISBN: 978-1-951568-12-2
Paperback ISBN: 978-1-951568-13-9

SMALL
BATCH
BOOKS

493 SOUTH PLEASANT STREET
AMHERST, MASSACHUSETTS 01002
413.230.3943
SMALLBATCHBOOKS.COM

For Kathy, Nora, and Emily

"Music is the language of emotion. Like that feeling in the pit of your stomach whenever you hear something that feels like it was custom-made for you. You go, 'Oh God, I can't believe anyone else felt like this before.' We're a language-based animal, and one of the more complicated things we've got in our toolbox is music. It speaks when nothing else can."

—singer-songwriter JOHN FULLBRIGHT

CONTENTS

PROLOGUE

ICTURE THIS. IT'S HARD FOR EVEN ME TO IMAGINE NOW. December 12, 2013. A rainy night in Columbus, Ohio. I am a corporate lawyer with BakerHostetler, one of the country's largest law firms, for which I once served as executive partner. I am the lawyer in charge of the firm's relationship with a Fortune 20 client. But tonight I am standing on the side of the stage of the historic Grand Valley Dale Ballroom, having just introduced Art Garfunkel to a packed house for a show my concert-promotion company, Zeppelin Productions, Inc., is promoting. In my introduction, I recognize Art as an inductee into the Rock & Roll Hall of Fame, of which I am chair of the board.

Looking out over hundreds of enraptured faces, I realize I have brought enormous joy to all these people. That's not a sensation most corporate lawyers ever experience. But it is an emotion I've felt many times since 1995, when I began presenting "national act singer-songwriter" concerts in Central Ohio. And I get the same feeling when I watch people walk through the doors of the Rock & Roll Hall of Fame in Cleveland.

I HAVE ALWAYS HAD A passion for rock & roll. But what is it about certain music that creates the joy I saw on those faces? I think it's the "connections." For me, it all starts with the *song*, and a well-written song creates connections in so many ways: through its lyrics and melody, through its rhythm and rhyme.

First and foremost, rock & roll connects us with our emotions. Love, joy, and celebration. Loss, sadness, and longing. The primal instincts of sex and anger. We connect with memories of our past and aspirations for our future.

Rock & roll connects us with people. It creates a sense of community, bridging ages, races, genders, and nationalities. (After extensive international travel, I can confidently report that rock & roll is the common language of the world.) It inspires us to action and it calms us down. It is the voice of protest and the call to harmony.

Rock & roll connects us to friends, old and new. I have made and kept some of the best friends in my life through rock & roll— as we hear, see, and honor both the music and the people who make it. Later in life, my involvement with the Rock & Roll Hall of Fame, including chairing the board for three years, has provided me with opportunities to hear, see, and honor the musicians and the music in ways I never could have imagined.

It is impossible to overstate the extent to which the music has contributed to my family connections. The shared experiences with my wife, Kathy; my parents, in particular my mother; my kids, Nora and Emily; and my brother, Jim, and his wife, Lisa, are some of the highlights of my life. I know our family isn't unique in sharing those experiences through music.

Finally, rock & roll connects the fans and the artists. It absolutely happens through recorded music, but it *really* happens with live music. It's been a special privilege for me, as a promoter, to connect (and be a connector) with both the fans and the artists. I've made friends among the ticket buyers—the folks on my Zeppelin mailing list of more than one thousand, whom I affectionately call the "Music Fans"—and I've made friends among the artists themselves. (By the way, once an artist graces the Zeppelin stage, he or she becomes an "Artiste" in my parlance.) And I've brought the Music Fans and the Artistes together.

MY PASSION FOR MUSIC, MY experience as a concert promoter, and my engagement with the Rock Hall have provided me with stories to tell—many stories, and tell them I do, replete with opinions to offer, obscure facts to reveal, and, always, music to foist on the willing (or sometimes not-so-willing) listener.

Over time, a number of friends have suggested, "You should write a book." I wasn't convinced. But in late 2016 and 2017, Kathy and I had a series of health issues and I had time on my hands. I began to assemble my thoughts and . . . write. It was fun. I enjoyed dragging up the memories and jumping into the research to bring them to life. The project also distracted me from the state of the world, which seemed to have gone wildly askew.

Progress was slow. Then came March 2020. The pandemic. Talk about a world gone askew! And talk about time on my hands! For the next few months, I wrote, edited, and wrote some more. While I was immersing myself in the memories of music past, I am afraid music present came to a screeching halt—at least *live* music, which has been so important to me and the people I care about. Obviously, those people include the musicians, whose economic and emotional well-being depends on playing for their audiences. But there are also the venues, especially those small, independent venues that are the lifeblood of the industry; the agents, managers, and road crews; the waitstaff and bartenders. The ripple effect goes on and on.

And to make it clear, the loss isn't just the money, although that's important. My singer-songwriter friend Chuck Prophet recently posted an essay online that says it all. After his wife asked if he was going to be okay, he went outside, sat down in his road-weary Ford

Econoline . . . and cried. I can assure you he isn't the only Artiste, capital *A* or otherwise, who has done that since March 2020. Or venue owner. Or agent. Or . . .

Then there are the fans. Thankfully, there is still recorded music. Many of us have "rebooted" our turntables. For some of us, CDs never went out of fashion. My seven thousand iTunes songs have been "random shuffled" multiple times over the past months. I have even finally accepted streaming services.

However, there is *nothing* like live music. And although viewing online my favorite artists playing on their living-room couches or in their kitchens is fun for a while, it simply isn't the same for the fans—or the musicians. Yes, a crowd becomes energized by a great show, but I can assure you it's often a fraction of the energy felt by the performer, whether entertaining twenty people or twenty thousand. That feeling, that rush, is why they do it. And, for the moment, it isn't there.

I DON'T KNOW WHAT'S ON the other side of COVID-19. Maybe by the time folks read these words, we will be back experiencing our favorite singer-songwriter in the confines of an intimate venue, or seeing our favorite Rock Hall inductee in a major arena. Or maybe not. Time will tell.

In the meantime, for your reading pleasure, here are my notes from sixty years of rock & roll fandom, including twenty-six as a promoter and sixteen as a member of the Rock & Roll Hall of Fame board. I hope my stories distract you for a moment from the world gone askew, trigger some fond memories of your own, and convey some of that joy I saw on those faces at Valley Dale.

On that note, the question is: How did a passion for music so impact a kid from Euclid, Ohio—a corporate lawyer from Columbus—that I ended up promoting shows and chairing the board of the Rock & Roll Hall of Fame? That's what you are about to hear.

MUSIC IN MY LIFE

ONE

My Big Bang

AM NOT SURE WHEN I GOT MY FIRST TRANSISTOR RADIO. I CLEARLY recall lying in bed with it next to me on the pillow as I listened to Cleveland Indians games, including the night in June 1959, when Rocky Colavito hit four home runs against the Baltimore Orioles. I am also unsure when I first listened to rock & roll on that radio, but I distinctly remember when it first *spoke* to me: December 1961. Sixth grade. I was ten years old, closing in on eleven. (Yes, I skipped a grade.)

It was Dion. "The Wanderer." He, and the song, spoke volumes to me. Melodically. Rhythmically. But especially lyrically. As if it were custom-made for me. A ten-year-old kid in Euclid, Ohio, somehow connecting with a twenty-one-year-old Italian-American from the Bronx singing, *"I'm the type of guy who will never settle down. . . ."*

For Christmas that year, I wanted nothing but rock & roll records. My mother went to a record store and, with counsel from the proprietor, got me a mix-and-match collection of 45s and a handful of 33s. I don't recall what all was in the mix. (When I went to college seven years later, I was too embarrassed to incorporate those early records into my "sophisticated" album collection, so my

3

mother donated them to a local hospital's charity flea market.) My parents also got me a Webcor Music Man record player. Baby blue with detachable speakers. I was in heaven.

To be clear, music hadn't been a part of my childhood. I never took lessons of any type. My elementary school music teacher made fun of my singing, ultimately asking me to narrate the sixth-grade Christmas program to get me out of the choir. On the other hand, my parents did play music around the house. My father, John, born in Glasgow, Scotland, in 1917, and mother, Betty, born in Cleveland in 1923, favored show tunes, Sinatra, and Como—and, especially, my father's beloved Kenneth McKellar, a classic traditional Scottish tenor. And every year my father took us to Cleveland's Public Auditorium to see Scotland's Black Watch Pipes and Drums when they made their annual visit to the States.

The Scottish heritage was important to my father. At the age of nine, in 1926, he immigrated to the United States with his mother and three siblings. My grandfather had preceded them three years earlier, and once settled in Chicago and gainfully employed with Addressograph-Multigraph, he summoned the rest of the family to the States. When A-M moved to Euclid, Ohio—the first suburb east of Cleveland—in the early thirties, so did the Wightmans. My mother met my father just before the war, and they were married in 1946. Three years later they bought my mother's childhood home from her parents. That red brick house at 117 East 212th Street in Euclid, a few hundred yards from Lake Erie, was where they lived when I was born in 1951. My brother, Jim, came along in 1957. My mother lived there until she died in 2005, eleven years after my father passed away.

Back to music. By early 1962, one record dominated my brand-new turntable: Dion's *Greatest Hits*. I discovered songs I had been too young to catch on first release. With the Belmonts, Dion perfected the doo-wop sound of "I Wonder Why" and the classic harmonies of "Where or When." I was especially drawn to the plaintive cry of "No One Knows" and "A Teenager in Love." Dion had already started a solo career, and my new LP contained his first hit without the Belmonts, "Lonely Teenager." I also discovered "Runaround Sue," which had just preceded "The Wanderer" onto the charts. Perhaps most significant of all, I realized Dion actually wrote some of the songs. So began an almost sixty-year fascination with singer-songwriters.

Dion stayed with me. The sound that first caught my ear continued through 1962 with "Lovers Who Wander," "Little Diane," and "Love Came to Me." I have to say, though, that even as a kid I cringed when, later that year, I bought his first record on his new label, Columbia, and heard Mitch Miller's team trying to turn him into a nightclub singer. Oh, he had a hit off the album with what I now know was a remake of the Drifters' "Ruby Baby," but the rest of it sounded like . . . adult . . . music.

Dion pretty much disappeared from the public eye for a few years in the mid-sixties. What I didn't know then was that he had serious substance abuse issues, including a heroin addiction that had plagued him since he was a kid in the Bronx. What I also didn't know until many years later is that he recorded, in 1965, one of the great lost rock & roll albums, *Kickin' Child*, which wasn't released in its entirety until 2017.

Although I lost track of Dion for a while, he popped up in my life periodically thereafter. He was one of only two rock & roll artists (Bob Dylan was the other) whom the Beatles included in the collage on the album cover of *Sgt. Pepper's Lonely Hearts Club Band* in 1967, a fact I duly noted at the time. In 1968, Dion scored a huge comeback hit with "Abraham, Martin and John," and I saw him live for the first time while attending Duke University in early 1969. He was solo acoustic and told the audience in a self-deprecating way how many of his songs had been "stolen" from blues chord progressions by artists like Jimmy Reed.

Forty-some years later, early in my tenure on the board of the Rock & Roll Hall of Fame, then-CEO Terry Stewart, with whom I had shared my fascination with Dion, invited me to a small dinner with Dion and famed rock journalist Dave Marsh. It was one of my first brushes with "stardom." I was a little tongue-tied, and I couldn't get much of a word in with the loquacious Marsh sitting next to me. However, I subsequently met Dion on the floor of an induction ceremony, where I had the chance to tell him how much he meant to me, sentiments he accepted graciously.

Things often come full circle in my life. In March 2016, I made what has become an almost annual pilgrimage to the South by Southwest (SXSW) music festival in Austin. Late one night, in a small, balconied meeting room at the venerable Driskill Hotel, Dion appeared with an acoustic guitar, accompanied by Jimmy Vivino on electric guitar. At age seventy-six, he looked and sounded great. The night ended with Dion leading two hundred fans, packed into the small room, in a rousing sing-along of "Runaround Sue." It was rock & roll at its finest.

A year later, in 2017, that unreleased 1965 album, *Kickin' Child*, finally saw the light of day. Some of the songs had appeared as one-offs on various collections over the years, but this was the first time the album could be heard in its entirety as Dion had intended. The backstory is fascinating. Dion was working on the album with Tom Wilson, the famed Columbia Records producer, trying to migrate his sound from the label's desired nightclub entertainer to what Dion envisioned as pioneering electric folk rock. In fact, that unreleased album included songs written by Bob Dylan (including an early "It's All Over Now, Baby Blue"), Tom Paxton, and Dion himself. During the project, Dion suggested to Wilson that he try that same electric approach with Dylan, for whom Wilson was simultaneously producing a record. The rest is history—Dylan's *Bringing It All Back Home*, his first record with electric instruments, and everything that followed. How different might the future of rock & roll and, certainly, Dion's career have been if that sound had first emerged publicly from Dion rather than Dylan?

NOT ONLY DID DION GO missing from my musical life in the early sixties, to some degree rock & roll went missing from the U.S. music scene as well. The phenomenon has been chronicled in countless places, not the least of which is Don McLean's "American Pie." But suffice it to say, a plane crash, the army, prison, a call to the ministry, and a marriage to a thirteen-year-old cousin had taken a number of the pioneers of rock & roll out of the spotlight. I was too young to know what I was missing, with no appreciation for the "Big Bang" of the 1950s—artists like Buddy Holly, Elvis Presley, Chuck Berry, Little Richard, and Jerry Lee Lewis, who found ways to splice the roots of country music and the blues into rock & roll.

Yet my musical tastes were being sufficiently honed that I could identify what I liked. In my own inimitable fashion, I began to immerse myself into rock & roll, listening to AM radio incessantly when I wasn't spinning records on that Webcor Music Man. My bedroom was the third-floor attic of our house, so I was isolated from the rest of the family and could listen to music when I should have been sleeping or doing homework. There, I experienced my own Big Bang.

At the time, there were Cleveland stations playing rock & roll like KYW, which had a disc jockey known as "Jerry G." But the primo rock & roll station was WHK, with Johnny Holliday doing the afternoon drive time. (Holliday went on to successful radio gigs in Chicago and San Francisco before turning to sports broadcasting in the Washington, D.C., area.) I did more than just listen. I found Demshar's, a record store within walking distance of my house that sold *Billboard* magazine. I bought it regularly, studying the charts and identifying commonalities among songwriters (who were Goffin-King?), producers, and labels. I made my own top forty list each week, and just like *Billboard*, I kept track of where each song was the prior week and how many weeks it had been on my charts. I would love to be able to look at those charts now and see how my musical tastes were evolving, but, alas . . . maybe Mom at work again?

My first year of immersion into rock & roll, 1962, was a challenge for a burgeoning rocker. The top five songs on *Billboard*'s Hot 100 for the year included instrumentals like Mr. Acker Bilk's "Stranger on the Shore" (actually, a great song, although hardly rock & roll) and David Rose's "The Stripper." But for every Bobby Vinton or Pat Boone entry on the Hot 100, there were also songs that caught my ear like Ray Charles singing Don Gibson's "I Can't Stop Loving You" and Cindy Walker's "You Don't Know Me," both off Charles' blockbuster album *Modern Sounds of Country and Western Music*. (The latter song, I learned later, has a cowrite attributed to Eddy Arnold, not the first or last time a singer insisted on a writing credit if he was going to record the song.) For every soppy Shelley Fabares or Richard Chamberlain number, there was Bruce Channel doing "Hey! Baby." I was especially drawn to the Everly Brothers' harmonizing on "Crying in the Rain," a duo from the Big Bang trying desperately to hold on to stardom. That harmony sound would remain a personal favorite for decades to come.

There were songs that caught my ear from Black artists, especially Sam Cooke and acts on a relatively new label out of Detroit called Motown. I also favored hits by Joey Dee and the Starliters, which later evolved into one of my favorite bands, the (Young) Rascals. And a brand-new group from the West Coast, called the Beach Boys, grabbed my attention. I spent time in Fort Lauderdale that summer with my grandparents, where I was fixated on a catchy ditty by Tommy Roe called "Sheila," which I now realize sounds suspiciously like Buddy Holly's "Peggy Sue." Roe later did a number of songs that I found to be almost unlistenable, but I loved this one.

My favorite song of 1962 walked the musical tightrope between the popular movie theme songs of the day ("Moon River," by Cleveland's own Henry Mancini, was huge that year) and the first great "folk music scare" of the rock & roll era (the Kingston Trio, the Highwaymen, and Peter, Paul and Mary all hit the year's Hot 100). I loved the unique voice of Gene Pitney. The first Pitney single I heard was (another) movie theme song, "Town Without Pity," and I liked his hits that followed. And although I didn't know it then, he wasn't "just" a singer but a very talented musician who could play several instruments and harmonize with himself, multitracking his vocals on such songs as "(I Wanna) Love My Life Away." I was really impressed when I learned he had written "Hello, Mary Lou" for Rick Nelson and, get this, "He's a Rebel" for the Crystals, as well as penned some of his own hits. I had no idea then that the real money in the business is from songwriting, but I was amazed that artists could be so talented as to perform their own material *and* write for others. My fascination with singer-songwriters continued to grow.

So, the big reveal: My favorite song of 1962 was Pitney's "The Man Who Shot Liberty Valance." The film by that name is one of the great Westerns, starring John Wayne, Jimmy Stewart, and Lee Marvin as Liberty. Hal David and Burt Bacharach, who had written other hits for Pitney, crafted this one on commission to be used in the movie. The song perfectly captured the film's plot and tone, and apparently everyone loved it—except the guy who mattered most: John Ford, the director. He rejected it and, believe it or not, the song never appears in the movie.

Gene Pitney's career soon faltered in the U.S., though he continued to write excellent songs and clearly had an ear for great songwriters. He was one of the first singers to record a song by a very young Randy Newman, "Just One Smile," which later appeared on Blood, Sweat & Tears' debut album. At the beginning of the British Invasion, he became friendly with the Rolling Stones and cut an early Jagger-Richards song. His career never wavered in Europe, where he remained a star; he recorded records in Italian, Spanish, and German, and continued to score hits in the U.K. long after his popularity had faded in the U.S. And my Pitney fandom would never cease.

In the late nineties, we had a summer associate at my law firm, BakerHostetler, whose college roommate was Pitney's son. When I somehow discovered the connection, I asked him to see if Gene would entertain a phone call from a "corporate lawyer in Columbus, Ohio, with a passion for music." Gene consented and I called him one afternoon at his home in Connecticut. He couldn't have been nicer. I told him what his music had meant to me over the years and asked if I could get him to Columbus to do a show, which my Zeppelin Productions would promote. When I described the gig and the venue, he said it sounded like fun, but that typically he didn't perform as a singer-songwriter. He was usually backed by an orchestra. That wasn't in the cards for my songwriter series, but just talking to him on the phone was a thrill.

Gene was inducted into the Rock & Roll Hall of Fame in 2002, just before my time on the Rock Hall board, and he died suddenly of a heart attack in 2006 at the age of sixty-six, leaving behind his childhood-sweetheart wife of forty years and three sons. I'm sorry I never got to meet him in person.

BY THE END OF 1963, I was listening to music wherever I could find it on the radio dial, stations broadcasting both locally and in far-flung places, thanks to clear channel stations I could catch after hours. WHK was still around in Cleveland (although replaced within a couple of years by WIXY-1260), but I discovered CKLW—50,000 watts coming across Lake Erie from Windsor, Ontario; WBZ in Boston; WLS in Chicago; and, of course, WABC in New York City with the great DJ Cousin Brucie.

In addition to Gene Pitney, artists like Roy Orbison resonated with me at that point, as did some wonderful one-hit wonders of the time (songs like "Rhythm of the Rain" by the Cascades). But nothing really captivated me as Dion had a couple of years earlier. I may have bought a few albums (the Beach Boys, for sure), but not many.

That would all change with the British Invasion in 1964. By mid-January, I was spinning the dial on that transistor radio every night trying to find songs by the Beatles. I bought *Introducing . . . the Beatles*, released by Vee-Jay on January 10, and *Meet the Beatles*, issued by Capitol on January 24. I was ready to be *invaded*.

There are a few moments in time for which we baby boomers can remember exactly where we were: The deaths of JFK, Martin Luther King Jr., Bobby Kennedy, and John Lennon. Certainly, 9/11. But one of those moments is where we were at 8:00 p.m. on February 9, 1964, when the Beatles first appeared on *The Ed Sullivan Show*. I was alone upstairs in my parents' bedroom watching a little black-and-white TV. The Beatles did five songs. They opened with their own "All My Loving," but their second song, featuring Paul, was "Till There Was You" from the Broadway musical *The Music Man*. Much has been written about how the Brits gave us back our music, usually focusing on early rock & roll, the blues, and rhythm & blues. That night, the Beatles also gave us back a show tune—a nice one, for sure, but it probably says as much about Paul's musical taste as anything. Before *Ed Sullivan* ended, the Fab Four had played their three initial U.S. hits: "She Loves You," "I Saw Her Standing There," and, of course, "I Want to Hold Your Hand." The world, and my world, had changed.

Throughout 1964 and 1965, I began to buy albums at an increased pace, a sickness that continues to this day. It should be noted that the early records by the Beatles, the Rolling Stones, and others were just collections of songs, not in any way "albums" produced or held together in a thematic or conceptual way. In fact, many of their albums released in America were quite different from those issued in Great Britain.

It is particularly interesting to think about how many cover songs they did. The Stones recorded acoustic and electric blues classics. The Beatles did Carl Perkins and Buck Owens. Both bands covered 1950s rock & roll and Motown. They cut songs by artists relatively unknown to the mainstream American public, like Alabama country-soul singer Arthur Alexander. At the end of the day, the British groups really did give our music back to us—both through cover songs and via their own original material heavily influenced by the likes of the Everly Brothers, in the case of the Beatles, and Chuck Berry, in the case of the Stones.

I once heard Steve Van Zandt from the E Street Band speak at SXSW. His basic theme was how the great rock & rollers learned their craft by playing the songs of others and discovering how those songs work onstage and in the studio. Steve discussed the years the Beatles, Stones, and other British Invasion bands spent as cover bands in the clubs of England and Europe. Just a few years later, Bruce Springsteen, Steve, and many more fledgling musicians were doing the same thing in American bars, now covering those very British rockers. With zero musical talent of my own, I was content to buy and spin records, but a number of my friends and thousands of other kids across the U.S. were banging away in garages and basements learning to play "Satisfaction" and "She Loves You."

By early 1966, the Beatles had released my favorite of their LPs, *Rubber Soul*—a true album, not just a collection of songs designed to be released as singles. Recorded in a series of sessions over just a two-week period, the album reflected the influences of the band's recent visits to the U.S., including the folk-rock sounds of the Byrds and Bob Dylan and the melodic rhythm & blues of Motown. In '66, most of the key players in the British Invasion had

MY BIG BANG | 13

released greatest-hits LPs, after appearing on the U.S. charts for a couple of years. I bought them all. Night after night, I would retreat after dinner to the basement, where my Webcor Music Man now resided. Throwing darts, overhand and hard, I'd attempt to work out my teenage angst while listening to greatest-hits collections from the Stones (*High Tide and Green Grass*), the Yardbirds, and the Kinks.

My favorite, *The Best of the Animals*, dominated my turntable. It included the traditional folk blues the band had turned into a massive hit, "House of the Rising Sun"; original material like "I'm Crying"; two John Lee Hooker songs; a version of Sam Cooke's "Bring It On Home to Me" (albeit without Sam's call and response with Lou Rawls); and a cover of Fats Domino's "I'm in Love Again." But the album's real strength was its songs that spoke to everyone from a fifteen-year-old pre-college high school kid in Euclid, Ohio, to working-class folks like the band itself, to GIs in Vietnam. There was Barry Mann and Cynthia Weil's "We Gotta Get Out of This Place"; "It's My Life," written by another and lesser-known Brill Building duo, Roger Atkins and Carl D'Errico; and an absolute killer version of a song written for and first recorded by Nina Simone, "Don't Let Me Be Misunderstood."

Years later, in March 2012, I sat in the front row when Bruce Springsteen delivered a marvelous keynote address at SXSW. He spoke lovingly about all types of music, but when he got to the British Invasion—and after he'd spoken about the Beatles—he said, "For me, it was the Animals. For some, they were just another one of the really good beat groups that came out of the sixties. But to me, the Animals were a revelation. The first records with full-blown class consciousness that I had ever heard."

Bruce asked if anyone had an acoustic guitar, and of course, someone did. With that, at a podium in front of a few hundred spellbound fans, he began to strum and sing, "*In this dirty old part of the city / Where the sun refuse to shine . . .*" When he'd finished

"We Gotta Get Out of This Place," Bruce said, "That's every song I've ever written. That's all of them. I'm not kidding. That's 'Born to Run,' 'Born in the USA,' everything I've done for the past forty years, including all the new ones. But that struck me so deep. It was the first time I felt I heard something come across the radio that mirrored my home life, my childhood."

Bruce went on at great length about the Animals. How they weren't good-looking; they were "aggression personified." He described Eric Burdon, the lead singer, as "your shrunken daddy with a wig on"; Eric's voice as "Howlin' Wolf coming out of a seventeen- or eighteen-year-old kid." And then Bruce simply read all the words to "It's My Life," starting with, *"It's a hard world to get a break in . . ."* and ending with *". . . show me I'm wrong, hurt me sometime / But someday I'll treat you real fine."* Bruce said, "I love that."

So did I in the mid-1960s, and I still did in *my* mid-sixties.

One last Bruce story—for now. He illustrated what Steve Van Zandt had said just a couple of years earlier in his own SXSW keynote address: how the great ones learn from the masters. Bruce said, "Youngsters, watch this one. I'm going to tell you how it's done, right now." This time, he strummed and sang the beginning of "Don't Let Me Be Misunderstood," and morphed it directly and seamlessly into "Badlands." "It's the same fucking riff, man," he concluded. "Listen up, listen up, youngsters, this is how successful theft is accomplished."

In June 2013, we held our annual Rock & Roll Hall of Fame board retreat in Chicago. That was the meeting at which I was elected chair of the board. We always have great music at our retreats, and in Chicago, not surprisingly, we had a collection of blues performers who were going to give us a private show as they rehearsed for some bigger shindig. Beforehand, a few of us were invited downstairs, where the musicians were hanging out, to meet Mayor Rahm Emanuel, who was stopping by to thank us for holding our meeting in his city. (By the way, short, slender, missing a finger, and in what looked to be a very expensive suit, he had a demeanor that suggested I wanted to be on his side, not the other.)

Meeting the mayor was cool, but meeting Eric Burdon was *really* cool. Yes, Eric was there to do a couple of songs with the band. I met him, shook his hand, and got to tell him that he and the Animals were my absolute favorites of the British Invasion. We didn't exactly establish a deep, meaningful relationship, but I did meet him—one up on Gene Pitney.

At times, my teenage angst probably bordered on what today would be diagnosed as outright depression. You couldn't pay me to go back to high school, other than for the music of the time.

In the summer of 1965, there were two unexpected deaths in my family, my father's older brother and my maternal grandmother. At fourteen, I had my right knee casted for a month in a misguided attempt to treat Osgood-Schlatter disease (which had caused a painful, hard lump below my knee); the only benefit of the "treatment" was to thicken my medical file for presentation to the doctor at my draft physical seven years later, which I failed for just that issue. As a result, I missed a summer of tennis and my high school's fall season. I also struggled mightily adjusting to the large pond of 3,500 students.

Most of 1966 wasn't much better. Tennis was a big part of my life, and although I got my game back in gear, I missed most of the summer, including tennis, when my family took my now-widower grandfather on an extended driving trip all over the western United States. My grandfather and I sat in the backseat for 7,500 miles, playing cards on the center armrest. A great trip, but no rock & roll—and not what a fifteen-year-old boy would have picked for his summer.

Thankfully, things improved a little in 1967. I was elected to some high school leadership positions. My tennis game went from good to better. And by year's end, I had been accepted to Duke University on an early admission application and was about to "get out of this place." With 1967 came the Summer of Love. Well, not for me. I spent it on the tennis court in the day and dangerously skateboarding down steep hills with my friends in the evening, at least until one friend stepped off his board at high speed and snapped his leg. But I also spent the summer—and the whole year, for that matter—immersing myself in an explosion of new music. There may have never been a music year quite like 1967.

The year started for me when a friend's father, who worked for an appliance distributor that also distributed records, gave me a handful of new releases he'd picked up at the office. One of them was *Fresh Cream*. I'd read about how fans scrawled CLAPTON IS GOD graffiti all over London, and I knew Eric had been an original member of the Yardbirds. But oh wow, this power-trio thing (Clapton, bassist Jack Bruce, and drummer Ginger Baker) kicked off a whole new sound. The second wave of the British Invasion continued to give us back our music—the album included Robert Johnson's "Four Until Late" and Willie Dixon's "Spoonful"—but there was a new edge and an emphasis on musicianship. I was off to the races.

I listened to progressive-rock shows on a university radio station, either Case Western Reserve or John Carroll, whose airwaves just barely reached Euclid. (Cleveland's WMMS, one of the first progressive-rock stations in the country, didn't go to that format until August 1968.) My friend Dave DiBiasio's cousin in Detroit introduced him to some underground sounds, and another pal, Dick Clark ("Ace"), was fascinated with soul music, especially Otis Redding. But I mostly shifted my source of music discovery from the radio to record stores, hanging out and studying album covers and liner notes, locating commonality among producers and musicians. By December I had bought dozens and dozens of new albums, including some I'd missed previously from bands like the Paul Butterfield Blues Band and the Blues Project. I took great pride in being on the very cutting edge of music. Some of my "discoveries" became popular among the masses—big hits of 1967 included the debuts of the Doors and Jimi Hendrix, not to mention the second Cream album, *Disraeli Gears*, all of which had huge hit singles.

I also bought and sang the praises of lesser-known releases like the first Velvet Underground album, with Nico, which had a peelable banana on the Andy Warhol–designed front cover; Love's *Forever Changes*, a vastly underrated record to this day; and *Electric Music for the Mind and Body*, from Country Joe and the Fish. (I had the thrill of meeting Joe at a Rock Hall Music Masters tribute to Janis Joplin thirty-two years later.)

There were some great radio singles in 1967. During the summer, "The Letter" by the Box Tops was everywhere, as were Bobbie Gentry's "Ode to Billie Joe" and the Beatles' "All You Need Is Love." Later in the year, the Who scored their first U.S. megahit with "I Can See for Miles," although I had picked up several of their earlier 45s: "My Generation," "The Kids Are Alright," "Pictures of Lily," "Happy Jack," and my favorite to this day, "Substitute." And Van Morrison's first post-Them solo hit, "Brown Eyed Girl," was a catchy song he later dismissed. I guess he thought it wasn't an appropriate precursor to his stellar subsequent albums, *Astral Weeks* and *Moondance*. (Van, who I only saw once in concert—in October 1974, with my then girlfriend/future wife Kathy Little and a smallish crowd at Veterans Memorial Auditorium in Columbus—has a well-deserved reputation for being a challenge. I once asked a veteran music television producer who was the most difficult person with whom he ever dealt. He said there was no close second.)

The epitome of that San Francisco Summer of Love sound was Jefferson Airplane, with both "Somebody to Love" and "White Rabbit." I must say, I wasn't the world's biggest Airplane fan. I bought and enjoyed *Surrealistic Pillow* but none of their subsequent albums, and I never saw them live. However, in 2016, for my last meeting as chair of the Rock Hall board, which I hosted at the new BakerHostetler offices in Cleveland, we invited Airplane cofounder and lead guitarist Jorma Kaukonen to be interviewed by Jason Hanley, the Rock Hall's vice president of education, and play a few songs in our conference room. Jorma was smart, friendly, and articulate, and I got to spend time with him while he was with us.

Fast forward a year or so and Jorma and I crossed paths again. At my suggestion, the Rock Hall conducted a "Roadshow" in Columbus. The original objective was to heighten the profile of the Hall in Central Ohio and give three local CEOs, who are Rock Hall trustees and musicians, a chance to play with the house band of a resident theater company called Shadowbox. The invitation-only event for local Rock Hall supporters, friends, and community leaders has been a resounding success. For our third year of the Roadshow, we decided to get an inductee to play music with our trustees and thought of Jorma. He lives in Meigs County, Ohio, where he and his wife operate the Fur Peace Ranch, a music workshop and camp. To make it worthwhile for Jorma, I agreed to promote two concerts in Columbus the night before.

The whole experience was wonderful. The two sold-out shows were in the intimate environs of Natalie's Coal Fired Pizza and Live Music, my regular promotion venue at that point. Jorma performed solo acoustic, not repeating a song or story during the performances. The next night we had a fun Rock Hall evening at Shadowbox, where Jorma strapped on an electric guitar, played "White Rabbit" with the band and our trustees, and then did a Hot Tuna song (his other band over the years), including an extended, breathtaking solo.

Who would have thought in the summer of 1967 that fifty years later, I'd be onstage three times in a twenty-four-hour period introducing Jorma Kaukonen to intimate audiences in Columbus, Ohio? Better yet, I was hanging out with him, getting to know him, and hearing fascinating stories about life and music in San Francisco at a time when I was still a high school kid in Euclid.

A year later, I brought Jorma back to Natalie's for another two-show evening. He was on the verge of releasing his memoir, *Been So Long: My Life and Music*. His wife, Vanessa, gave me a galley proof of the book and we discussed having Jorma do a signing at my friend Linda Kass' bookstore, Gramercy Books, in the Columbus suburb of Bexley. Shortly thereafter, Linda called and said she and Vanessa had worked out Jorma's bookstore "gig," but they wanted me to interview him in front of an audience. I had done a similar event with the author Holly Gleason some time earlier, so I was comfortable with the concept and agreed.

On November 15, 2018, Jorma and I sat on stools in front of a (small) packed house at Gramercy Books. I'd read the book twice, taken lots of notes, and prepared an interview outline, albeit one he had never seen because Vanessa didn't show it to him even though I'd sent it to her. I asked him questions and picked some selections from the book for him to read. He brought his guitar and played three songs, including his classic "Embryonic Journey." Linda arranged to have the show videotaped with a two-camera setup. It was a delightful evening, all the more impressive when I saw the well-produced and edited video. A true highlight in my musical "career."

During the interview Jorma said, with humorous disbelief, that he couldn't believe I had never brought Hot Tuna to Natalie's, something I hadn't considered feasible. Shortly thereafter, I called Vanessa. She knew Jorma had made the comment and was expecting my call. Sure enough, we found a date when Jack Casady, the other key member of Hot Tuna (and Jefferson Airplane's bassist), was available and booked the acoustic duo into Natalie's for the evening of March 26, 2019. They agreed to do two shows, we jacked the ticket prices, and sold both shows out in a heartbeat. When Jack arrived, he couldn't have been nicer, but I could sense the skepticism. What had Jorma gotten him into? A guy who had played 20,000-seat arenas and festivals for hundreds of thousands was about to play a hundred-person capacity "pizza joint." Let's just say both shows were magical, and it was clear Jack and Jorma were enjoying themselves. Afterward, Jack was effusive about the experience, and the next morning, literally, Vanessa called and said the guys wanted to know when they could book the gig again—which we did just seven months later.

"'LIVE MUSIC IS BETTER' BUMPER stickers should be issued." That's a great Neil Young line from "Union Man" on his 1980 album *Hawks and Doves*, and it's true.

I was late arriving to the live music experience, notwithstanding the fact that Cleveland has always been a great live music town. I didn't see the Beatles when they played there in 1964 and 1966. I didn't see the Stones in 1964. I certainly made up for it with a vengeance, but I was late to the starting line. One of my biggest musical regrets of the 1960s is that I never made it to either La Cave, the legendary folk club at East 106th Street and Euclid Avenue that operated from 1962 until 1968, or Leo's Casino, the equally legendary soul club at East 75th Street and Euclid Avenue, which was open from 1963 until 1972. In both instances, I respected my parents' wishes that I not go into those perceived (and, in those days, for real) dangerous neighborhoods. I had friends who went to both, including to Otis Redding's very last show on December 9, 1967, at Leo's. (He was tragically killed that night flying to Madison, Wisconsin, from Cleveland's Burke Lakefront Airport.)

The first concert I attended, other than school dances after Friday night football games, was on Thanksgiving 1966. I remember it because I left the house with a Browns vs. Cowboys football game on national TV and walked to the Euclid Rollerdrome. Uncharacteristically, alone. Must have been that teenage angst. What I don't clearly remember is whom I saw. For years,

I thought it was the James Gang with a very young Joe Walsh on lead guitar. But recently I told the story to Michael Belkin, a fellow Rock Hall board member and the son of Mike Belkin. (Mike and his brother Jules, as Belkin Productions, dominated the promotion business in the Midwest for forty years and were instrumental in the James Gang's career.) Michael seemed doubtful, and he called and put me on the phone with his friend Jim Fox, the band's drummer.

I shared my recollection with Fox, and he said it wasn't true. He recalled no such gig and, in fact, said the only time the band was booked in Euclid was for a high school dance that was canceled because of bad behavior by some students. Furthermore, he said Walsh didn't join until 1968, replacing lead guitarist Glenn Schwartz, who went to California to form Pacific Gas & Electric (the band, not the utility). As an aside, there is a famous story of Eric Clapton and Schwartz jamming at La Cave one night and Eric saying Glenn was the finest guitar player he'd ever heard.

In retrospect, it must have been the Choir I saw that night at the Euclid Rollerdrome. They and the James Gang were the dominant local bands of the era, with the Choir having a smash regional hit in late 1966 with "It's Cold Outside." When I got to Duke in September 1968, I was surprised to learn it had been a hit in North Carolina too.

Although I didn't go to La Cave or Leo's Casino, I did discover the Hullabaloo clubs, first in Mentor and then in Chesterland. There, I recall seeing a fledgling Bob Seger, who had a regional hit in Detroit with "Heavy Music," which we heard blasting across the lake on CKLW. (I hope no one establishes that Seger never played in one of those clubs.) One band I definitely saw in the Hullabaloo clubs was the Poor Girls, an all-girl, straight-up rock & roll band from Akron. I was smitten, including by the music. I still remember the drummer beating her sticks on the microphone stand to start their version of the Four Tops' "Reach Out." I wonder if a young Chrissie Hynde in Akron saw them and was inspired to front her own rock & roll band?

Sometime during my senior year at Euclid High School, the Key Club, of which I was a member, sponsored a fundraising dance. I talked the club into letting me put it together. I made contact with the Poor Girls, either through an agent or, as I recall, I just got a phone number from a band member after a Hullaba-loo show. Regardless, I secured their services, we sold a bunch of tickets to see a band that hardly anyone at Euclid High had heard of, and it was a fantastic evening. It was also the start of my concert-promotion "career"—and a forerunner of things to come almost thirty years later.

IN THE SUMMER OF 1968, I received a couple of real lessons about the importance of a well-crafted stage show to fully realize the power of live music. At that point, I was a major record collec-tor and had gone to a number of concerts. But in June 1968, shortly after our high school graduation, six or eight of us (yes, all guys—1968 wasn't my "summer of love," either) went to see the Temptations at the Penthouse Club in the Versailles Motor Inn at East 29th Street and Euclid Avenue. We put on coats and ties and ventured into a true nightclub environment. The Temptations were doing two shows that night and we bought tickets for the first one. We settled in at our table and were treated to one of the most polished choreographed shows of all time. There was nothing like the Tempts circa 1968.

Near the end of the show, there was a pause. One of the Tempts came forward and, choking back tears, said this was the first night in years he had been on the road without his wife, who was back in Detroit and seriously ill. He said he wanted to dedi-cate a song to her, and he broke into an almost solo version of "You'll Never Walk Alone." He couldn't complete the song. He broke down sobbing. It was just too much for him. But, fear not, the other Temptations were there to console him and, with their support, the group finished the song and the show. We were beside ourselves. What incredible good fortune to be present at such an emotional moment! Certainly, a once-in-a-lifetime event in the history of rock & roll.

The show ended, and, as the crowd began to file out, the maître d' came over to our table, told us the second show wasn't sold out, and asked if we wanted to stay. How could we say no, especially after that rare moment of emotional spontaneity in the first show? Heck, the Tempts needed our support.

The second show began. Again, it was extraordinarily well choreographed. Everything in the second exactly like the first, including . . . at that very same moment in the show, that very same speech about the ill wife, the very same tears, and ultimately the very same sobbing. And the very same rescue by the other Tempts to finish the song. *The very same everything*. We'd been duped. But oh, what a show!

I now know that all the drama wasn't onstage. In doing a little internet research trying to pin down the date of that show, I learned that the Temptations actually did a ten-night stand at the club from June 14 to June 23, 1968. Their lead singer, David Ruffin, was already in trouble for his cocaine use, unreasonable personal demands, and unreliability. One night during the engagement, he was a no-show, having scooted off to New Jersey or someplace to visit a girlfriend. That was the last straw for the other Tempts, who fired him on June 27 and immediately replaced him with Dennis Edwards. Quite honestly, I don't know if we saw Ruffin that evening. Regardless, we saw an amazing show—and did I say it was perfectly choreographed?

A few weeks later, I was at the other end of the musical spectrum. On July 14, 1968, a bunch of us went to see the Who at Musicarnival on the east side of Cleveland. Believe it or not, it was under a tent, in the round, and held only about two thousand people. I vividly remember two aspects of the show. First, my friend Roy Larick, a year ahead of me in school and a photographer for the Euclid High yearbook, put on a suit and tie, made phony credentials to hang around his neck, and walked onstage with his camera equipment like he knew what he was doing. He spent the whole show cross-legged, ten feet from the band, and captured some fantastic live-action rock & roll pictures. I wonder where those photos are now? Second, after playing a wildly intense set, the Who suddenly went into one of their famous rampages. Smashing equipment. Guitars. Amps. Speakers. Screeching feedback. Drums kicked over. They left the stage.

The crowd had come knowing what to expect. That's what the Who did. So two thousand of us began to file away, heading to our cars, only to have someone come over the speaker system and tell us that was the end of the first set and they'd be back after an intermission. And they were.

Another perfectly choreographed show.

TWO

Changes

L IFE WAS FULL OF CHANGES FOR ME IN 1968, PERSONALLY AND musically.

On the personal front, by the time the year was over, I'd gone from being a successful (although not particularly happy) high school senior in Northern Ohio to a struggling freshman in North Carolina. I again had trouble adjusting to the new pond. (Hmm, there's a theme here, and the first year of law school was yet to come.) Among other things, I'd gone to Duke to play tennis, and it was a challenge adjusting to clay courts and kids who played the game twelve months of the year. I'd experienced neither in Cleveland, where we didn't even have indoor courts at the time.

Yet I made great friends in my freshman house right from the start, especially John Collins, a.k.a. "the Moose," whom I met the first week of college. He was appropriately so christened about the sixth time he knocked something off a shelf in his dorm room. Moose and I bonded on multiple levels, including, but not exclusively, around music. He was also a huge sports fan and had arrived from Texas with the only television on the floor. Every afternoon, I would sprint into his room to watch the Mexico City Olympics, earning a nickname that stays with me to this day among my fellow

25

Dukies—variously "Mr. Olympics," "Ollie," the "Big O," or just "O." Moose and I became friends for life.

The year 1968 was a tough time to be a frizzy-haired northerner in the South. During the height of both the Vietnam War and the civil rights movement, kids with no drawl weren't particularly welcome off campus in a tobacco town like Durham. Life at Duke didn't get better until I had a car and could drive the ten miles to Chapel Hill, a true college town as the home of the University of North Carolina.

Music has helped me survive relatively dark periods of an otherwise charmed life, and that included my freshman year at Duke. And much of that music was discovered during 1968. By the early part of the year, I had found a couple of new Cleveland-area record stores where I hung out and learned about the rapidly changing scene: Record Rendezvous, which opened a location in Richmond Mall, and, especially, the Music Grotto, downtown near Cleveland State and the old arena. Perhaps most important, in late 1967, I purchased at the Grotto an early issue of a brand-new music rag, part newspaper and part magazine, *Rolling Stone*. It offered unparalleled information about my musical obsessions—and I read every word. My mother cut out a little form from that issue and ordered me a subscription for Christmas. In many ways, that subscription, which continues to this day, changed my life.

I continued to buy new records with a passion, but one day stands out in particular.

For senior year spring break in 1968, my parents took my brother and headed to Saint Louis to visit family friends, leaving me home alone because I had tennis matches that week. Some kids might have used that opportunity to get in trouble. However, my friends and I went to the Music Grotto, bought albums, and stayed up all night at my house listening to them. I can still remember that visit to the Grotto and the records I bought.

First, the proprietor told us that Jimi Hendrix (who had played in Cleveland a few days earlier, on March 26) had stood in that very store and claimed that the best new band out there was called Traffic, featuring Steve Winwood, the teenage phenom from the Spencer Davis Group. So I bought their U.S. debut, *Dear Mr. Fantasy*. (That was actually their second U.K. album.)

Second, I was a huge fan of the Paul Butterfield Blues Band and thought (and still do to this day) that their album *East West* featured some of the greatest electric guitar playing ever, by my favorite guitarist, Mike Bloomfield (a notion recently confirmed by Jorma Kaukonen). I was sorry to learn that Bloomfield had departed the band, but Paul had added horns, and I bought the band's new LP, *The Resurrection of Pigboy Crabshaw*.

Third, I was told not to despair, Bloomfield had formed his own band with a collection of all-star musicians, including horns, so I picked up the brand-new release by Electric Flag, with one of the great album covers (at least in the eyes of a seventeen-year-old boy), a barely clad hippie chick ethereally superimposed over photos of the band.

And finally, I knew about Al Kooper, his role in recording Bob Dylan's "Like a Rolling Stone" (when he accompanied his buddy Bloomfield to the recording session and, uninvited, sat down at the organ and played the now iconic chords that give the song its distinctive sound) and especially his work with the seminal progressive-rock band the Blues Project. He, too, had put together a band with horns, calling it Blood, Sweat & Tears, and I bought their first album, *Child Is Father to the Man*, which remains one of my favorites.

So on that day alone, I had firmly placed myself on the cutting edge of the music scene. None of those albums scored significant chart success and clearly none of them spawned hit singles. (Although I could argue that each had songs that *should* have been hits, whether it was "Paper Sun," by Traffic, "One More Heartache," by Butterfield, the Flag's "Over-Lovin' You," or BS&T's "I

Can't Quit Her.") But maybe it was just as well, because I now had music that most of my circle had never heard, including friends I made when I arrived at Duke in September.

I constantly sang the praises of that first Blood, Sweat & Tears album—throughout the summer of '68 and at Duke in the fall. When I came home for Thanksgiving break, I spotted a little ad in the *Plain Dealer* promoting the band's gig on Friday night at the WHK Auditorium on Euclid Avenue. My friend Ace and I drove down and took our seats on the aisle with what seemed like just a few dozen people.

Lo and behold, there was an opener: a band from Detroit then known as the Psychedelic Stooges with a lead singer I later learned was named Iggy Pop. They were loud, raw, and scary. Iggy fell face first onto the stage, microphone pole in hand, without catching himself. I can still picture his bloody face. At one point, Iggy saw a good-looking young woman sitting on the aisle just a few rows across from and behind me. He crawled across the stage, down the stairs, and up the aisle, closing in on her on his hands and knees. As she realized he was coming her way, she got up, screamed, and ran out of the hall.

The Stooges (as they were later called) wrapped up, and after a much-needed intermission, the curtains opened and there was BS&T. *Only without Al Kooper.* The lead singer was now big-voiced Canadian David Clayton-Thomas, and although they did a few songs off *Child Is Father to the Man*, most of the music was unknown to me. (But they did play Traffic's "Paper Sun.") A fine band, their showmanship was quite polished.

Just a few weeks later, BS&T released their second album, the first with Clayton-Thomas; it went straight to the top of the charts, generating three top five singles. I must say, the album did wonders to enhance my reputation as a music aficionado, since I had been championing the band for months, but truth be known, it was a somewhat different sound than the one I'd been praising.

As far as another artist from that major record purchase in spring 1968, I'd been a fan of Steve Winwood going back to his days in the Spencer Davis Group; through his on-again, off-again relationship with Dave Mason and the Traffic ensemble; and during his short-lived super-group, Blind Faith, with Eric Clapton, Ginger Baker, and Ric Grech. Although he faded from my sight for a while, Winwood would make a successful comeback in the eighties as a kind of middle-of-the-road solo artist.

In the summer of 2007, Rock Hall CEO Terry Stewart got a call from András Simonyi, the Hungarian ambassador to the United States. Terry, at first, thought somebody was pulling his leg, but in fact it was the ambassador. It turned out Simonyi's tenure was ending and he would soon return to Hungary. Before he left, he wanted to pay tribute to the Rock Hall and, especially, rock & roll—which he thought was instrumental in the fall of the Iron Curtain. He wished to host an event at his home in D.C., where his best friend would be in attendance—Steve Winwood.

So on July 20, 2007, Terry and a handful of us from the board went to the ambassador's residence. It was a great party attended by politicians (including Ohio senator George Voinovich) and journalists (such as CNN correspondent Wolf Blitzer). Steve didn't play any music, but he and the ambassador spoke to the group and explained their relationship. Apparently, in 1968 or so, Traffic performed in Budapest. At the end of the show, they were paid in Hungarian currency and learned for the first time that they were prohibited from taking it out of the country. They had to spend it all there. So Winwood, age twenty, spent a few days in Hungary, where he met a local contemporary, now the ambassador, and struck up a lifetime friendship.

Over the course of the evening, I chatted with Steve, a friendly guy married to a Tennessee native, whose daughter attended Vanderbilt's medical school. I had only seen Winwood once in concert, on October 16, 1971, the day during my senior year at

Duke that Moose and I took the LSAT (Law School Admission Test). It was also Moose's twenty-first birthday, and I gave him an industrial jug of Cribari wine as a present. After the morning exam, we started consuming it, drinking throughout the day and evening, attending a Duke football game that afternoon, followed by that night's Traffic concert in Cameron Indoor Stadium (the iconic home of our basketball team).

As a college freshman with quite a sophisticated record collection, I was still saddled with my vintage portable Webcor Music Man. I received as much teasing about my Webcor as I did compliments about my taste in music. (My parents came to the rescue the following year when they bought me a high-end KLH component set that was much more appropriate for my stature as a music aficionado.) Nevertheless, whether playing albums on my Webcor or on Moose's slightly more advanced system, we truly bonded over music, sharing many of the same tastes as we explored outside the mainstream of AM radio. We also began a lifetime of seeing concerts together, including two memorable shows freshman year, in the spring of 1969.

On March 1, 1969, Moose and I got to see Janis Joplin at Cameron Indoor Stadium. But it wasn't just Janis. The Chicago blues harmonica legend James Cotton opened for her. He sounded great, especially to a couple of self-proclaimed purists like Moose and me. Sad to say, the eight thousand Dukies in attendance weren't purists, and they booed, heckled, and chanted, "*We want Janis!*" throughout James' performance. Finally, he gave up and retreated. The crowd cheered as he left the stage, not demanding an encore, but expressing pleasure that he was finished.

Outraged, Moose and I left our seats in the bleachers and sprinted down front, up the steps stage left, and behind the curtain. We found James backstage, nicely accosted him, and conveyed our apologies for the behavior of our fellow Dukies. James shook our hands—Moose and I still remember his small, stubby fingers—and talked with us for a while. I told him I was from Cleveland, and he said he had played La Cave a number of times. Then, as we conversed, there was a flurry of activity, and walking right by us, heading for the stage, were Janis and her band. She brushed right up against me. She was attractive, with a noticeably acne-scarred face. What a thrill!

Moose and I headed back to our seats and watched Janis put on a high-octane show with her seven-piece group, later called the Kozmic Blues Band. Her amazing energy was fueled in no small measure by bottles of Southern Comfort continuously handed to her by kids standing in front of the stage. She would take a swig and keep on singing.

Speaking of high energy, about six weeks later (on April 11), Moose drove us to nearby Raleigh (he was the only one on our freshman floor with a car) to see the Jimi Hendrix Experience at Dorton Arena. *Talk about a thrill!* An exciting show—but not the only excitement of the evening. On the way back to Durham, we came over a rise in the road, and just on the other side were two kids standing in the street hitchhiking. Moose missed them, but decided to look back over his right shoulder and give them a piece of his mind. With that, we rear-ended a car stopped at a red light. I don't think Moose ever hit the brakes. Fortunately, the guy saw us coming in his rearview mirror and took his foot off his own brakes. We sent him flying through the intersection. Moose's car was totally smashed. I had to crawl into the backseat to get out the rear door. We were lucky no one was killed.

Janis and Jimi weren't so lucky. Within about eighteen months, in the fall of 1970, they were both dead. At the age of twenty-seven. Yes, members of the "27 Club"—along with Brian Jones of the Rolling Stones, Jim Morrison, and decades later, Kurt Cobain and Amy Winehouse. Tragic.

———

A FIVE-DAY STRETCH IN EARLY 1970 perfectly summarizes the evolution of my musical tastes. On April 8, Moose and I returned to Dorton Arena, this time to see Led Zeppelin. I knew the band as an outgrowth of the Yardbirds and, in fact, had tickets to see them at Musicarnival in Cleveland the prior summer as the opening act for Vanilla Fudge. But I didn't go. As much as I loved music, I stayed home that evening to watch Neil Armstrong walk on the moon. That, by the way, was also the day when I asked the foreman at the nail factory where I was working that summer, and where I had been required to join the union, if we could have the next day off to celebrate the anticipated success of our fellow members of the International Association of Machinists and Aerospace Workers. He just stared at me, incredulously.

Anyway, by the end of 1969, Led Zeppelin had released their first two albums, which met with critical and commercial success, combining a deep sense (and thievery) of roots music, especially the blues, with a sound that can only be described as a precursor to heavy metal. Their Raleigh concert started late, but oh, did they make up for it. I now know that bootlegs from that show are legendary, and for good reason.

For starters, it was louder than anything I had ever heard. Moose and I were in folding chairs on the floor, not too far back, but by the end of the concert, hundreds of us had walked on the chairs to rush the stage. Completely and utterly into the show, Led Zeppelin improvised solos, jumping all around and exhausting themselves and the audience. Near the end, with the crowd going crazy, the band kept huddling onstage and appeared to be discussing what other songs they knew and could play. In addition to their own material, they did a bunch of old rock & roll songs. I was never the biggest Led Zeppelin fan, but that night was special.

Just a few evenings later, on April 12, I saw Tom Rush on the Duke campus. Solo acoustic. At that point, I had his album *The Circle Game*, which had been released in December 1968, and remains a "desert island disc" in my book to this day. It not only includes one of Rush's rare compositions, the classic heartbreak song "No Regrets," but it also introduced many listeners to the work of three young singer-songwriters: Joni Mitchell, James Taylor, and Jackson Browne. Actually, I already knew about each of them one way or another. Judy Collins had a hit and won a Grammy in 1967 with Joni's "Both Sides Now." There was some buzz around Duke about James Taylor, in part because his father was the dean of the medical school at the University of North Carolina. I already had both his first album, the Apple release from late 1968, and *Sweet Baby James*, a then-obscure record released a couple of months before the Tom Rush show. The real mystery to me was Jackson Browne. I only knew about him from an entry in Lillian Roxon's classic 1969 *Rock Encyclopedia*, which said, "Some things take a long time to happen . . . and it's clear that when he does happen, when he is good and ready, the wait will have been worth it." She turned out to be right, but at the time I had no idea who or what she was talking about.

Tom Rush introduced me to the singer-songwriter world, at least in terms of an intimate concert performance. He sang exquisite songs, and he talked about the songwriters and their work. It was a whole new experience for me. I owe him a lot.

THOSE FIVE DAYS IN APRIL may have said a lot about my evolving musical tastes, but I'm not sure I've ever had a week of music more powerful than the one I experienced in summer 1970.

First, there was the Who. It was the second time I'd seen them, only now they played Cleveland's venerable Public Auditorium, on June 27, 1970. It wasn't just the Who, however. In what Jules

Belkin described to me forty-five years later as the single worst billing ever by Belkin Productions, the Who came to Cleveland on their *Tommy* tour with a show opened by Cleveland's absolute favorite local band, power trio the James Gang featuring Joe Walsh, and a relatively unknown James Taylor, solo acoustic.

Tommy had been released a year earlier to critical and commercial acclaim, and the Who's live shows were legendary. The James Gang had broken out of Northeast Ohio with a couple of nationally successful albums, and Walsh was already viewed as something special. The eight-thousand-plus fans were at a fever pitch to see these two electric acts. Into that environment strolled James Taylor, with a stool and an acoustic guitar. I might have been the only person in the place who knew who he was. He opened with the Beatles' "A Little Help From My Friends," clearly hoping he could get some. He didn't. I have no idea what else he did, or tried to do, but the crowd never quieted down. It made the Dukies' treatment of James Cotton look polite.

At some point, James slunk off stage. (No, I didn't run back to apologize this time.)

Out came the James Gang and then the Who. It was a powerful, powerful performance. Extraordinarily bright white lights flashed out at the crowd from behind the stage in sync with the music. The Who did some of their early classics, but mostly it was *Tommy*, start to finish.

I'm not sure if my ears had stopped ringing when I returned to Public Auditorium on July 3 to see Crosby, Stills, Nash & Young. Let me set the context a little. The first Crosby, Stills and Nash album was released the summer before, in 1969, and immediately became a regular on my turntable from the day I bought it. In those days, that first CSN album; Blood, Sweat & Tears' *Child Is Father to the Man*; and *Buffalo Springfield Again* were my three favorite albums. Stephen Stills was part of two of those records, and when Neil Young joined CSN for *Déjà Vu*, released just a few months before this show, it was almost more than a fan like me could handle.

Then, there was Kent State. On the evening of May 4, 1970, I received a call at Duke from my mother. She told me she had heard that day from the mothers of two of my high school classmates, one of whom had been in the crowd of protesters and another of whom had been in a National Guard unit on the scene. Those National Guard units were kids from Northeast Ohio who signed up to avoid going to Vietnam. High school friends were shooting at high school friends. That's a spin about that tragic day that I've never heard told. Anyway, you probably know the story. After hearing of the shootings, Neil Young immediately penned "Ohio." The band rehearsed it a few times and on May 21 they recorded it live in just a couple of takes. It was mastered and rush-released as a single, and despite being banned on many radio stations, rose up the charts.

Crosby, Stills, Nash & Young's Public Auditorium concert was almost two months to the day after the shootings. I remember it like it was yesterday. It was the first time I had ever seen my (already) musical hero, Neil, live. CSN opened the show, seated and acoustic, with "Suite: Judy Blue Eyes," Stills' collection of short songs written for Judy Collins. Neil then wandered onto the stage with his own stool, sitting down and immediately going into one of my absolute favorites, "On the Way Home," from Buffalo Springfield's *Last Time Around*, albeit sung on record by Richie Furay. (A song, by the way, which was the last song I played every time I left Duke to return home to Euclid.) By night's end, CSN&Y had played many of the songs from their two albums. Stephen and Neil had traded searing guitar solos on Young songs like "Cowgirl in the Sand" and even "Southern Man," which didn't appear on record until Young's *After the Goldrush* was released later that year. Most important, they played "Ohio," just thirty miles from the location of that American tragedy sixty days earlier. People in the crowd were singing along at the top of their lungs with tears streaming down their faces.

Talk about the power of rock & roll.

THE SUMMER OF 1970 WASN'T over for me.

I am not sure how I even heard about the Mariposa Folk Festival, but later that July, Dave DiBiasio, Ace, and I got into my mother's Mercury Monterey (with the roll-down back window) and headed for Toronto. While most kids our age smuggled illegal substances across the international border in 1970, we stopped in Buffalo (where the drinking age was eighteen) and bought beer. And while most of the other kids camped on Toronto Island, where the festival took place, we stayed in a fancy downtown hotel. Dave, who is still a fine musician, took his guitar, and we checked into the Royal York quite certain that everyone mistook us for performers.

Mariposa was an eye-opener for me. On an island accessible solely by ferry, the festival promoters only sold seven or eight thousand tickets, so the crowd was totally manageable. (I hadn't even considered going to Woodstock or any of the other megafestivals of that time.) Numerous small stages hosted workshops and performances throughout the day. Then, in the evening, the main stage featured performances by better-known artists.

We had a blast. The music was varied and wonderful: blues performers like Bonnie Raitt's mentor, Mississippi Fred McDowell, and Chicago bluesman J.B. Hutto with his band, the Hawks; the Cajun fiddler Doug Kershaw, who sang "Louisiana Man"; Canadian folkie/rocker David Rea, who played guitar for Gordon Lightfoot, Joni Mitchell, and Ian and Sylvia and cowrote Mountain's hit "Mississippi Queen"; and David Bromberg, a guitarist who played for years with the folkie (as contrasted with the "outlaw") Jerry Jeff Walker, among others. (Bromberg's extended version of Jerry Jeff's "Mr. Bojangles," complete with commentary, is a classic.)

Evening headliners that year included James Taylor and Joni Mitchell, seen strolling hand in hand around the grounds during the day. "Fire and Rain," the single off *Sweet Baby James*, was making its way up the charts, and James received a much warmer reception from the folkies at Mariposa than he had a few weeks earlier in Cleveland. He also did a great song written by his brother Livingston, called "In My Reply," recorded a couple of years later by Linda Ronstadt.

The highlight of the weekend was Joni Mitchell's Sunday evening performance under the stars. She wore a beautiful bright yellow dress. Joni was already a goddess in Canada, especially in Toronto, where she'd started her career, and she captivated the crowd with her voice, unusual guitar playing, and dulcimer. It was the only time I ever saw her in concert.

Each night, we returned to the hotel, Ace fell asleep, Dave pulled out his guitar, and we emulated the folkies we'd seen that day. I had actually written lyrics for a song or three that summer, he had some tunes, and you would have expected nothing less—they meshed perfectly, at least to us. Thankfully, there are no recordings or other remnants of that collaboration, but we did have fun.

And we did have folkies to emulate. It seemed like every day, six or eight times, the same duo would show up and crash somebody's workshop: Ramblin' Jack Elliott and Bobby Neuwirth. It appeared to me they were enjoying some mind-altering substance, and probably not beer smuggled in from Buffalo. Although I am sure they warbled through other songs over the weekend, the only one I remember is "Me and Bobby McGee." They did it on one stage after another. I had never heard the song, although it had been a moderate-sized country hit for Roger Miller the year before. (Janis' version—her only number one song—wouldn't be released until after her death a few months after Mariposa.)

Many years later, in 2015 to be exact, I promoted a show at Natalie's that included Ramblin' Jack. For years, other Artistes had urged me to bring him to Columbus, but I was always reluctant, given his reputation for . . . rambling. (In his day, he was a heavy drinker and, shall we say, unreliable.) But he was out participating in a kind of story performance show with a woman named Nell Robinson. A mutual friend, Joanne Gardner, had prevailed upon me to bring Nell and the show to town.

The performance was fine. Jack's handler kept him to one glass of bourbon after the show, and my family and I listened to Jack tell one great story after another. At one point, I told Jack about seeing him and Bobby Neuwirth a multitude of times that 1970 weekend at Mariposa. He totally remembered the event. However, when I recalled Jack and Bobby telling the audience they had just come from Gordon Lightfoot's house and that Gordon had taught them "Me and Bobby McGee" (Lightfoot had a number one country hit with it in Canada that year), he said that wasn't so. In fact, Jack knew exactly when he had first heard the song—and he proceeded to tell the story.

A couple of years before that Mariposa weekend, Jack had been in a Nashville hotel room when he heard a knock on the door. He opened it and a scruffy guy stood there with a guitar. No case or anything, just a guitar. The guy told Jack that Johnny Cash had sent him over to meet Jack and sing him a song or two he had written. They went into the room, Jack sat down, the guy disclaimed his own guitar-playing abilities, and then—Kris Kristofferson strummed and croaked his way through his new song, "Me and Bobby McGee."

In the great folk tradition, it is interesting how songs get passed from person to person. Gordon Lightfoot may not have taught "Me and Bobby McGee" to Ramblin' Jack, but in doing a little research to sort out the times and places, I learned that Bobby Neuwirth taught the song to Janis, who then recorded it right before she died.

Yes, music helped me make it through my first two years at Duke, and I needed help. I made great friends and had lots of fun along the way, but I was really homesick at first. (To think I sang "we gotta get out of this place" about Euclid?) The academics didn't do much for me, or me for them, placing into advanced Spanish on a standardized test and then getting a D- from Señor Torre only because he knew I "tried." And I continued to struggle with tennis, ultimately quitting the team at the end of the season. It all took its toll.

On the other hand, music also helped me enjoy my junior and senior years, which were much improved. As a junior, I was elected president of my residential house and speaker of the student legislature. I had that car and could drive to Chapel Hill. I also kicked in academically; got my tennis game back in gear, winning both the intramural singles and doubles championships both years; and although I missed Moose when he headed off to England our junior year, I continued to go to some memorable concerts.

I experienced great live music in those years. I remember one show in particular. I was on the floor—front row, center—to see the Byrds and Poco at Cameron on November 21, 1970. It's almost hard to conceive of the talent that had been in Buffalo Springfield: Stills. Young. Furay. When the band finally dissolved for good, Richie went off with Jim Messina, who had played bass and produced much of the third and final Springfield album, and formed Poco, taking that country-rock sound up another notch.

Richie grew up in Yellow Springs, Ohio, and attended Otterbein University, a school located in the Columbus suburb of Westerville and on whose board of trustees I served many years later. He has a great voice and wrote a couple favorites of mine along the way, including "adolescent" classics like "Sad Memory" and "First

Love." Poco was first-rate that night. High energy. An excellent stage performance.

Richie was also great forty-eight years later when we brought him to the intimate Natalie's venue for two shows, one on a Sunday afternoon and one that evening. In his mid-seventies, he was as nice as could be. He looked (in an Otterbein T-shirt) and sounded fantastic and was joined by his daughter, who also had a wonderful voice and stage presence. The set lists for both shows were great, filled with Buffalo Springfield and Poco classics. He even honored my request between shows to do "On the Way Home" in the evening set. A truly magical evening.

That 1970 Duke show also included the then-current version of the Byrds. To this day, I really can't judge anything other than what sounds good to me. I can't tell you much about the technical musicianship on stage. But that night I thought the Byrds were simply mailing it in. I may be unfair. Obviously, prior incarnations of the band had been on the cutting edge of folk rock, psychedelia, and country rock, respectively. Heck, *Sweetheart of the Rodeo* is an absolute groundbreaker of the latter, and Gram Parsons, a motivating force behind that album, was in many ways the godfather of the Americana music I love. And although Parsons was gone from the band by 1970, founder Roger McGuinn was still there and so was Clarence White, a much-revered guitarist. But they unenthusiastically did a bunch of old Byrds songs because that's what the crowd wanted to hear. They didn't appear to take the songs seriously. From the front row, I could tell. At one point, McGuinn sang, "with one hand waving free," and took his hand off the guitar and waved to the crowd.

Between songs, being a nineteen-year-old smart-ass, I sarcastically asked aloud, "Why don't you do 'Louie Louie'?" McGuinn heard me, laughed, told the crowd someone wanted them to do "Louie Louie," and they broke into it for a few seconds. Thank goodness he had a sense of humor.

Literally one week later, on November 28, Ace and I continued a great concert streak in Cleveland. Home for Thanksgiving, we saw Derek and the Dominos live at the Allen Theater.

Eric Clapton and Duane Allman formed the band in April 1970; they recorded their classic album *Layla and Other Love Songs* in August; and they did a handful of U.S. dates between late October and December 2. Duane only played the last couple, so we didn't see him, but we did see a live version of one of the great rock & roll albums. (If pressed, I've been known to say that "Layla" is the best rock & roll song ever.) I actually don't remember a lot about the show that night. I do remember that Lee Michaels opened, just him on guitar and his huge drummer, Frosty, banging out songs like "Do You Know What I Mean?"

What I do know is that "Layla" became a go-to song for me as a tennis player. I was back playing serious tennis, especially in the summers, and I would psych up for big matches by lying on the floor, listening to that song through headphones.

I've never met Eric Clapton, although I remember seeing him at my first Rock Hall induction ceremony at the Waldorf-Astoria in 2005. I was actually prepared to introduce myself to him that night because I had a "hook." Eric had married a woman from Columbus, and they were part-time residents of the city. Friends had posted Facebook pictures of Eric standing in the back of the Woodlands Tavern watching the performance of a very young Gary Clark Jr. Other friends had breached the anonymity of Alcoholics Anonymous to tell me Eric had attended local meetings, something he wouldn't mind because he is a huge proponent of the program. One of the best sightings was by my good Columbus friend, the late Bob Barnett, a.k.a. "the Dancing Bear," who was sitting in the waiting room of Northwest Family Practice one day trying to identify this bookish-looking older man with a young wife and kid. Finally, the nurse came to the door and announced, "The doctor is ready, Mrs. Clapton."

Then in 2006, I went to see Bob Dylan at the old Cooper Stadium, once home of the minor-league baseball team the Columbus Clippers. Halfway through his set, the opening act, Jimmie Vaughan, said he had a friend who was living in Columbus. Without ever mentioning his name, he brought Clapton onstage to play guitar on four or five songs.

Although the opportunity never presented itself that night at the Waldorf, there came a time a few years later when it seemed like I was going to meet Eric for sure. In 2009, the Rock Hall did a Music Masters tribute to Janis Joplin. One of the performers was the excellent singer and guitarist Susan Tedeschi. At the after-party, she hung out with the family. It was a beer- and wine- only event, but my sister-in-law, Lisa, kept running downstairs to the restaurant to keep Susan supplied with her drink of choice, mojitos. At some point during the early hours of the morning, I told Susan about the shows I promoted in Columbus, the cool venue I was using at the time (the Maennerchor), and suggested that she and her husband, Derek Trucks (who had recently toured as part of Clapton's band), should do a show there. She said they were on. Definitely. Then she said if I promised not to promote it, and if they could coordinate with his Columbus residency, they would bring Eric. I have witnesses. She said it. I was beside myself. She gave me her personal e-mail address, told me not to go through her agent, and to e-mail her directly.

I waited a few weeks and sent the e-mail, reminding her who I was and what she had said. No response. I waited a few more weeks and tried again. No response. Sigh. So near, yet so far.

One last part of the story: I got a call a week or so after the Music Masters from my good friend Greg Harris, now Rock Hall CEO, but then the relatively new vice president of development. He said, as I knew, that a young pitcher for the Cleveland Indians was at the after-party and had been on the periphery of my discussion with Susan. He had seen her give me her personal e-mail address. The pitcher wanted Greg to call me and get the e-mail address so he could leave her tickets next time the Indians played in Boston, where she lived. I declined.

I HAVE NUMEROUS PICTURES IN my mind from that 1971–72 era. Some clear, some a blur. A truly magical moment was the Johnny Cash television show that aired on February 17, 1971. Cash usually filmed his show at Nashville's historic Ryman Auditorium, and from the summer of 1969 until the spring of 1971, he presented artists ranging from Bob Dylan to Louis Armstrong and everything in between, including Derek and the Dominos. For that February night in 1971, however, he went to Vanderbilt University and did a show with an antidrug theme. His guests included Linda Ronstadt, James Taylor, and Neil Young. I watched that show transfixed. James did "Sweet Baby James," "Fire and Rain," and "Country Road." He joined Johnny in singing "Oh, Susannah." Linda sang a song or two. Cash sang Kristofferson's "Sunday Mornin' Comin' Down." But the killer for me was seeing Neil do "Needle and the Damage Done," which wouldn't be released on record for another year, and the obscure "Journey Through the Past."

What we now know is that, while in Nashville, Neil went into the studio and cut a bunch of songs that would appear a year later on his megahit album *Harvest*, including his only number one single, "Heart of Gold." The backup singers on that song, who just happened to be in town, are James and Linda. Many years later, I had the privilege of having dinner with Rosanne Cash, Johnny's daughter, and I told her that story. She didn't know it.

Speaking of James Taylor . . . again . . . on March 4, 1971, I drove over to Dorton Arena . . . again . . . to see James with a co-bill unknown to many, Carole King. By this time, being the obsessive fan, I was well familiar with Carole. Totally into songwriters, I knew the many, many hit songs she had written during the sixties.

I also was one of the six people in the country (don't let the facts get in the way of a good story) who owned her first album, *Writer*, which had been released in May 1970. I'm sure I stumbled onto it because I noticed the band included James Taylor and many of the folks from *Sweet Baby James*, who now joined them on the road.

This tour is legendary. James had rocketed to the top of the charts and was on the cover of the March 1 edition of *Time* magazine just a week before the show. (Oh, how I loved—and still love—being ahead of the musical curve.) When Carole's *Tapestry* was released on February 10, I bought it immediately and foisted it on the friends I dragged to the show. We all were enthralled the entire evening.

Truth is, they did that tour again. 2010. Almost forty years later, I saw them at the Schottenstein Arena in Columbus. A horrible venue (I've been known to complain about the parking, among other things), but the show was as magical as it was in 1971.

Unfortunately, the 1970–71 school year didn't end on a high note. Well, maybe it did musically, but that's the rest of the story. I don't share well. My kids say I never learned to share because I skipped kindergarten. Although I may have never been a good sharer, I think some of it later in life has to do with May 1971.

I brought a car to Duke my junior year. A Ford Galaxie 500. Candy-apple red. My mom drove it for a year or two, and then it was mine. I was pleased and proud to have it. The school year was wrapping up, and my roommate needed to take a bunch of stuff to the airport to ship home. He asked if he could borrow my car. I never let anyone drive my car, but that time I said yes. On a rainy afternoon, he pulled out of East Campus in front of an oncoming vehicle that never hit its brakes. T-boned. I think my roommate was bruised and battered, although he never revealed it in his emotionally distraught state. But the car was crushed. Windows blown out. Roof buckled. The old-style, tank-like frame was intact, but it would take a couple of weeks to repair the damage. So I stayed in my dorm room for a week or so before they threw me out. Luckily, I was going to live off-campus my senior year and had access to that house while waiting for the car. No one was around most of the time, which was a new experience for me.

Back to music. One day after everyone had left campus, I walked to the Record Bar in downtown Durham. There was a new album by Rod Stewart. I was a huge fan. I knew him a little from the Jeff Beck Group, but I loved his first album (nobody else had it that I knew), notwithstanding what I thought was a horribly muddy production. And his second album, *Gasoline Alley*, was one of my absolute favorites and had been a staple on my turntable the prior summer.

I bought the new one, *Every Picture Tells a Story*, and brought it back to my dorm room and then to what would be my home for the next school year, 112 West Trinity Avenue. I played it nonstop for days. Music can get you through most things. "Wake up, Maggie, I think I got something to say to you. . . ." I finally made it home to Euclid with my repaired automobile. On July 10, 1971, I saw Rod Stewart and the Faces at Public Auditorium. The Faces (at that point, Rod with Ronnie Lane, Kenney Jones, Ian McLagan, and, of course, Ron Wood) were at the peak of their power-sloppiness. They did Faces songs, but they also played songs off Rod's albums, including the new one.

Trust me, all eyes were on Rod Stewart. Talk about stage presence. I never saw Sinatra, but I always heard that when he hit the stage, you knew he was in command. Rod was in command. Sometimes, probably just to be provocative, I've said that was the best rock & roll show I have ever seen.

THREE

Musicians in My Life

THERE ARE A NUMBER OF MUSICIANS WHO HAVE A SPECIAL meaning in my life because they kept popping up in various sundry and important ways.

One of those is Boz Scaggs. I distinctly recall when I first heard Boz. Well, actually, I had heard him before—I just didn't realize it was him—playing guitar on Steve Miller Band's *Sailor* album and singing the closing song, "Dime-a-Dance Romance," which he wrote. I also didn't know then that he was a grad of St. Mark's School in Dallas, where some of the Moose's siblings attended.

When I first heard his new solo album, simply called *Boz Scaggs*, he caught my ear immediately. I was hanging out in the Record Rendezvous at Richmond Mall in late August 1969, right before I went back to Duke for my sophomore year. His album was playing over the store's sound system. I asked who it was, and they handed me the LP jacket. At the time, I probably didn't know the significance of the Muscle Shoals studios and the session musicians who played there. I am confident I had no idea who Duane Allman was, who appeared naked (there was a hat strategically placed) on the inside of the fold-out jacket. I did note that *Rolling Stone*'s cofounder and editor Jann Wenner produced the record, which was cool, not realizing that would be the only album (that I know of) that Jann ever produced.

Oh man, the music sounded terrific. Great songs, killer rhythm section, amazing guitars, and that distinctive Boz voice. I played *Boz Scaggs* over and over again. It is one of those albums—and there aren't many—I had to replace because I wore it out. Boz was prolific, turning out one fine album after another, sliding from that roots/folk/blues sound through more power rock & roll and finally to a jazzier smooth sound. He released two albums in 1971, including a favorite of mine, *Moments*, and another one in September of 1972.

In many ways, I associate Boz Scaggs with law school. I'd graduated from Duke in spring 1972 with a major in political science and went to law school at The Ohio State University that fall. I played all my Boz records for my new friends there and have a vivid memory of the Dancing Bear being blown away by the extended thirteen-minute song on the first album, "Somebody Loan Me a Dime," with breathtaking guitar work from Boz and Duane Allman.

Ah, that first year of law school. No need to recount another period of relative depression on my part, but notwithstanding making some wonderful friends, it was one of the darker periods in my life. A nadir of that school year was when Boz came to Columbus on April 19, 1973, and I couldn't get anyone to go with me to see him. I ended up dragging along a friend from high school who was in grad school at Ohio State. He had no knowledge or appreciation of music, and may have never been to a concert in his life. He had no enthusiasm for this show before, during, or after. I picture Boz that night at the Ohio Theater in front of a couple hundred people at most. He had a straight-up, scruffy-looking rock & roll band behind him. They were loud, ragged, and fabulous.

Kathy and I started dating in September 1973, my second year in law school. Actually, we met the prior fall, when that same Dancing Bear fixed her up with my extraordinarily conservative first-year law school roommate. Kathy was finishing up her undergraduate education at Ohio State before starting a career as a social worker. He brought her to a party, and the next morning I told him how much I liked her. He didn't—because Kathy "drank, smoked, and swore." She later maintained it was because she had a cold. Regardless, she was my kind of girl, even if it did take another year for us to go out—and a few more before we married. Thankfully, Kathy shared my passion for music from the beginning. When we were first dating, we would meet at the Scioto Trail, an old roadhouse on Route 33 in Columbus halfway between our respective apartments. We sat and talked in a booth with a jukebox at the table. "Tennessee Waltz" was E-7 and it became "our song."

Anyway, I quickly introduced Kathy to that first Boz Scaggs album. Boz remained completely under the mainstream radar, and I loved singing the praises of an artist who was unknown to anyone in my circle of friends. Boz didn't appear in Columbus again until May 5, 1976. Kathy and I were there, of course. Once again, I picture the show at the Ohio Theater with another small crowd. Boz was still unknown to the masses, but that didn't last long.

I had told Kathy about seeing Boz three years earlier, and I'm sure I described that scruffy-looking group of hippie musicians and their raw rock & roll sound. My surprise at this show was a little like the Blood, Sweat & Tears concert in 1968, albeit without the Stooges as an opener. Onstage this time were a small orchestra, backup soul singers, and Boz—in a tuxedo. He was out supporting the just-released *Silk Degrees*. It peaked at number two, spent 115 weeks on the *Billboard* 200, was certified five times platinum, and spawned one hit single after another. Boz was a star, and I had known him "when."

Boz's career didn't sustain at that level. The albums that followed over the next few years were good, but he had settled into a smooth blue-eyed soul format that didn't have the edge of his earlier music. I also think Boz went through a difficult divorce and custody battle. As I remember reading later, he shut down his career for most of the 1980s, staying at home to take care of his kids. He didn't record for almost ten years and didn't tour at all. Instead, he founded a live music venue in San Francisco, Slim's, where he served as the maître d' many nights of the week.

Boz stayed in my life in the eighties and beyond, however. That first album had introduced me to the music of Jimmie Rodgers, the "Father of Country Music," in the form of his song "Waiting for a Train." It became a road-trip sing-along song for years, and for some reason it later became a bedtime song when my daughters, Nora and Emily, were little. Almost every night, I sang that song to them as I rubbed their backs and put them to sleep. (Little did I know that decades later, I'd do the same with my grandson, Gavin.)

I've never met Boz and I haven't seen him live since that night in 1976, although he did resume his career over the past couple of decades and has occasionally toured, sometimes as part of a "revue" composed of late-seventies contemporaries like Donald Fagen and Michael McDonald. I did, however, make it to Slim's. In 2015, the Rock Hall held its board retreat in San Francisco. We rented out Slim's for the evening and asked my friend Chuck Prophet and his band, the Mission Express, to entertain our trustees and guests. He did, it was wonderful, and Chuck told me that he and his wife, Stephanie, had held their wedding reception at Slim's.

I don't think Boz is still involved with Slim's, and he certainly wasn't there that evening, but I'd listened to him enough and read about him so much over the years that I felt his presence.

ONE DAY IN LATE SUMMER 1970, I made another record store run that resulted in a bulk purchase. By then, I was really delving into the singer-songwriter thing, especially after the recent trip to Mariposa. Among the albums I bought that day was Jesse Winchester's debut. I am not sure why it jumped out of the bin and into my hands. He lived in Canada at the time—maybe we heard about him in Toronto? Possibly, I noted that Robbie Robertson from the Band produced the LP? Maybe I noticed that David Rea, who we had just seen at Mariposa, played guitar? I know now what I didn't know that day: Jesse was living in Canada because he fled America to avoid the draft at the height of Vietnam. My friends and I laughed at the gatefold album sleeve illustrated with his photo on all four sides, thinking it an ego trip rather than—as it was intended—a symbolic Wanted Poster for draft dodging.

Jesse was one of the best songwriters of our time. His debut alone included "Yankee Lady," "Brand New Tennessee Waltz," and "Biloxi," among others that he performed magnificently—and which were later covered by countless artists. It was a remarkable album, as were those that followed. But due to his legal status, Jesse couldn't tour America to promote his records, so he developed a cult following at best. Eventually, Jesse and his U.S. fans benefited from Jimmy Carter's amnesty for draft evaders, and he finally returned to perform here in early 1977.

The first time I "saw" Jesse was on a *Midnight Special* television show in June of that year. A phenomenal ninety minutes of TV: Little Feat, Bonnie Raitt, Emmylou Harris, an extraordinary performance by Neil Young, and Jesse, who seemed positively joyful. Shortly thereafter, I got to see him in person on his amnesty tour at Bogart's in Cincinnati. "Joyful" doesn't adequately describe his stage demeanor. He sounded and looked great, and—who knew—he even *danced* great. Kathy and I fondly remember his performance of "Rhumba Man"—people shouldn't be allowed to have that much fun.

I remained a fan of Jesse's throughout the years. I bought his CDs, all of which included a gem or three or more. I saw the December 16, 2009, episode of Elvis Costello's television program, *Spectacle*, with guests Neko Case, Sheryl Crow, and Ron Sexsmith sitting on stools next to Jesse while he sang his breathtaking

"Sham-a-Ling-Dong-Ding." The camera did a closeup of Neko near the end of the song and captured tears rolling down her cheeks. Elvis was speechless. Ah, again, the power of rock & roll.

At SXSW in March 2013, I attended a showcase put on by the Keith Case & Associates agency. I knew some of the performers in attendance and met with Lee Olsen, a KCA agent with whom I had worked. I told him he had one of my dream acts, Jesse Winchester. Jesse had been diagnosed with cancer of the esophagus in 2011, and although he was reported to be in remission, I presumed there wasn't much of a chance of getting him to Columbus. Lee said he'd check. Within days, I had a call from Lee. Jesse said yes! He would drive by himself from his Charlottesville home and do a one-off show for the Music Fans.

We packed the Grand Valley Ballroom on May 2, 2013. I picked Jesse up at the hotel. He clearly wasn't well. Cancer was back, and he was undergoing a clinical trial in Virginia. That night, he had trouble getting up and down the stairs to the "greenroom" on the balcony. He had to take my arm, and when we got to the top of the stairs, he had to stop and catch his breath. When the show was over, he asked me to take him back to his hotel. I believe he truly enjoyed the evening, but he was exhausted.

Onstage, Jesse was fabulous: gentle, almost fragile, but strong of voice, both singing and telling stories. An absolutely charming Southern gentleman. An honor and privilege to present him, it was a highlight of my "musical life." He only did a show or two after that one. He died April 11, 2014, of bladder cancer. Five months later came the posthumous album *A Reasonable Amount of Trouble*, a deeply moving collection of songs about living and dying.

A SECOND ALBUM I PICKED up that day in 1970 was *Willard*, by John Stewart. I do remember why I bought that one. The back cover credits said "produced by Peter Asher"—James Taylor's producer—and the musicians included Carole King and much of the band from *Sweet Baby James* (and later *Tapestry*). Within days, I returned to buy his previous release, *California Bloodlines* (1969), which became the most-played album in my collection. It remains, with one exception, my top desert island disc. There is no other album I have given so often as a gift—dinner parties, weddings, whatever. I gave it to Kathy for our first Christmas in 1973 (along with a Janis Joplin biography; it is always about the music). Unfortunately, at this writing, *California Bloodlines* is out of print and unavailable other than as a rare copy in used record stores or on eBay. Even a 1994 CD reissue, on the German label Bear Family, combined with songs from *Willard*, can't be found. What a tragedy.

Born and raised in Southern California (apparent from much of his music), John Stewart teamed up with actor Tim Robbins' father (really) to form the Cumberland Three folk group. In 1961 he replaced Dave Guard in the Kingston Trio. He recorded a dozen albums with the Trio, many very successful commercially, before that version of the group disbanded in 1967. That year, John had his first hit—as a songwriter: "Daydream Believer," by the Monkees (later a hit by Anne Murray too). The lyrics convey how reality sets in after the initial blush of romance. Stewart told a great story about the record company demanding the Monkees change the words from "Now you know how 'funky' I can be" to . . . "happy." Stewart squealed. It made no sense. But if he wanted them to record it, he had to agree. Reluctantly, he did. The rest, and hundreds of thousands of dollars of royalty checks later, is history.

In 1968, Stewart began a solo career and, among other things, toured with Robert Kennedy, warming up the crowd during his presidential campaign. That experience was also reflected in some of his early albums, especially *Willard*. In February 1969, Stewart headed to Nashville and recorded *California Bloodlines* with Music City's primo studio musicians, many of whom were playing on Bob Dylan's *Nashville Skyline*, which was being recorded in the same studio at the same time. Stewart's album is simply a master-piece of songwriting, singing, and playing. Not one bit of filler.

Critics loved it. It received "album of the year" and top ten list awards. Over the years, rock, country, folk, and pop artists covered its songs. The Lovin' Spoonful scored a minor hit with "Never Goin' Back." *California Bloodlines* also made a tremendous impact on the next generation of singer-songwriters. Many of the Artistes who have performed at my Zeppelin shows mention it—and Stewart—with reverence. But back in 1969, *California Bloodlines* flopped completely, as did all but one of the albums John Stewart recorded over the decades.

I first saw John live in October 1975, when I visited the Moose in Los Angeles, where he was then working. We had both taken our respective bar exams and were awaiting the results. Fortuitously, Stewart was doing two shows on one night at the legendary Palomino Club in the Valley. We stayed for both shows. Stewart was everything I could have expected and more. I already had placed him on a musical pedestal, and he just rose higher.

Throughout the seventies, John continued to turn out albums, some better than others, but all strong. He developed a significant cult following in different pockets around the country, including Phoenix. *The Phoenix Concerts* live double album found some limited commercial success. But he bounced from one major label record deal to another, never selling even close to expectations. That changed for one brief moment, maybe for the best for John, financially, but causing me another concert surprise.

Throughout the decade, I had introduced his albums to numerous Columbus friends. So when it was announced he would be at Bogart's in Cincinnati, I rounded up a crew and headed off to see this wonderful singer-songwriter. Unbeknownst to me, John had signed with the Robert Stigwood Organisation (Clapton, the Bee Gees, et al.), and they had teamed him with his lifelong admirer, Lindsey Buckingham, to record an album (*Bombs Away*

Dream Babies) with a Fleetwood Mac–type sound. That night, when he hit the stage with a full band and dressed in an all-white suit, it wasn't the same John Stewart I had listened to for ten years. I was stunned and disappointed. But guess what? The album was a huge hit, with a top five single, "Gold," and two other top forty hits. John's follow-up album, *Dream Babies Go Hollywood*, fell flat, and within a year or two, he returned to his solo career, making his own albums and writing great songs, including the likes of "Sweet Dreams Will Come," which he sang with Nanci Griffith, and the extraordinary "Runaway Train," which was a hit for Rosanne Cash.

In the late eighties and early nineties, Les Hershorn ran the Dell, a small club in Columbus. With excellent musical taste, he brought in musicians ranging from a teenage Alison Krauss and the Union Station to a Guy Clark/Townes Van Zandt duo show. I began to suggest performers to him, he'd bring them in, and I'd help sell tickets. Les was also a John Stewart fan, and in the late eighties he brought John to town. Les invited Kathy and me to come early, and we met John while he had dinner before the show. That was the first time I had ever met a "star"—certainly someone who had been so important in my life.

That night, I began to learn that musicians are just people. He was a nice guy. We talked about many things, including music. After I ran through my list of favorite singer-songwriters, he told me I needed to expand my horizons. He wrote down on a place mat a list of musicians I needed to listen to. (I kept the place mat for years, but I don't know what happened to it. I do remember Sting was on it.) Ultimately, John excelled that night, and the crowd loved him.

In March 1995, I promoted my first "national act singer-songwriter show" in Columbus with Tom Russell. It was such a success and so much fun that I decided to continue. Determined to book only those performers whose music I loved, my next choice was John Stewart. I am not sure how I reached out to him in those pre-internet days; I vaguely recall he had an agent in Oregon. One way or another, I booked him to do a show at the Columbus Music Hall. I didn't print tickets and I have no records to help me pin down the exact date, but on a summer night in 1995 we did our second Zeppelin Productions show. The concert went well, but for a guy (me) who did this just for fun, the experience was a little disappointing. John sent his sidekick Dave Batti to do the sound check while he stayed in the hotel. I picked John up and drove him to the gig, but he was clearly doing a concert like others he'd performed thousands of times, and there was no special energy offstage. After the show, a friend of his from Wisconsin who had driven down for the evening whisked him away. Hanging out with the promoter isn't a requirement of the gig, but it's nice to feel at least a little camaraderie with the Artiste. It wasn't there that night.

Nevertheless, I remained a John Stewart fan until he died. He continued to tour, although I never saw him in concert again. I bought some of the one-off independent CDs that he sold from a mailing list, to which I remained a subscriber. At some point, he was diagnosed with early Alzheimer's, and in 2008 he died of a brain aneurysm at the age of sixty-eight.

BY THE TIME I STARTED promoting concerts in 1995, I had gained a deep appreciation for the traditional country music that had primarily hailed from Nashville for decades, not to mention the more recent phenomenon of "Americana" or "alt-country" or whatever you want to call the music coming out of places like Austin. But I must concede that during my four years in North Carolina, I didn't spend much time listening to country music radio, even though it dominated the airwaves in that part of the world. However, I did have a handful of country music experiences then and shortly thereafter that make for some interesting stories and helped set a personal platform for the music I would come to love down the road.

First, in the spring of 1971, I rounded up a handful of Duke friends and dragged them to Raleigh to see Merle Haggard. I'm ashamed to say we did it more as voyeurs than as music fans, and I'm confident that collection of long-haired college boys and short-skirted girls weren't exactly welcome in a crowd of Merle fans, but we lived to tell about it. I can't pin down the exact date of the show, but suffice it to say, Merle was riding a string of number one hits, the two most recent of which had been "Okie from Muskogee" and "The Fightin' Side of Me." (That would be . . . "if you're running down my country, son, you're walking on. . . .")

Whether or not Merle was serious about his apparently conservative political viewpoint (he implied he wasn't in later interviews), I can assure you the crowd was *very* serious. When he got to those songs on the set list, a giant American flag unfurled behind him and the crowd sang along at the top of their lungs. Regardless of politics, I was blown away by the music of Merle and his band, the Strangers.

In 1994, my friends Tom Russell and Dave Alvin coproduced the Merle Haggard tribute *Tulare Dust*, an album that in many ways was a crystallizing moment in what became the Americana music scene. We could debate forever what *Americana* means, and whether it really defines a music genre at all, but it is meant to encompass music and artists with genuine roots in traditional country music and blues, with some rock & roll influence, who don't get aired on the standard radio formats. *Tulare Dust* features many of my favorite artists of the time (and many who went on to become Zeppelin Productions' Artistes, like Tom, Dave, Joe Ely, Rosie Flores, Steve Young, and Katy Moffatt) covering Merle Haggard songs. Thanks in part to *Tulare Dust*, I was converted from a voyeur to a Merle Haggard fan.

My second interaction with a country music performer occurred at the other end of the concert spectrum when, on November 3, 1971, Kris Kristofferson visited Duke. By that time, he had enjoyed a number of hits as a songwriter, including "Sunday Mornin' Comin' Down," "Help Me Make It Through the Night," "For the Good Times," and, of course, "Me and Bobby McGee." But he was unknown as a performer. I had picked up the first issue of his self-titled debut, later re-released with a new cover and title. With a single exception, I bet I was the only person on the Duke campus who had it.

That exception was the one Duke professor with whom I became friends, Bob Krueger. Krueger was born and raised in New Braunfels, Texas, and shortly after I graduated, his father died and Krueger returned home to run the family car dealerships. Ultimately, he ran successfully for the House of Representatives, came close to knocking off John Tower in a Senate race, and ended up as the ambassador to Burundi during the Clinton administration. Long before he did any of those things, Krueger had studied at Oxford, where he made good friends with a Rhodes scholar named Kris Kristofferson. I don't know how much Krueger had to do with Kris coming to Duke, but I know he was a factor.

When Kris played that night, he was dressed in all leather. Let's just say he didn't seem to be lacking in self-confidence. His opening act and his backup band at the time were a collection of big-time Nashville studio musicians. They were fine, but Kris really couldn't sing very well, and it was not the best concert I ever attended. I do remember Kris telling the small crowd that at Oxford it was Krueger who was the singer and songwriter, not Kris.

Another venture into traditional country music arose out of a five-week-plus camping trip Moose and I took around the West in the summer of 1973, after our first year of law school. We listened to music day and night on that trip, but with the exception of singing along to the Allman Brothers' "Ramblin' Man," incessantly played on the radio all summer, music wasn't a big part of the experience. We saw a singer-songwriter named Jim Post at a famous little club in San Francisco called the Drinking Gourd, but surprisingly we didn't enjoy any other live music during the entire trip. But we did visit a Berkeley record store while in the Bay Area. Though thousands of miles from our turntables, we both bought albums, including *Hank Williams' 24 Greatest Hits*. Moose recalls we wanted to see if Hank's "Ramblin' Man," listed on the jacket, was the same song we'd heard the Allmans do for the last five weeks. We ended our trip in Chicago, staying at the very nice home of our friend and my Duke tennis doubles partner Wade Copeland, whose father was the president of Swift Meats. I asked if we could play that Hank Williams record to answer our burning question about "Ramblin' Man." Not the same song, but it turned out that Mr. Copeland was a Louisiana native and knew all Hank's music. We put on the record, and this sophisticated, big-time businessman just let loose, singing along and dancing around the room. When I returned to Columbus, that Hank Williams album became a treasure in my record collection, played regularly for years to come.

Finally, one of my all-time favorite music experiences arose from a visit to the Ashland County Fair in September 1975, a few months after I earned my J.D. from Ohio State. My friend and two-year law school roommate, Bill McIntyre, moved to Mansfield, Ohio, following law school graduation to take a job with a small law firm. (Not the same roommate who dated Kathy once during our first year of law school.) He'd only been there a few months when he called and asked if Kathy and I wanted to come up and see Dolly Parton at the Ashland County Fair, just north of Mansfield.

Kathy and I jumped at the chance. Already a big fan, I had seen a few of Dolly's television shows with Porter Wagoner when I was at Duke. I now regularly listened in the car to AM country radio, which played a number of her solo hits, after she officially split from Porter in 1974, and I had a wonderful "best of Dolly" album. One of the things that impressed me about Dolly was that she wrote her own songs. Among other great ones, she had a number one country hit in 1974 with a song she wrote about her breakup with Wagoner, "I Will Always Love You." Apparently, Elvis wanted to record the song, but would only do so if she succumbed to Colonel Parker's demand that Elvis and company get half the publishing. Dolly said no. Subsequently, she charted with it multiple times, and as recorded by Whitney Houston, it became the biggest-selling single by a woman in music history. Millions of dollars of royalties later, I am sure Dolly is glad she hadn't done what Cindy Walker did when she gave up part of the songwriting credit (and publishing royalties) for "You Don't Know Me" to Eddy Arnold.

Kathy and I headed to Mansfield, picked up Bill, and drove to the Ashland County fairgrounds for what was to be an outdoor concert with the Statler Brothers opening. On the way, the heavens opened up. A torrential rainstorm. When we got to the fair, we learned the decision had been made to move the concert from the outdoor stadium into the animal barn.

So, yes, with animals all around, we saw the Statler Brothers and Dolly Parton (and her Family Band) play on the back of a flatbed truck while hundreds of fans sat around on bleachers, hay bales, or whatever. It was truly one of the most memorable music experiences of my life.

In many ways, my musical life changed in November 1973, when Moose called from Austin, where he attended law school at the University of Texas, and insisted I buy *Viva Terlingua!*, a new album by Jerry Jeff Walker. I knew a little about Jerry Jeff. I remembered seeing a late-sixties LP in the record store bins by his New York–based band, Circus Maximus. And during his Greenwich Village folkie days, he released the solo album *Mr. Bojangles*, with a title track that became a hit for everyone from the Nitty Gritty Dirt

Band to Sammy Davis Jr. At Mariposa, I heard David Bromberg do a long narration about his years of playing it every night with Jerry Jeff and the terrible things they'd do to the song in the dressing room after the show. But in 1973, I didn't know much about the burgeoning Austin music scene, notwithstanding the fact that Moose and I had spent that whole summer driving and camping around the West. (He must have spent too much time studying during his first year of law school.) I bought the record, put it on, and from the very first song, "Gettin' By," to the last, the album was a classic. It really did change my musical life.

For starters, it introduced me to Guy Clark, with his "Desperadoes Waiting for a Train." More than ten years later, it gave me another song to sing to the kids at bedtime—Michael Martin Murphey's "Backslider's Wine," which I later heard by Gary Stewart. (I have no idea why I sang that one to the girls, but imagine my surprise when Emily, at the age of three or so, started singing it in the checkout line at the grocery store, replete with the line "I fell down on a barroom floor.")

The emotions on the album ran from the partying of Jerry Jeff's "Sangria Wine" to the sadness of his "Wheels." He reprised a song he had recorded on an earlier album, "Little Bird," an absolute favorite of which I heard Jerry Jeff tell a crowd at the Dell in Columbus years later was "written for a girl from Euclid, Ohio." (I've always wondered *who?*) The album included Ray Wylie Hubbard's "Up Against the Wall, Redneck Mothers," a song that Ray told the Music Fans at a Zeppelin concert he had grown to hate 363 days out of the year. ("But those other two days, when I walk to the mailbox . . .") And the last song on the album was Gary P. Nunn's (he wrote it and sang it) "London Homesick Blues," which not only became the theme song for the *Austin City Limits* television show, but also was one of my mother's favorite songs.

I quickly learned that *Viva Terlingua!* wasn't the first album Jerry Jeff had recorded after relocating to Austin, so I bought his self-titled, more polished LP from a year earlier. All but a pair of the songs were Jerry Jeff originals, and those two were by this still-mysterious-to-me Guy Clark, including "That Old Time Feeling" and one of my future favorite sing-alongs, "L.A. Freeway."

Jerry Jeff is one of those singer-songwriters who kept popping up in my life, at least for a while. When I was in Los Angeles in the fall of 1975, when Moose was at work, I would drive my Ford Pinto rental around the west side of L.A., often ending up in Tower Records on Sunset Boulevard. There, I bought Jerry Jeff's *Ridin' High*, playing it nonstop that week and discovering Chuck Pyle's "Jaded Lover," another fab sing-along. (Just ask the guys with whom I took golf and white-water rafting trips in the 1980s.)

Jerry Jeff would even be part of my honeymoon: Kathy and I got married on June 19, 1976, and we had a first-class wedding trip planned for New Orleans. About two weeks before the big day, we realized it wasn't in our budget. (We had also made expensive plans to attend the Montreal Olympics the next month.) So we changed our honeymoon to three nights in Cincinnati, 110 miles down I-71. It turned out to be a wonderful trip. We took in the zoo, Kings Island amusement park, and a Monday night Reds vs. Dodgers game. And in a completely unanticipated development, a look at the Sunday paper revealed that Jerry Jeff Walker was playing at Bogart's on Tuesday. We decided to stay an extra day and, truly out of money, moved for our last night from the relatively expensive Carrousel Inn to a Red Roof Inn on the north side of town.

On Tuesday evening, we headed to Bogart's, our first of many visits there over the next ten years or so, and saw Jerry Jeff and the Lost Gonzo Band. They were fantastic. Great songs, hot band, and Jerry Jeff in top form. And continuing that small world thing, the opening act was a young singer-songwriter named Katy Moffatt, who would show up in my musical life in a big way twenty years later. She opened for Jerry Jeff on that whole tour, and although I can honestly say I only vaguely remember her that evening, she was certainly there, as confirmed by her own memory and my internet research.

A year or two later, Jerry Jeff came to Columbus to play Zachariah's Redeye Saloon, a campus-area bar that hosted live music. By this point, I was a huge fan and had foisted Jerry Jeff's music on countless Central Ohio friends. I rounded up a bunch of them, and on a hot summer night we headed to Zachariah's.

Hot is the operative word. It felt like 110 degrees in the place. We sat there sweating and downing cold drinks, waiting for the 8:00 p.m. show. Waiting past 8:30, 9:00, 9:30. It must have been 10:00 when they finally hit the stage. The band played a song or two, then a very inebriated Jerry Jeff came out sweating, stumbling, struggling, and finally simply leaving. He walked off the stage and didn't come back. We had waited for two hours or more for what seemed like a fifteen-minute "show." We left in abject disappointment, only to find out later that at some point after he exited the stage, he'd put on a great show—acoustically, in the alley behind the bar. *Sigh*.

The only other time I saw Jerry Jeff live was when Les Hershorn brought him to the Dell in the late eighties. Still a huge fan, I bought all his records and continued to introduce his music to friends. We had another large contingent in attendance that evening. A few of us arrived early for the sound check and tried to convey our admiration. He really wasn't interested. He was sober, as far as I could tell. But he was a grouch onstage, at one point telling one of my friends in the crowd to quit fooling around with a cowboy hat. I must say, he did play a fine show that night. Tom Russell told me early on to "separate the art from the artist," and Jerry Jeff was a perfect example of the need to do just that.

When I started promoting shows, I put Jerry Jeff on my list of favorites to bring to town, albeit with some trepidation. Notwithstanding my brief experience at the Dell and, honestly, the personal concerns about Jerry Jeff I'd picked up from the media and from other musicians, I did reach out once to his wife, Susan, who booked him, about coming to Columbus. Granted, he wasn't touring much, so it would have been something of a one-off, but she quoted me a price that was a large multiple of anything I was paying anyone at that point. He never did a Zeppelin Productions show, and sadly, he passed away in late 2020.

On the other hand, Guy Clark did do a Zeppelin show. I had seen Guy live a couple of times, and he was always something of a dream act for me when I started Zeppelin Productions. The first time I saw Guy live, Kathy and I were in New York in the 1980s, on another hot summer night, and he happened to be playing at a small club in the Village. Naturally, we went. I think it was the legendary Gerde's Folk City, but I'm not sure. It was downstairs and oozed an atmosphere to rival Zachariah's—unbearably hot.

Before the show, I saw Guy sitting by himself at the bar drinking a Rolling Rock; I went up, introduced myself, and suggested he needed to come to Columbus. He was suitably unimpressed, not really rude, but gruff and pretty dismissive. I'm not sure whether I pursued it or if Les did it on his own, but at some point thereafter, the Dell hosted a Guy Clark/Townes Van Zandt duo show. In retrospect, that was an exceptional night, especially given Townes' failure to make it through many a show in his time (including a later solo performance in Columbus). The fact that Townes was sober enough to get through this one was wonderful, although I recall he did most of the show sitting on a stool, rocking back and forth with his eyes closed.

Many years later, I worked through Guy's agent at Keith Case & Associates, and on April 1, 2004, Zeppelin Productions produced "An Acoustic Evening with Guy Clark" at the Columbus Music Hall. Not unlike John Stewart, it was clear Guy had done thousands of shows and this was just one more. He sent his guitarist, Verlon Thompson, to do the sound check. I picked Guy up at the hotel, he was wonderful onstage, and then I took him back. But he really didn't have much to say. No warm-and-fuzzies at all. None-theless, I have to admit, it was an honor to have met him and produce a show with one of the founders and true patriarchs of that whole Americana sound.

FOUR

My Rock Pantheon

WHEN PUSHED TO NAME MY FAVORITE ARTIST OF ALL time, I have been known to say, "There is no one I would drive farther to see, pay more to see, or have seen more often than Neil Young." And if I were told I could have just one album on a desert island, it would be Neil's *Tonight's the Night*.

Neil first caught my ear in early 1967 via Buffalo Springfield's debut album, initially released in December 1966. Shortly thereafter, band member Stephen Stills wrote a song about a riot on the Sunset Strip following the closing of a nightclub. (Not exactly the fact pattern that would inspire Neil's "Ohio" a few years later.) "For What It's Worth" was released as a single and by March became a top ten hit without even being on the LP. So the album was re-released with that song added; a friend and I each bought it that spring—my copy had the song and his didn't.

It was Neil who really grabbed my attention, not just his unique vocal style, but especially his songwriting, including several originals sung by Richie Furay. The Springfield recorded two more albums before their demise: *Buffalo Springfield Again* in November

1967 (still one of my favorites) and, the following July *Last Time Around*, with a pair of Neil's classics, "On the Way Home" (sung by Richie) and "I Am a Child." By the time of the latter's release, the "band" had transitioned to simply a trio of excellent solo performers in the form of Steve, Richie, and Neil.

I became obsessed with Neil's music. He spoke to me—the combination of wonderful lyrics, some direct and others hopelessly enigmatic, and fabulous melodies. He could rock with the best of them, but there was also evidence of the great acoustic singer-songwriter to come. Neil's first solo album hit the streets in January 1969, and I bought it right away. In fact, I have the version that really bothered Neil. He had the sound remixed and it was re-released soon thereafter with a slightly different cover.

But Neil was just getting started. By May, he had released *Everybody Knows This Is Nowhere*, recorded live over a two-day period with his new band, Crazy Horse, including classics like "Cinnamon Girl," "Cowgirl in the Sand," and "Down by the River," all of which he said he wrote in one day while in bed with a 103-degree fever. I loved the album, couldn't stop playing it, and foisted it on everyone that summer and, especially, when I returned to Duke for my sophomore year. Almost as amazing to me: the single release of "Cinnamon Girl," backed with the solo acoustic "Sugar Mountain," recorded live in Ann Arbor a few years earlier. "Sugar Mountain" became one of my jukebox staples, and the song inspired his friend Joni Mitchell's "Circle Game." The two sides of that 45 rpm record say all that needs to be said about Neil's musical spectrum, although that presupposes his music is actually linear enough for a spectrum.

By August 1969, within three months of the release of the Crazy Horse album *and* the stellar Crosby, Stills and Nash debut, Neil had joined CSN, and Crosby, Stills, Nash & Young were performing at Woodstock. I stood in line waiting for the Record Bar in Durham to open that day in March 1970 when their debut as

CSNY, *Déjà Vu*, was released. By summer, the album hit number one and they were filling arenas like the show I saw in Public Auditorium on July 3.

As CSNY rolled in the gold, Neil went into the studio with a mix-and-match group of musicians (including a young guitar player he'd just met in Washington, D.C., Nils Lofgren) and cut another classic, the aptly named *After the Goldrush*. Released in September 1970, it only further cemented Neil's critical and commercial success. It also cemented my reputation as a music connoisseur since I had been raving about him to my friends for a few years. That fall, Neil embarked on a solo acoustic tour. Recordings from those shows, originally intended for a live album, weren't officially released until four decades later, but bootlegs made the rounds for years (including one once loaned to me by guitarist Andrew Hardin, an album he taught himself to play from). It was during that tour, that I saw Neil on the Johnny Cash television show in February 1971, furthering my infatuation.

Throughout that year, Neil recorded a number of new songs he'd been performing on tour, many cut in Nashville with studio musicians he dubbed the Stray Gators. On February 1, 1972, *Harvest* was released, yielding the only number one song of Neil's career, "Heart of Gold." The album itself also topped the charts and stayed on my turntable that last semester at Duke. Neil's reaction, as he said describing "Heart of Gold" in the liner notes of his 1977 retrospective, *Decade*, was that the song "put me in the middle of the road. Traveling there soon became a bore, so I headed for the ditch. A rougher side but I saw more interesting people there."

Head to the ditch he did, into a very dark period for Neil and his music. In the fall of 1972, while rehearsing for a tour, Neil fired a dysfunctional Danny Whitten, the Crazy Horse lead guitarist who was wracked with drug issues. Shortly thereafter, Whitten overdosed; then on June 4, 1973, Neil's roadie Bruce Berry also died of an overdose. The guy who had written "The Needle and the Damage Done" lost two close friends to drugs in a matter of months.

Neil turned to the music. He assembled a group of his musician friends, including Nils Lofgren, and fueled by tequila and who knows what else, Neil and a band he dubbed the Santa Monica Flyers recorded—essentially live in one day (or night)—much of what became *Tonight's the Night*. It opens and closes with two different versions of the title track, Neil singing, *"Bruce Berry was a working man, he used to load that Econoline van."* One cut features Danny Whitten singing his own "Come on Baby Let's Go Downtown," live with Neil and Crazy Horse at the Fillmore East in 1970. Neil wrote the rest of the songs—dark, brooding, melodic—and often sung out of key and clearly under the influence. The powerful album wouldn't see the light of day until 1975; Warner Bros. refused to release it at first. But that didn't keep Neil from going on tour with the Flyers to "promote" it. And for the first time (other than the CSNY arena show in 1970), I got to see Neil Young live.

On November 18, 1973, Neil and the Santa Monica Flyers played Mershon Auditorium, a three-thousand-or-so-seat venue on the Ohio State campus. I recall the show billed as the "Tonight's the Night" tour and the scheduled start time as midnight. A solo Nils Lofgren opened the show. I knew him from my incessant reading about Neil and by virtue of Nils' own band, Grin, whose debut LP was constantly on my basement turntable at 112 West Trinity Avenue (my off-campus abode during senior year at Duke). Nils was magical that night, slipping and sliding gracefully around the stage, on guitar and keyboard. He played new solo material and some of those great Grin songs, including my favorite, "Like Rain."

Decades later, Kathy and I actually spent significant time with Nils and his wife, first hanging with them at a party before a Rock

Hall tribute to the Rolling Stones, when he played in the house band, and later at events in connection with his induction into the Rock & Roll Hall of Fame as part of the E Street Band. He's as genuine in person as he seemed onstage that night in 1973.

After Nils' Mershon set, the stage and auditorium went dark following the break. When the lights came up, barely, Neil and the band were onstage. There was a palm tree and the wooden Indian that has accompanied Neil onstage ever since. The crowd clearly came to hear "Heart of Gold," "After the Goldrush," and "Cowgirl in the Sand" but got . . . *Tonight's the Night*, beginning with the title track, start to finish. An "album" that wouldn't even exist for another two years.

Neil didn't speak to the audience all night until just before the last song, when he said, "Here's one you've heard before." The crowd, most of whom were in a state of shock trying to process what was happening, burst into an applause of relief, only to have Neil and the band perform again the opening number, just as the album would do two years later. "Bruce Berry was a working man. . . ."

It was a special night for me—one I will always remember. My favorite artist, then and now, doing a totally unique performance of what are, in fact, great songs. Dark and brooding, for sure, but melodic and accessible, even on the first listen at a concert. It was also one of my first dates with Kathy, and what a test it must have been—a weekday, midnight concert with a very unpredictable Neil Young doing an entire set list of songs no one had ever heard. I guess I passed the test.

Neil stayed in the ditch, at least for a while, with another album of introspective songs, *On the Beach*, released in July 1974. Although slightly more polished than the still unissued *Tonight's the Night*, it continued to alienate his mainstream "Heart of Gold" fans. Even the critics seemed mystified, although the album is now considered something of a classic. I loved it from the first time I heard it, from opener "Walk On" to closer "Ambulance Blues," with the autobiographical "I guess I'll call it sickness gone, it's hard to say the meaning of this song," which kind of sums up Neil at the time.

By the summer of 1974, Neil had returned to CSNY, who embarked on rock & roll's first major stadium tour. I saw them with Kathy and my brother, Jim, still in high school, on whom I'd been foisting music since the late 1960s. It's our common bond to this day. CSNY headlined the World Series of Rock at Cleveland Municipal Stadium on August 31, 1974, with openers Jesse Colin Young, Santana, and the Band. Seated on the upper deck and parallel to the stage, we didn't have the best acoustics, but we got to see the comings and goings backstage, including volleyball games among the musicians and crew.

My passion for Neil's music continued. By the mid-seventies, he was beginning to climb out of the ditch, which was clear the next time I "saw" him, in June 1977, when Kathy and I tuned in to *The Midnight Special*, that late-night TV show where we first saw Jesse Winchester. Typically filmed in Burbank, on this night the show featured Neil and Crazy Horse taped live in London a couple months earlier. The then unreleased "Like a Hurricane" was like nothing I'd ever seen on television—almost ten minutes long, Neil going crazy on guitar, an electric fan blowing his hair back. And what an amazing song! On first listen—and to this day.

In the fall of 1978, Kathy and I took a driving tour of New England, catching both the peak colors of the fall foliage and on October 2 the release of Neil's new album, *Comes a Time*, a return to the mainstream with a set of accessible, well-produced songs, featuring backup vocals by Nicolette Larson. We bought the cassette, listened to it incessantly on our travels, and sang along, especially to one of the first covers I'd heard from Neil—Ian Tyson's "Four Strong Winds." That same year, Neil embarked on a lengthy tour, which he called Rust Never Sleeps, ultimately releasing an album of the same name in July 1979. Once again, he started and ended the album (and the shows) with the same song, first an acoustic "My My, Hey Hey (Out of the Blue)" and then an electric "Hey Hey, My My (Into the Black)," the lyrics of which remain a staple of the rock world. The LP also includes perhaps my favorite Neil Young song, sing-along or otherwise, "Powderfinger."

After an extraordinarily prolific decade, Neil took a break from the road and studio, presumably dealing with the challenges of having (with two different mothers) two children with cerebral palsy. That circumstance led to his album *Trans* and the tour in support, with Neil singing through a vocoder, a device that heavily distorted his vocals. Neil said it helped him communicate with his kids, but it wasn't particularly effective in communicating with his audience, including Kathy and me; we found it weird. We saw him at the Richfield Coliseum on February 21, 1983, with daughter Nora seven months in utero—a scary experience to be with a very pregnant woman surrounded by a mass of dope-smoking people.

The 1980s were tough years for most Neil Young fans. His new label, Geffen, actually sued him for breach of contract, claiming Neil was making music "unrepresentative of himself." At one point, Neil recorded a fairly hard-core country album, which Geffen rejected. Not to be deterred, Neil went on the road with his country band, the International Harvesters. Kathy and I saw them open the "remodeled" Agora in Columbus, now called the Newport, on September 11, 1984, and they were great. Geffen finally released a revised version of Neil's country album, *Old Ways*, eleven months later, in August 1985.

Just as the decade came to an end, Neil repeated his magic from ten years earlier, re-signing with Warner Bros. and releasing *Freedom*, his first outstanding album since *Rust Never Sleeps*. Once again, he opened with an acoustic version of a now-classic song, "Rockin' in the Free World," and closed with the electric take. *Freedom* received an excellent response from relieved critics and fans alike, including me, and the subsequent tour with Crazy Horse was tremendous.

During the course of his career, Neil has been as prolific and creative as any rock & roll artist. Although not always successful, artistically or commercially, he has consistently pushed the envelope, musically and otherwise, often in support of causes he is passionate about.

Throughout it all, I have remained a fan. I can't begin to recount the number of times I have seen him live over the years, with a full band and solo. I saw him frequently at Polaris (later Germain) Amphitheater in Columbus and at Riverbend in Cincinnati. Once, he appeared at Polaris with Crazy Horse as the headliner for the traveling H.O.R.D.E. festival. He agreed to the tour only if he could set up a giant Lionel train display under a tent at each site. He had helped purchase Lionel out of Chapter 11 because his sons could operate the trains. Neil and one of his sons ran the trains before each show as hundreds of fans watched.

In one of the more uncomfortable evenings, Kathy; my brother, Jim; and his wife, Lisa; and I saw Neil solo acoustic at the E.J. Thomas Hall in Akron where, halfway through his second or third song, he stopped and told chattering people in the front row that he would pay them twice what they'd paid for their seats if they would leave. (They didn't, and after the intermission, he sort of apologized.) We also attended the very strange Greendale tour, where he and the cast performed the entire "musical." Another time, Kathy and I flew to Toronto to see the last show of a tour, where rumor had it that he was about to release his "archives," thinking we might be treated to an evening of classics. Instead, we only heard a bunch of new songs about cars. In 2002, Kathy and I took in the reunited CSNY tour, where Neil was the only one even passable, the others just sounding awful.

Twelve years later, in early 2014, Neil played a series of solo acoustic shows at Carnegie Hall in New York and the Dolby Theater in Los Angeles. Kathy and I went coast to coast to see both. In New York, on January 9, everything sounded fabulous: his voice, the guitar, the harmonica, pianos—both the baby grand and the upright. But the key to the show was the set list. We got old Buffalo Springfield along with some of his solo staples and rarities. He also did two covers, including Phil Ochs' "Changes." (Ochs graduated from Mohawk High School in Columbus and briefly studied at Ohio State.) Neil said Ochs "didn't have the makeup for the long run," gently mentioning that he had hung himself, which may not have registered with much of the crowd. Neil's second cover was "Needle of Death," by Bert Jansch, who Neil described as the "best acoustic guitar player" ever. (He added that Jimi Hendrix was the best he ever heard on the electric guitar.) During that song, he briefly turned his back to the audience, singing to the wooden Indian onstage with the spotlight on it for a few seconds. A poignant moment for those few of us who had seen the unforgettable Tonight's the Night tour where that Indian held a prominent place onstage. Finally, he ended the set with his "hit song," dedicating "Heart of Gold" to "my sweetheart—she's in the house," a reference to his new girlfriend, Daryl Hannah.

On March 29, we completed the Neil Young coast-to-coast double by seeing him at the Dolby, this time with daughter Nora in tow. He was even better than in New York. The set list was similar, but with a few stunning additions. Neil was softer, warmer, and calmer, and more talkative and engaging with the crowd. He did "Changes" again, but his second cover was a killer, introduced with the words: "When I was first starting out, there was a songwriter in Canada. Wrote lots of great songs." Then he did a transcendent version of Gordon Lightfoot's "If You Could Read My Mind." The thirtyish group next to us went crazy over the song, trying to figure out who "Gordy" was—as Neil called him. Twenty seconds into "Flying on the Ground," from the Buffalo Springfield debut, he stopped and said, "I just remembered. I wrote this song two blocks from here. I need to start it over. But that's not bad." *Wow!* Neil concluded to a standing ovation, and as he returned for the encore, he switched guitars at the last minute. He started to sing and play: *"They were hiding behind hay bales. . . ."* "Thrasher!" The first time live in thirty-six years! A song about a lot of things, including, as he once admitted in an interview, Crosby, Stills and Nash: "They were just dead weight to me. . . ." Finally, he finished with "Long May You Run," an ode to a car. But like most of Neil's songs, about so much more.

I've never met Neil, although I did have a couple of close calls, beginning in January 2002. I drove up to Cleveland late one evening in a horrendous snowstorm for our law firm's New Partner Program, which was to begin the next day. Close to midnight, I pulled up in front of the Ritz-Carlton in a blizzard. With no doorman out front, I began getting my bag from my trunk. A large white van pulled up behind me and the driver emerged with a guitar case in hand. Out of the passenger side stepped . . . Neil. He looked at me, smiled, and from five feet away said, "Hi, man." By the time I gathered my things and went inside, he was gone. It turned out that CSNY had rented the Wolstein Arena at Cleveland State to rehearse for their upcoming tour and they were all staying at the Ritz. Over the weekend, the other three were spotted a time or two in the hotel. But no additional Neil sightings.

Then on March 14, 2005, Neil inducted the Pretenders into the Rock & Roll Hall of Fame. I had been on the board for less than a year, but I'd become good friends with then-CEO Terry Stewart, who appreciated my passion for music. I sprung for a ticket to the ceremony, held in the ballroom at the Waldorf Astoria in New York. After inducting Chrissie Hynde and the band, Neil joined them onstage for a rousing version of "My City Was Gone." After the ceremony, I made my way to the hotel's Bull & Bear restaurant for a private after-party hosted by Jann Wenner, spending a few late-night hours seated at the northeast corner of the Cheers-type square bar. (More about that evening later, especially my first meeting with Bruce Springsteen.) For two-plus hours, Neil and his second wife, Pegi, sat less than ten feet away in a booth with another couple. I didn't have the nerve to bother him. I had heard and read enough to know I risked getting the "bad Neil." It turned out I had excellent judgment. That very night, Neil began to experience headaches and blurry vision. Within two weeks, he had surgery for a brain aneurysm.

NEIL WASN'T THE ONLY CALIFORNIA-BASED artist who caught my ear in the early seventies, nor was he the only one we saw at Mershon Auditorium in those days. On March 4, 1974, Kathy and I witnessed two very young, up-and-coming performers on a double-bill in that auditorium's relatively intimate confines: Jackson Browne and Linda Ronstadt. The first of numerous times I've seen Jackson over the years, but it was my only time catching Linda.

At that point, Jackson had already released two albums, the first of which included the hit "Doctor My Eyes" and one of my favorites to this day, "Looking Into You." The second, 1973's *For Everyman*, was equally good and included another of my faves, "These Days," the Tom Rush version of which I had worn out in the depressed days of my first year of law school. It also included Jackson's version of "Take It Easy," the hit he'd written for the Eagles. He was only months from releasing my favorite Jackson Browne album, *Late for the Sky*, so he probably played songs from it that night.

Like Jackson, Linda was already a successful recording artist, although neither were the megastars they would become in just a few years. (Heck, they were double-billing at Mershon.) I had loved her music since her hit with the Stone Poneys in late 1967, a great version of Michael Nesmith's "Different Drum." Linda and the band had played at Duke in the spring of 1968, and the students were still buzzing about her performance when I got there in the fall. Linda had embarked on a successful solo career, first with some country-tinged albums, one of which included another of my jukebox staples, "Long, Long Time," and then a series of wonderful records under the production and tutelage of Peter Asher. In fact, like Jackson, when we saw them in concert, she was just months from releasing my favorite, *Heart Like a Wheel*. My guess is we heard songs from that record too. The show was mesmerizing, and I'm sure everyone in the crowd fell in love with one or both of those beautiful people.

Just two months later, we were back in Mershon to see another California act, the Eagles. Again, I had their first two albums, both produced by Glyn Johns. (Decades later, Kathy and I would donate money to dedicate a plaque to Johns, a Rock Hall inductee, which sits in the sidewalk outside Public Auditorium in Cleveland.) In fact, the second album, *Desperado*, had been a turntable mainstay since its release a year earlier. This tour was promoting *On the Border*, continuing the string of hits written by the band and friends like Jackson Browne, J.D. Souther, and Jack Tempchin. It was the first of many times I saw the Eagles over the years, and I felt the same way I did every time I saw them—it sounded just like playing the records, for better or worse.

In those years, the California sound resulted from a commonality of producers (Peter Asher, for one), songwriters, and studio musicians, including keyboardist Craig Doerge. He played in the Section, a band that in whole or in part backed up folks like James Taylor, Jackson Browne, and various combinations of Crosby, Stills and Nash for years. Craig was close with the late Bill Schweitzer, my friend who managed BakerHostetler's Washington, D.C., office. They met in kindergarten, roomed together at Trinity College in Connecticut, and remained close through adulthood. Our firm merged into the Los Angeles market in 1990, and shortly thereafter, Bill invited me to join him at dinner with Craig and his wife, Judy Henske. I certainly knew who Craig was from my years of scouring album liner notes. But although I knew Judy's name, it wasn't until I did my homework before dinner that I discovered she had not only been a relatively big name in the Greenwich Village folk circles of the early sixties, she had also been romantically involved with Woody Allen and inspired his character Annie Hall. (Judy was born in Chippewa Falls, Wisconsin, etc.) Oh, and she had also been married to Jerry Yester from the Lovin' Spoonful.

At the restaurant, I was a good boy for about twenty minutes until I started firing away at both of them, especially Craig, for insights about my heroes. Conceding now that I have no idea how his relationship ended with either, Craig suggested neither Jackson Browne nor James Taylor were folks you wanted to invite for dinner, at least in their early days. At one point, I asked Craig to identify the one artist who was most respected by others—with whom other artists would most want to work. He didn't hesitate: "Neil Young." I knew it!

After we left the restaurant, we headed to Santa Monica, and at 1:00 a.m. we strolled the Promenade. Judy, who's six feet tall, and I were walking ahead of Craig and Bill. We were shoulder to shoulder and she had her arm around me. We had been together for hours, mostly talking music. At one point, after I made some obscure musical reference, she stopped, stepped away from me, threw up her hands, and said, "I have been in this business for thirty years, and I've never met anyone who knows as much about music as you!" That really made my night.

I HAVE TO ADMIT THAT Bruce Springsteen ranks right up there with Neil Young in my rock & roll pantheon. And the truth is, although I may not have seen Bruce as often as I've seen Neil, and I may not have traveled quite as far to see Bruce as I have Neil, I have paid more to see Bruce (on Broadway) than I have paid to see any rock & roll artist. Ever.

Now, having said that, I have to confess I missed the Boss coming out of the box. And having missed him at first, my rock &

roll snobbery made me a little late to the party altogether. I felt if I hadn't discovered him, he couldn't be all that good. I saw his first two 1973 albums, *Greetings from Asbury Park, N.J.* and *The Wild, the Innocent & the E Street Shuffle*, in record stores, but I never bought them. Honestly, I don't even remember hearing them at the time. Each album only sold 25,000 or so on release, so chances are I didn't even know anyone who had one. I also missed the classic quote from Jon Landau in the May 22, 1974, issue of Boston's *The Real Paper*, when he famously wrote, "I saw rock & roll future, and its name is Bruce Springsteen."

Finally, my big miss was *Born to Run*, released in late August 1975. It rose to number three on the charts, and in the last week of October, Bruce was on the cover of both *Time* and *Newsweek*. With my rock snobbery in full bloom, I wanted nothing to do with this new star who had snuck by me to the top of the charts. Even when my good friend Bob Barnett, the Dancing Bear, played the album for me, I refused to fully commit myself to fandom, notwithstanding the fact that the music was really special.

Then I saw him live—for the first of many times: February 16, 1977, at Veterans Memorial Auditorium in Columbus. The Dancing Bear dragged Kathy and me there. By the end of the night, I was a complete convert, having never seen anything like it: fantastic music from *Born to Run*; compelling material from the first two LPs, including my introduction to "Rosalita"; and songs from the yet-to-be-recorded *Darkness on the Edge of Town*. But also songs that wouldn't see the light of day for decades on compilations like *Tracks* and, especially, wonderful cover songs. I didn't know all the music, but it didn't matter because of the unbelievable energy in the venue and, especially, onstage, as Bruce jumped and slid, up and down and sideways, for hours. Nonstop.

That was the "lawsuit tour," because Bruce's recording career was severely interrupted by litigation with his former manager, Mike Appel. When *Darkness on the Edge of Town* was finally released, in June 1978, almost three years after *Born to Run*, I was ready. I now had "discovered" Bruce and grabbed the album the day it was released, playing it constantly for anyone and everyone. "Favorites" have as much to do with the circumstances in which you first hear the music, and in many ways, *Darkness* continues to be my favorite Bruce album.

I have so many Bruce memories. Sitting in a huge thunderstorm on the breezeway at 3529 Snouffer Road (our little house in the country in what was then the far northwest side of Columbus), listening to the famous August 9, 1978, concert from the Cleveland Agora, broadcast live on eight stations around the Midwest. I saw him twice in a suite at the Schottenstein Center with football star and now-announcer Chris Spielman and his late wife, Stefanie, both huge Springsteen fans. (Stef and I became close friends through our mutual service on the foundation board for the James Cancer Hospital at Ohio State.) And Kathy, Jim, Lisa, and I caught what was Bruce's next-to-last show with the Big Man, Clarence Clemons, as Bruce wound down his 2009 tour. I still remember the two of them standing on the back of the stage in Cleveland, the rest of the band having departed after multiple encores, and seeing Bruce soak up the adulation. Bruce appeared to be contemplating just one more song when Clarence gently put an arm around him, took the guitar away, and led him down the steps.

I've experienced Bruce solo, with the E Street Band (with and without Steve, with and without Nils . . . yes, that same Nils), and with his non–E Street bands. I saw him headline the 2012 SXSW Festival, just after he delivered his brilliant keynote address and as he was getting ready to kick off the first tour after Clarence had died, albeit ably replaced by Clarence's nephew Jake. Throughout the last four decades, there haven't been many Springsteen tours where I didn't catch him somewhere—Columbus, Cleveland, Cincinnati. Sometimes, it's multiple times on the same tour.

In 1995, he performed at the Rock & Roll Hall of Fame grand opening concert, where he and his band served as the house band for many artists, including an aborted show-ender with Chuck Berry. And he paid tribute to Woody Guthrie at the initial Rock Hall American Music Masters program in 1996. In 2009, at the Rock Hall's twenty-fifth anniversary concerts at Madison Square Garden, he not only played his own songs but also joined the E Street Band backing up other performers.

I've never been as impacted by Bruce, though, as I was on January 11, 2018, when we had the privilege of seeing *Springsteen on Broadway*—a privilege in multiple respects. Kathy had a rough 2017, with five months of chemotherapy after an ovarian cancer diagnosis. (Post-treatment prognosis is better than good when the word "cured" is used.) And although the tickets were close to impossible to get on first release, I had become friendly with Jon Landau, Bruce's longtime manager with whom I serve on the board of the Rock & Roll Hall of Fame Foundation. He was kind enough to provide us with access to two fifth-row, center-aisle seats for the show. I had read Bruce's autobiography, *Born to Run*, which now has a place on my "shelf of honor" (my absolute favorite books), and I'd heard plenty about the show. But until you saw it, you really couldn't fathom how this one-man musical used songs to tell Bruce's life story and convey his insights into humanity and the world. As I said in a Facebook post after the show, "First in his book, now in this show, and probably always in his music (but maybe we didn't know it), he provides such transparency into his life, mind, soul, and heart that it helps us understand things about ourselves. This couple of hours was as powerful and captivating as it gets. It was an honor to be a part of it."

By the way, that autobiography is special to me for a number of reasons, but one of them is the jacket photograph. You see, some number of years ago, when Kathy and I wandered through Soho, we stumbled into the Morrison Hotel Gallery, with an exhibit of dozens of Springsteen photos taken by Frank Stefanko. I bought and had framed a striking picture of Bruce leaning on the fender of his Corvette, probably taken during the cover shoot for *Darkness on the Edge of Town*. I proudly hung it on a wall in my home office, only to be stunned when the exact picture appeared on the jacket of his memoir.

From time to time, people ask if I have met famous people in the course of my dabbling in the music business and, especially, my involvement with the Rock Hall. The obvious answer is . . . yes. But meeting Bruce is probably at the top of the list. I've met him twice, initially on the evening of March 14, 2005—or, actually, early the next morning. The same night that I had the foresight to *not* introduce myself to Neil Young, I had the judgment to do so to Bruce. He inducted U2 that evening at the Waldorf, and like most of the inductees and presenters, he attended Jann Wenner's private after-party at Bull & Bear. I sat at the bar next to Samuel L. Jackson, chatting with Dan Aykroyd and ogling everyone from Bono to Paul Shaffer. At about 2:00 a.m., I spotted Bruce, who had been talking with folks all evening, standing quietly with his arms folded leaning against the bar. I made my move and had my line—my hook—ready. I walked up to him, stuck out my hand, and said, "I'm Alec Wightman, I'm on the board of the Rock & Roll Hall of Fame and I just want to thank you for all you've done for the Rock Hall." He kept leaning back, arms folded, and nicely, but barely, acknowledged my presence with a brief handshake. Then . . . the hook: "I have a good friend, Tom Russell, who once showed me a longhand letter you wrote him congratulating him on a new CD." Bruce stood up straight. His eyes lit up. He said, "I remember writing that letter. Do you know Tom and I have never met?" I said I did, but added that Tom would be getting an e-mail from me at 3:00 a.m. telling him that I met Bruce. With that, the attractive redhead standing next to Bruce stuck out her hand and said, "I'm Patti Scialfa." I replied with a smile. "I know who you are." I shook her hand, said I didn't want to disturb them any longer, and we parted with smiles all around.

The second time we met was April 10, 2014, at another of Jann's after-parties, this time in a private room at Barclay's Center following Bruce's induction of the E Street Band.

That evening was special all the way around, but at some point well into the party, Bruce was standing alone, again leaning—this time on a pillar. He had what looked to be a bodyguard keeping people away from him. (Jon Landau later told me that wouldn't have been someone in Bruce's employ because he doesn't use them.) Once again, in my tux, I confidently walked up to him, shook his hand, and this time had a more meaningful Rock Hall line: "I'm Alec Wightman and I am chair of the board of the Rock & Roll Hall of Fame." With that, he stepped up, smiled, and thanked *me* for what I'd done for the Rock Hall. I motioned Kathy up, made the introduction, and the three of us chatted for what seemed like twenty minutes and was probably ten. I again told him the Tom Russell story, he again remembered the letter (although I'm not sure he remembered our prior meeting), and he couldn't have been nicer.

THROUGHOUT THE LATE 1970S, THE 1980s, and early 1990s, I not only followed big stars like Neil and Bruce, I also discovered the wonders of small venues. We were blessed to have three of them within driving distance: Bogart's in Cincinnati and in Columbus, the Dell and a true "dive bar with live music," Stache's, in the north campus area.

Kathy and I made regular pilgrimages to Bogart's. In addition to seeing favorites like Jerry Jeff Walker and John Stewart, we also saw unbelievable talents like Tom Waits. That one was another "surprise" show. We took friends expecting to see the balladeer from "Heart of Saturday Night," but were greeted instead with the strange beat persona that Waits has adopted and maintained.

We also saw a very young Rosanne Cash at Bogart's, with a band featuring an equally young lead guitarist, Vince Gill. And on at least one occasion, maybe more, we saw a Texas-based singer-songwriter who epitomized the sweet spot of my musical tastes, Nanci Griffith. She did a song called "St. Olav's Gate" on my favorite album of hers, *Last of the True Believers*, which introduced me to the music of its writer, Tom Russell.

Stache's was, in fact, a true dive with little redeeming value other than the musical taste of its owner, Dan Dougan. The list of bands that played there would take your breath away. Stache's highlights for me include Richard Thompson with a full band on the Shoot Out the Lights tour (with Linda Thompson) and a very young Jimmie Dale Gilmore, also with a full band, who simply blew the place away with a superb encore, Townes Van Zandt's "White Freightliner Blues." I would love to know who was in the band that night.

At some point in the mid- to late eighties, Les Hershorn opened the Dell in a tiny space on Parsons Avenue on the near east side of Columbus. Les had great musical taste, meaning it coincided with mine, and he brought talents like John Stewart, Guy Clark, and Townes Van Zandt to town. When he hosted a teenage Alison Krauss with her band Union Station, she got so frustrated with the sound system that she turned it off, the band came down from the little stage, and they finished the show in true acoustic fashion.

One of my favorite evenings at the Dell was an appearance by Kinky Friedman, whom I had become a big fan of, primarily through his mystery novels that featured the Kinkster as the protagonist. That night, he had his sidekick, Cleve, in tow, who appeared regularly in Kinky's books. Throughout the evening, Kinky would shout out to him for one thing or another, referring to Cleve as his "homosexual lover." At the break, I approached Kinky with his most recent hardback to get him to sign it and then wandered over to a surprised Cleve and asked him to do the same. Cleve flipped open the book and said he'd sign on the page where he made his first appearance, did so, winked, slapped the book shut, and handed it back to me. When I got back to my seat, I flipped through to the signature page and found Cleve had written, "Alec, meet me in the men's room."

The Dell gave me my first opportunity to (sort of) promote a show—or two. Les and I regularly compared notes, and he brought a number of folks to town based on my recommendation and enthusiasm. Having been introduced to Tom Russell's music from Nanci Griffith's cover of "St. Olav's Gate," on which Tom sang backup vocals, I chased this intriguing songwriter down the rabbit hole. (Sometimes I just searched for a commonality of producer or studio musicians or whatever.) I found the Tom Russell Band's *Road to Bayamon* (on vinyl) in 1987. Nanci's liner notes said his band (which included Andrew Hardin and Fats Kaplin, both of whom would become great friends and an ongoing part of the music in my life) was "an assemblage of the best honky-tonk musicians I'd ever heard east or west of the Hudson." Tom lived in Brooklyn at the time, and Nanci's liner notes went on to say, "They've played joints in New Jersey and out on Long Island that you wouldn't set foot in to use the pay phone," calling them "the best 'country' band in America." Famed critic and musicologist John Lomax III also contributed liner notes to *Road to Bayamon*, writing, "Tom Russell is one of the finest singer-songwriters in the world."

Based on that record alone, I agreed. His 1989 follow-up, *Poor Man's Dream*, which I initially bought on cassette, was even better. However, nobody in Columbus, Ohio (or much of the rest of the world outside of New York and Norway, where he was a big star), even knew who he was. I talked to Les about Tom and somehow he reached out to him and booked a date. I told Les I would help sell tickets. I am sure Les advertised the show in the local rags and did his own version of promotion. But when showtime came, there were forty-six people at the Dell and every one of them was a friend of mine. I had sold every ticket. Les introduced me to Tom; Tom introduced me to Andrew, Fats, and the rest of the band; and they put on a show that exceeded even my high expectations. Yes, Tom was a fantastic songwriter, but he also was a great singer, somewhere between John Stewart and Johnny Cash in style and intonation, and the band rocked. "My" crowd loved them.

Tom and the band came back to the Dell one more time in the very early nineties. The crowd was similar in size and composition. Once again, he and the band were tremendous. Unfortunately, within months, the Dell was history and Les skipped town, reportedly owing hundreds of thousands of dollars to lots of folks, including the state taxing authorities. I later heard he'd set up camp somewhere in Hawaii and was still promoting shows, but who knows? And the Tom Russell Band was soon history too. The challenge of struggling on the road, economically and otherwise, took its toll, and a ten-year run came to an end. But at that last show at the Dell, I signed up for Tom Russell's *Dark Angel* newsletter. My signature on that little clipboard would change my life.

FIVE

Zeppelin Productions, Inc.

I'VE TOLD THE STORY A THOUSAND TIMES. . . .

In January 1995, the new issue of Tom Russell's newsletter, *Dark Angel*, arrived in the mail at my office. On the back page, a little box said something like, "If you know a venue in your town that would be appropriate for Tom, call this number. . . ." I put the newsletter on the corner of my desk and it sat there for weeks. Finally, and for no particular reason, I picked it up one day in late February and called the number. The guy who answered was an owner of Village Records in Shawnee, Kansas, who helped Tom with his bookings and for many years handled his mail-order merchandise. The guy (Corky, I believe) said, "You aren't going to believe this, but Tom has a Midwest run kicking off in a couple of weeks and he has a night open between Pittsburgh and Detroit. See what you can do."

I called every bar in Columbus with live music (including Stache's) and said, "If you bring Tom Russell to Columbus on March 8, I'll sell twenty tickets." (Always trying to manage expectations.) They basically all laughed at me. I called Corky back, got his answering machine, and left a message that I couldn't get it done. Maybe next time.

The next day, during a meeting in our firm's Cleveland office, I was handed a note that my secretary, who knew what I'd been trying to do, had phoned to tell me, "Tom Russell called." At that point, this was like hearing from Mick Jagger or Bruce Springsteen. I excused myself from the meeting and called Tom. He answered from his home in Brooklyn, reiterated that he had March 8 free, and urged me to do something in Columbus, even if it was at my house. *Something* was better than nothing. We talked for fifteen or twenty minutes about all kinds of stuff—maybe even baseball. But the bottom line was I couldn't really do anything on such short notice. I apologized, hung up, and called Kathy. "I just talked to Tom Russell," I said, and related the conversation. Kathy didn't hesitate, she just said, *"You have to do this."*

I knew a place called the Columbus Music Hall, an old renovated firehouse at the corner of Parsons and Oak, just around the corner from the Dell. It was owned by a nonprofit controlled by Becky Ogden, a schoolteacher and patron of the Columbus music scene. I had attended concerts at the Music Hall promoted by the then-fledgling nonprofit Six String Concerts. (Six String promotes fine singer-songwriter shows in an alcohol-free environment; their music tilts Northeast while mine tilts Southwest.) I called Becky, and sure enough, the Music Hall was available on Wednesday night, March 8. I took a deep breath and said I'd rent it for the evening. She told me it had a little sound system (who knew you needed a sound system?), and although she didn't have a liquor license, folks could BYO.

So . . . on eight days' notice, I rounded up ninety-nine people to see Tom Russell and his guitarist extraordinaire Andrew Hardin at the Columbus Music Hall. I literally knew every person in the room: Family members, friends, coworkers, and clients. Every person whose arm I could twist. I didn't print tickets. They just paid cash at the door.

The night before the show, the lawyer in me kicked in. I panicked ever so slightly. What if the place burned down during the show and everyone was killed? I needed to form a corporation to insulate myself from personal liability. (This is like the cobbler making flip-flops for his children.) What would I call it? Kathy reminded me that my "lucky word" since high school was *zeppelin*, a code word a group of friends used during our squirt-gun fight in a Boston hotel the spring of senior year. (I have no idea why we chose that word—it was before Led Zeppelin had formed.) Even in my family setting the word had magic; my kids knew when they knocked on a door, I would ask for the password and they would say "zeppelin."

The next day I formed the corporation, and that evening Zeppelin Productions, Inc., produced its first show: Tom Russell at the Columbus Music Hall. One of the great nights of my life! Oh, there were minor hiccups—like when Tom and Andy asked who was "running the sound?" I had no idea you needed someone to actually run that equipment. Thankfully, Andrew was perfectly capable, so he ran their sound check, moving back and forth from the stage to the soundboard.

The show itself couldn't have been better. In great form, Tom personalized things with lawyer jokes and shout-outs to me. Yes, it was BYO, and the crowd came with coolers filled with drinks. One young lawyer from our firm, who was sitting right in front of the stage, found a moment in a quiet, sensitive song to open his cooler and loudly pop the top on a beer. Tom christened him "Igloo boy" and ran with that one all night long. But most important, the music was extraordinary. I had told my family, friends, coworkers, and clients that Tom was "the finest singer-songwriter working in America today," and he lived up to the billing.

After the show, we headed to my "private club," a then relatively new bar/restaurant called Flatiron that had the finest jukebox ever, stocked by a guy named Charlie Jackson (who, two decades later, would open a venue called Natalie's). We ate, we drank, and we closed the place, but not before I bought Tom and Andy Flatiron T-shirts.

The next day, Tom and Andy were off to Detroit and I was reveling in my glory. I loved the show and hanging out with the Artistes. And honestly, I loved that I had done something that brought so much joy to so many people. I never, ever considered giving up my day job, but I did think this was too much fun to not do it again. Zeppelin Productions was in the concert-promotion business.

I quickly decided the first of what would ultimately be my two criteria for bringing artists to Columbus: I would only produce shows with "great music," defined solely as music I loved. It remains the first and most important criterion for me. That's why I immediately reached out to John Stewart, although he was still unknown in Columbus (which actually confirmed my status as a cutting-edge guy). I don't know the specific date of the show because it was another "friends and family" event and I didn't print tickets. But on an early summer night in 1995, we drew another nice crowd, and although the offstage experience was 180 degrees different from that with Tom and Andy (well, *120* degrees), the show was breathtaking, with a crowd blown away by this new listening room experience.

On a roll, my eyes got big. I thought I could *really* do this promotion thing. So I did two things, one of which saved me from big trouble, and another of which almost brought this new endeavor to a screeching halt.

First, feeling cocky, I called Doug Kridler, then head of the Columbus Association for the Performing Arts (CAPA), which operated a number of beautiful restored theaters in downtown Columbus. Doug has since become a good friend, but he didn't know me from a hill of beans in the summer of 1995. We had lunch and I unloaded on him with great enthusiasm about my new promotion business, ultimately asking him about renting one of those downtown theaters to promote bigger shows. He listened patiently and then asked if I had a gambling problem. Stunned, I quickly told him no. He said, "CAPA will rent you any theater you want, but you are having fun and not risking too much money. Why do you want to put yourself under that kind of pressure?" I said I didn't, putting that ambition to an end immediately, and forever. A bullet permanently dodged.

But I still thought I could move up the musical food chain. A big fan of Jimmie Dale Gilmore by then, I'd been dazzled by that Stache's show. I loved his most recent album, *Spinning Around the Sun*, which remains one of my favorites. (Even the famed music critic Robert Christgau rated it a rare "A," writing, "I doubt I'll hear a more gorgeous country record—maybe a more gorgeous record—anytime soon.") I don't remember how, in that relatively pre-internet day, I reached the William Morris Agency in Nashville, but I managed to speak with some twelve-year-old agent who cut a deal with me for a Jimmie Dale Gilmore show at the Columbus Music Hall on September 19, 1995. I signed a lengthy contract with an extensive rider and a very clear provision that the concert could only be canceled under certain circumstances and, then, on thirty days' notice. I know the date because this time I printed tickets and posters. I hung them around town and placed tickets for sale in a variety of outlets, including record shops and bookstores. I was really in the promotion business now.

Then something very unexpected happened. In late summer, about four weeks before the scheduled show, I opened the Sunday *New York Times* and guess who was on the cover of the *Magazine?* Jimmie Dale Gilmore. This was too good to be true. My relatively unknown Artiste, who I already had booked for a show, had been "discovered" by the national media. Ticket sales were not going to be a problem for Zeppelin Productions.

If it seems too good to be true, it usually is. Two days later, that twelve-year-old agent at William Morris called, and the first words out of his mouth were, "Alec, bad news. Jimmie isn't coming." I was incredulous. He said Jimmie had an offer to tour as an opener for Natalie Merchant and they were canceling my gig. I was irate. I pointed out we were inside the contract's thirty-day cancellation period. I told him I had spent money to print posters and tickets, and now I had to find a way to refund the tickets sold through independent outlets. I raised my voice and said, *"Jimmie can't do this!"* I at least wanted my expenses covered. The twelve-year-old laughed and said, "Welcome to show business," and hung up on me.

I was devastated. This wasn't fun. And although certainly not threatening to my lifestyle, it was expensive—and embarrassing. At some point, I called my new friend Tom Russell and told him the story. He was almost as upset as me. He pointed out that Jimmie probably didn't even know what had happened, placing blame on Jimmie's manager at the time, a name the twelve-year-old had invoked. Tom said guys like that didn't understand the damage they were doing to all the struggling musicians out there because they would drive aspiring promoters like me out of the business. I must say, I wasn't sure I wanted to try this promotion thing again. Tom felt so awful that he offered to come back to Columbus and "cover" the date. I accepted, pulled the tickets from the outlets, and converted the concert to another Tom Russell show. The silver lining in the cloud: I began to expand the audience (always known as the Music Fans) beyond friends and family.

On the day of the show, I went to the airport to pick up Tom and Andy. In those days, you could walk right out on the concourse and meet the passengers as they disembarked. I was waiting at the gate when the Artistes emerged from the plane, both wearing their Flatiron shirts. Yep, true friends had been made.

The show was even better than the one six months earlier. Among other things, the folks at Six String Concerts referred me to a young soundman who, like me, never gave up his day job. Mitch Hyde, "Mitch the Soundman," had real equipment and he began running expert sound for Zeppelin shows as he has done for twenty-seven years.

That night, after we'd retreated to Flatiron to postmortem the evening, I spoke with Tom about the experience, and in the course of our discussion, I developed my second criteria for Zeppelin shows going forward. Yes, "great music." But also, "nice people." And there was no better way to identify the latter than by getting referrals from artists who had done a Zeppelin show and understood the venue, audience, and promoter. I asked Tom to recommend others, and he said he would.

Looking back, I am confident Jimmie Dale had no idea what came down with that 1995 show. Many years later, we brought him to Columbus as a solo artist several times. And then, with his endorsement, we booked the legendary Flatlanders (Jimmie, Joe Ely, and Butch Hancock) on multiple occasions. Finally, we twice brought Jimmie with Dave Alvin. Jimmie has become a friend, we have shared many an evening, and I have never told him about the September 1995 episode. Nor have I related what happened in December 1995. Early that month, I got a call from the twelve-year-old agent telling me that Jimmie was going to do a short Midwest run and I could book a Columbus show between Christmas and New Year's Day. No way would I do a show in that time frame, plus I reminded him I wanted reimbursement for my expenses; again, the discussion ended acrimoniously.

Just a few days later, I saw ads for a Jimmie Dale Gilmore show in the offered time period—a fundraiser for Columbus' wonderful public radio station, WCBE. I did something wildly out of character. I called the twelve-year-old agent and disclosed for the first time something I never "use" in my personal life: I was an attorney, and if they didn't reimburse me for my out-of-pocket expenses for the September show, I would serve Jimmie with a small-claims court summons onstage during the show.

A few days later, I received a check for the expenses and four free tickets to the show. Jimmie was great, and afterward, my brother, Jim, ran backstage with a poster for the aborted September show and Jimmie signed it for him.

Thankfully, I didn't give up my day job. And with lessons learned, I realized I wanted referrals from one Artiste to another. I needed a Zeppelin Productions "family tree," and Tom Russell became its roots and trunk. He started me in the concert-promotion business, and by bailing me out when Jimmie Dale canceled, he kept me in it. From that point forward, many of the early Zeppelin artists were either direct referrals from Tom or, over time, indirect, as his friends recommended their friends.

From the beginning, Tom's Columbus shows were special. He's played twenty-five Zeppelin shows in twenty-five years, with no two alike. In part, that's because he is a prolific recording artist, and most of his tours support newly released albums. And his keen eye and quick wit always result in a spontaneity that can pick up on the events of his day or the dynamics of a particular audience. Having said that, for me, it is all about the songs. I've always introduced Tom as "the finest singer-songwriter working in America today" because over four decades, he has written hundreds of songs, with many of them favorites among different fans. His set lists and audience requests vary dramatically from night to night.

As for that initial "introduction," I was too nervous to take to the stage to introduce any of the Artistes the first couple of years. I only changed when Katy Moffatt dragged me onstage one night and made me do it. Some years later, after I'd done an apparently loquacious introduction, Tom told the audience that he remembered when I was too nervous to get onstage, and "Now Alec thinks he is Bill Graham."

I can't deny it, one of the things I most enjoy about Tom's performances is the way he personalizes each show. Yes, there are always multiple shout-outs to me, like telling the crowd I was his divorce lawyer (not true) when he returned from a Puerto Rican carnival gig and his ex-wife served him with divorce papers (that is true, I think). But he also worked the rest of the family into the shows, regularly dedicating songs to my mother or calling out to brother Jim near the end of a show, "Jim, pull the Lexus around." Jim replied, *"Wrong brother!"*

Tom became a good friend right from the beginning. We had lots of fun nights at Flatiron after the shows. I began to "road manage" him and Andy to their Cleveland gigs (Wilbert's, the Brick Alley, and ultimately the Beachland Ballroom), which consisted of driving and helping carry guitars. They would stay at my mother's house, a very unusual thing for Tom to do, and he and I remain tied to this day from our Ping-Pong matches in her basement.

A most memorable weekend was in September 1997, which started with Tom, Andy, and Katy Moffatt playing a Thursday Zeppelin show at the Columbus Music Hall. The next day, I drove the crew to Cleveland to perform in what is now called the Foster Theater at the Rock & Roll Hall of Fame for our law firm's Litigation Group retreat (long before I was involved with the Hall). Then, on Saturday, I drove us all to Catawba Island, about ninety minutes west of Cleveland. We caught a ferry to Put-in-Bay and were picked up in a boat and taken to Sugar Island, a private island owned by the Keny family from Columbus. There, on Saturday night, the Artistes did a show on the beach to celebrate our friend Karen Keny's fortieth birthday party. On Sunday, we were back to Wilbert's for another show. We were exhausted from the travel and the nonstop laughter of the weekend, including from a running joke created when Tom asked for Sun Chips at a drive-through restaurant and, when they said they didn't have any, he barked, *"Get some."*

A highlight of that weekend was my introduction to one of my favorite albums, Lucinda Williams' *Car Wheels on a Gravel Road*, almost a year before its release. Lucinda, who had been working on the album for years, was shopping it after her record company had gone bankrupt. Tom had a friend who worked at Sony Music, and he had given Tom a cassette with a rough mix of the songs in a different sequence than the final version. We were all blown away.

I remember another night at Wilbert's when I discovered Tom after the show in the back office with the owner, almost coming to fisticuffs to get paid what he was owed. Ah, the dirty underbelly of the music business. No wonder artists liked playing Zeppelin shows, where I paid them the guaranty before they ever hit the stage, plus sometimes more after the show if the crowd exceeded expectations.

Over the years, I've seen Tom perform in a variety of places around the country, ranging from the Bottom Line in New York to McCabe's in Santa Monica. (At McCabe's, he gave me a shout-out as chair of the board of the Rock & Roll Hall of Fame, always a rush, but especially so in that iconic venue.) I've seen him at such venues as the Birchmere in Alexandria, Virginia, and a small (but noteworthy) house concert in New York's East Village.

A favorite family experience was attending the 1999 Edmonton Folk Festival, where we were Tom's guests with full access privileges. The performers included Joan Baez, Iris DeMent, Nanci Griffith, Jimmie Dale Gilmore, and many other favorites, not to mention newcomers (at least to me) like the Canadian Laura Smith, who blew me away, and Dan Bern, who did the same for daughter Nora.

I've had some other interesting experiences thanks to Tom. In February 2001, I traveled to Juarez, Mexico (really), to discuss a possible affiliation between our law firm and a Mexican firm. At that point, Tom lived in El Paso, having moved there from Brooklyn a couple of years earlier. He picked me up at my El Paso hotel and took me on a driving tour of the area. The musical accompaniment was a rough mix of songs from what would become *Borderland*, an album that remains my favorite of his. He showed me places referenced in the songs, even pointing out the "three crosses by the roadside" mentioned in "Love Abides" from his prior album, *The Man From God Knows Where*.

Tom has continued to write and record, sometimes experimenting with new sounds and styles. For example, he recorded 2009's *Blood and Candle Smoke* in Tucson with members of the band Calexico, and he cut 2013's *Aztec Jazz* with a Norwegian jazz ensemble. In 2015, he released the ambitious *Rose of Rosecrae*, a fifty-two track Western folk opera, completing his storytelling trilogy that began with *The Man From God Knows Where* and included a . . . unique . . . album, *Hotwalker*. Often a bit outside the mainstream himself, Tom has an affinity for outsiders. But he also appeared many times on David Letterman's show, once performing a rare political composition, "Who's Gonna Build Your Wall?" which he wrote prophetically in 2008. Letterman is clearly a fan and also hired Tom to put a band together to entertain in Montana, where Dave has a home. A poster Tom created for the few Texas shows the band played as a warm-up to Montana hangs on my home-office wall.

That poster isn't the only piece of Tom's art on our walls. Over the past two decades, he became a prolific painter and is as entrepreneurial with his visual art as he is with his music. He gifted us one of his early paintings, *Real Blues*, and we have a number of his limited-edition prints. We also have an original painting of James Thurber, which Tom wanted us to have since Thurber was from Columbus.

After stints in El Paso and Santa Fe, Tom currently splits his time between Austin and Switzerland, having married Nadine, a beautiful and smart Swiss woman. As Tom tells the story, he told her on first meeting he was going to marry her. He did, in two ceremonies. First, in a civil ceremony in Elko, Nevada, in early 2008 (with Ian Tyson and Ramblin' Jack Elliott as his "best men") and in late June in a small stone church in Gstaad, Switzerland. Kathy and I went to the latter ceremony, during which Gretchen Peters stepped to the front of the church with her guitar and performed "Guadalupe," a then-new song that may be Tom's finest composition. While standing at the altar with his back to the congregation, Tom began to harmonize. A truly transcendent moment.

A very important person in my life, musically and otherwise, Tom was the debut Artiste at three Zeppelin venues: the Columbus Music Hall, the Columbus Maennerchor, and the Grand Valley Dale Ballroom. He has also played at and loves Natalie's. Directly or indirectly, he referred many other Zeppelin artists, especially in the early years, including Gretchen Peters, Dave Alvin, Steve Young, Eliza Gilkyson, and Katy Moffatt.

COMING HOME LATE ONE SUNDAY afternoon in January 1996, I saw there was a message on our answering machine. I pushed the button and heard this soft Texas drawl saying, "Hi, Alec. This is Katy Moffatt from Studio City, California, and Tom Russell says you and I need to talk."

I knew Katy and Tom had cowritten many songs, contributed to each other's records, and occasionally performed together. So it wasn't a complete surprise when I heard from her. I called her back, and at the end of a short conversation, I booked Katy for a show at the Music Hall on April 19. The Zeppelin family tree had begun to sprout.

It turned out I had known Katy's music for a long time without realizing it. Kathy and I had seen her open for Jerry Jeff Walker at Bogart's on our honeymoon in 1976, and in the mid-eighties, she opened for the Everly Brothers at the Ohio Theater in Columbus on their reunion tour. I, like most of the world, had missed Katy's two major label releases for Columbia in the seventies. But I owned her three most recent records: *Walkin' on the Moon*, a wonderful acoustic album coproduced by Katy and Andrew Hardin; *Child Bride*, an edgier one coproduced by Mark Linett and

Steve Berlin (which includes one of the finest vocal performances I've ever heard on John Hiatt's "We Ran"); and her latest release, originally called *The Greatest Show on Earth*, which she and Tom had coproduced.

The fate of that last CD is a tragedy. A classic of the Americana genre, the album, like all of Katy's records, garnered strong critical reviews upon its 1993 release. However, this one also developed commercial traction. Unfortunately, Ringling Brothers asserted that the title and cover, featuring a buxom brunette falling off a tightrope, was a copyright infringement, and her record company pulled the CD from circulation. The label eventually re-released it with a new cover and title, *The Evangeline Hotel*, but it never recovered its momentum in the marketplace.

My life is filled with coincidences (if there is such a thing), and in February of that year, after we had booked the show, I traveled to the Houston area (the Woodlands, to be exact) on business. I opened the daily paper and was surprised to see that Katy was appearing that night at Anderson Fair, a legendary acoustic music venue in the city. (Nanci Griffith memorialized the place in her song "Spin on a Red Brick Floor" and recorded a live album there in 1988.)

I rounded up the Moose, living in Houston at the time, and a young lawyer from our Houston office with whom I was working, and the three of us headed to the Montrose area of town where we set up camp in the intimate environs of Anderson Fair.

Before the show, I spotted Katy standing in the kitchen area. She is hard to miss with her distinctive red hair. I went back and introduced myself, catching her by surprise since she had no idea I would be there. We exchanged pleasantries and I returned to my seat. Katy played two sets, and late in the second set, she asked for requests. I shouted out, "We Ran." She heard me, paused, and then told the crowd she didn't think she could do it. I presumed it was because of the challenging vocal. Later she told me the vocal was easy; it was because of the even more challenging gui-tar parts. So she did another song, "Better Let Her Run," close in terms of the requested title. When she finished that song, without hesitation she went right into "We Ran" and nailed it. For many years thereafter, she did very few Zeppelin shows without doing that song. And Katy did many a Zeppelin show, starting just two months later.

That initial one, in April 1996, was the first concert for which I printed and sold tickets, other than the aborted Jimmie Dale show the prior year. This time, I sent out a sales pitch memorandum to friends, family, and others, beginning to establish a hard-mail list (later converted to e-mail) that since has grown to over a thousand: the "Music Fans."

Another Zeppelin "family tree" also began to take shape off-stage as we settled into a routine. I booked the Artistes and sold the tickets. Brother Jim handled the operations at the show (light-ing, taking care of the musicians' needs in the venue, etc.). Kathy and my mother took the tickets at the door. Jim married Lisa in the summer of 1995—he gained a wonderful wife and Zeppelin had someone to sell the merch. And of course, Mitch the Soundman became part of the family, at least for the evening. I can say quite honestly that the whole Zeppelin Productions enterprise has been a wonderful Wightman family event from day one.

We also settled into a routine for the day of the concerts. I would pick up the artist at the airport and take him or her to the hotel, and we'd often have dinner before the show. I'd chauffeur the performer to and from the venue. And for many years we'd almost always end the evening with our family and the Artiste at Flatiron. A post-show meal would be had, drinks poured (although a number of the artists were in recovery), stories told, and a CD left behind to make its way into the Flatiron jukebox.

Katy, like Tom and Andy, fell right into that routine with great enthusiasm. When she heard the guys were scheduled for a show on the Friday of Memorial Day weekend, and I was worried about ticket sales, she volunteered to fly back and perform for free just to be part of the evening's events. Tom agreed, and with her opening set and backup vocals, the show sounded even better than Tom and Andrew's appearances the year before. We also enjoyed a memorable post-gamer at Flatiron.

Katy became a regular member of the Zeppelin roster for many years. She performed solo and with other Artistes—Tom and Andy; just Andy; Rosie Flores; the late Steve Young; her brother, Hugh, author of some major country hits; and lesser-known performers like Denice Franke and Pat McLaughlin, the latter a longtime cowriter with the late John Prine and a member of his band. Katy also became an auxiliary part of the Wightman family, staying with my mother when performing in Cleveland and becoming close to Kathy and me, and Jim and Lisa.

One of my favorite evenings with Katy was December 31, 1999, when Kathy and I hosted a Y2K party at our home on Winstead Road. Katy flew in from L.A. to entertain a large contingent of friends and Music Fans on what could have been the last night of civilization as we knew it. At the very least, a massive failure of the electric power grid was possible, so we gave each guest a small flashlight on arrival. The Y2K part of things turned out to be a nonevent, but the party was fantastic. Katy finished up her set shortly after midnight with a surprise version of "Waiting for a Train," which I'd told her about singing to my daughters at bedtime.

Katy was also the impetus for my one and only venture into the record production business. Although I have contributed smaller amounts to help other artists fund recording efforts from time to time, I only once provided the full production costs for an album—Katy's *Fewer Things*. In 2008, nearly ten years had passed since Katy released her last album, *Loose Diamond*, on HighTone Records. (Actually, an intervening cowboy record appeared on Western Jubilee, which I thought was too out of the mainstream.)

As an aside, HighTone released many fine albums of the era, including by Tom Russell and Dave Alvin. The label's claim to fame, in many respects, was releasing early hit records by contemporary blues artist Robert Cray. In its later, struggling years, I got to know one of HighTone's owners, Larry Sloven, at least by telephone, and arranged for a lawyer in our Costa Mesa office to help with the sale of its catalog to Shout! Factory records.

By 2008, Katy's touring career had slowed dramatically and she thought it was in no small measure due to the absence of any new "product." I volunteered to finance a stripped-down, acoustic CD, to be produced by Andrew Hardin in the same vein as *Walkin' on the Moon* some twenty years earlier. The record turned out great. Andy did a fine job with the production, including adding some tasteful instrumentation from folks like Fats Kaplin, whose guitar playing was superb as always, and Katy was in fine voice. She selected a strong batch of songs, including one by the late Stephen Bruton, her high school classmate from Fort Worth who went on to play guitar for Kris Kristofferson, among others. She also did a song I suggested, Nick Lowe's "What Lack of Love Has Done," one I could "hear" Katy sing the first time I heard Nick's version a few years earlier. Unfortunately, despite a few strong critical reviews, the record didn't enjoy, shall we say, commercial success. But I can say there is one, and only one, record released on the "Zeppelin Productions" label. I did get a Zeppelin logo out of the effort. Katy (and Tom's) good friend John Yuelkenbeck designed one for the CD cover that I still use on the Zeppelin website and Facebook page.

TOM, ANDREW, AND KATY, ALONE or in combination, dominated those first few years of Zeppelin concerts. I did bring John Stewart in the summer of 1995 and a co-bill of Michael Fracasso and Greg Trooper in January 1997. But it was Rosie Flores who provided the next branch in the growing Zeppelin tree.

My introduction to Rosie wasn't unlike my first face-to-face meeting with Katy. In very early 1997, Katy suggested she make another visit to Columbus and bring her friend and sometime singing partner, Rosie Flores, with her. Knowing Rosie's music well from her albums of the prior ten years or so, I enthusiastically agreed, and we booked a show for June 1997.

Not long thereafter, I was in Los Angeles on business and saw that Rosie was playing at Jack's Sugar Shack at Hollywood and Vine. I rounded up a bunch of our law firm management, and we headed to Jack's. Before the show, I saw Rosie saying hello to people throughout the crowd. I went up to her, stuck out my hand, and opened with, "You don't know me, but—" Before I could get any further, she coolly interrupted, "I don't know you from a hill of beans." That was the last cool exchange Rosie and I ever had, as I managed to get out the rest of my intro and we quickly became friends.

By the way, a highlight of that evening came when Rosie called a friend in the crowd to the stage—and Emmylou Harris stepped up and joined Rosie in a version of "Pancho and Lefty" in memory of Townes Van Zandt, who had recently passed away. (Emmy was apparently in Los Angeles to visit her daughter at the University of Southern California.)

On June 4, 1997, Katy and Rosie did a wonderful show at the old Music Hall, ending the night at Flatiron as we were wont to do. Well, apparently the night didn't really end there. After I dropped them off at the Southern Hotel, the ladies headed to one of their rooms and called their mutual friend Dave Alvin, in Los Angeles. They told Dave he had to do this gig. Dave later told me he came to Columbus the first time at the urging of "two drunken girls."

That evening began a long series of Rosie shows in Columbus, every year for a while and sporadically to this day. For a number of years, Rosie maintained an annual tradition of coming in early September when she and my mother would celebrate their respective birthdays. Rosie's age was a little bit of a mystery for a while. Various sites on the internet had her listed as ten or so years younger than me, which didn't feel quite right. On one of those early visits, I "road managed" her and Katy to Cleveland for a show at Beachland Ballroom and we all stayed at my mother's house. The next day, as we were leaving Euclid, we drove by my high school and I said, "Euclid High, class of '68," which I knew was Katy's graduation year as well. Rosie immediately piped up, "Hey, that's my year too." Mystery solved.

Tom's and Katy's connections led to a number of other artists making their Zeppelin debuts in those early days, including the legendary Steve Young and the highly respected Nashville songwriter David Olney. Steve visited with us several times and was almost a mystical performer—a powerful singer, tremendous guitarist, and masterful songwriter. His best-known composition, "Seven Bridges Road," was popularized in the late seventies by the Eagles, but he wrote many others, including "Lonesome, On'ry and Mean," a hit for Waylon Jennings, and "Montgomery in the Rain," covered by Hank Williams Jr.

On the cutting edge of the alt-country/outlaw/Americana movement, Steve lived in Nashville in the early seventies and hung out with the likes of Guy Clark. (Steve appears in the cult documentary *Heartworn Highways*, with Guy, Rodney Crowell, Townes Van Zandt, Steve Earle, and others.) Heck, one of his early albums featured a young backup singer named Gram Parsons. Not only was Steve a captivating live performer, he was also captivating in a shy, quiet way at our post-show sessions at Flatiron. A self-described Zen Buddhist, he was a recovering alcoholic. (I think substance abuse played a role in derailing his early career.) Steve told us nearly surreal stories, including one about serving as a State Department representative to bring country music to the South Pacific islands. (Other friends of Steve told me they never heard that story.) He was also the only Artiste to engage in palmistry after a show, reading Lisa's future at Flatiron.

Steve didn't sustain his career in a meaningful way in Nashville. He ended up moving to the Los Angeles area, where he wrote a song about his new hometown, "Silver Lake." Dave Alvin and Jimmie Dale Gilmore humorously report that Steve told each of them he'd written the song specifically for him. Sadly, Steve and I had just reconnected about bringing him back to Columbus when he fell and suffered a head injury in October 2015, an injury that led to his death the following March.

Like Steve, David Olney was also a highly respected songwriter, especially among his peers. And like Steve, he originally emerged from the rock & roll world—Steve having played in the psychedelic band Stone Country and David with the Nashville rockers the X-Rays. David, unlike Steve, was certainly not in recovery, but he did have a soft spot for those musicians struggling with substance issues.

One of the more bizarre Zeppelin evenings was a Dave Olney show at the Music Hall in the late nineties. Unbeknownst to me, David showed up with a (sort of) singer-songwriter from Kentucky, whom David introduced as Paul K. David said Paul was a recovering heroin addict and he wanted Paul to open for him. (To this day, I don't do "openers" at Zeppelin shows unless foisted on me by the billed performer.) Before the show, Paul went into the courtyard behind the Music Hall and smoked a lot of marijuana. When he hit the stage, he had something of a meltdown as he sweated profusely and tried desperately to make it through a handful of not-so-good songs. Being sensitive to my reputation with the Music Fans (in those days, many people came to Zeppelin shows simply because they trusted me), I was really unhappy.

On the other hand, Rosie hit a home run when she sprung an unbilled artist on me—plus she had the courtesy of asking first. A couple of days before Rosie's September 10, 1999, show, she called and asked if she could bring a friend, Tammy Rogers, who I knew to be one of Nashville's premier fiddlers (and was later a founding member of the Grammy Award–winning blue-grass group the SteelDrivers). Of course, I said yes, and Rosie and Tammy blew the crowd away, as they did a second time when they returned the following September. After one of those Rosie/Tammy shows, I asked Tammy the question I asked most of the Artistes post-concert. "You now know me, the gig, and the audience. Is there an artist you would recommend for a Zeppelin show?" Without hesitation, Tammy said, "Kieran Kane."

Directly or indirectly, then, Rosie gets credit for two important branches of the Zeppelin tree: first Dave Alvin and then, via Tammy, Kieran Kane (and, as we soon discovered, Kevin Welch and Fats Kaplin).

DAVE ALVIN'S FIRST ZEPPELIN PRODUCTIONS appearance was an acoustic show at the Columbus Music Hall on July 1, 1998. He then rattled the walls of the Hall on his second visit, in the fall of 2000, accompanied by the full complement of Guilty Men, including the late, great Chris Gaffney. Over the next twenty years, Dave returned to Columbus many times and in many modes—solo; duo with Rick Shea or Chris Miller; with the Guilty Men, the Guilty Women, and the Guilty Ones; with brother Phil; and with Jimmie Dale Gilmore.

I learned a lot about Dave on his first visit. I put him up in a swanky downtown hotel, as I did with all the Artistes in those days. It was an attraction of the gig for many of them. Dave told me after the show that he really didn't like staying in nice places and preferred a Red Roof Inn. I thought it was because he could smoke in the room or something, but I later learned it was because the floor plans were all identical and he could find the bathroom in the middle of the night.

Dave quickly settled into the Zeppelin routine, enjoying the gigs and the post-show Flatiron meals. When Red Roof built a "high rise" (five or six floors) next to the Flatiron, he was in heaven.

Dave's desire for consistency manifests itself in a variety of ways. Over time, he developed one absolute requirement in his contract rider—Bud Light. No craft beer. Nothing fancy. Somewhat like the Red Roof, he wants to know exactly what he is consuming. Dave likes a beer or two before the show, and a couple during and after. He wants to know what he is putting in his body, especially in terms of alcohol content. Bud Light it is.

On that second visit, Gaffney, who was Dave's best friend until the day he died of cancer, sold the product and joined the band onstage with his accordion for a song or two. I mistakenly thought Gaffney road managed Dave's tours at one point, but he set me straight: "If Gaffney had been my road manager," said Dave, "we would have missed a lot of shows in order to stop at whatever bar caught his fancy. It once took us fourteen hours to make the eight-hour drive from L.A. to Tucson so that he could hit bars in Cabazon and Blythe, California, as well as Quartzsite and Gila Bend, Arizona. In his defense, though, they were definitely interesting bars."

That Guilty Men show was on a Sunday night and Flatiron was closed, so I took the whole crew to the Blue Danube in the north Ohio State campus area. It was a "meat, two sides, and a beer" place if there ever was one, and the boys loved it.

Dave is an extraordinary guitarist, whether he bangs on his electric or plays an acoustic. His singing has grown better over time, and today he is first-rate. But part of Dave's magic is his stage presence. When he hits the stage, he is in command. And Dave does like to be in command. With his tough-guy persona, he can give you a look that makes you melt. Having said that, he is truly as nice as can be under that exterior.

Dave has made me melt at least once. Before one of his solo shows at the Maennerchor, Dave did an afternoon in-studio performance at WCBE-FM. Sitting in the tiny broadcast studio while getting ready to go on the air, he played and sang one of my favorite songs, John Stewart's "July, You're a Woman." He did it perfectly start to finish. After the interview, I asked him about it. He said it was one of his favorite songs, too, and recounted the story of watching TV as a youngster with his mother in Southern California and seeing Stewart play it on local television. I asked Dave if he would sing it that evening and he said no, that he had never done it before an audience and wasn't about to begin.

That night, Dave played a typically stellar show. When he returned to the stage for the encore, without saying a word, he went right into "July." Thirty seconds in, he went blank. Forgot the words. Totally. Not a good feeling for a perfectionist like Dave. He moved from embarrassed to angry, turned to face the side of the stage where I stood, and growled for the whole crowd to hear, *"That's your fault, Alec."*

Notwithstanding that faux pas, Dave and I became good friends. He is one of the few Artistes who have played multiple shows at all four Zeppelin venues—the Music Hall, the Maennerchor, Valley Dale, and Natalie's. They are all very different places and he has embraced each one. And "July, You're a Woman" has become a theme in our relationship, just like Red Roof and Bud Light.

In November 2011, Dave made his first appearance at Valley Dale. Although he was on the road with the Guilty Ones (no longer the Men because Lisa Pankratz was on drums), there was some conflict with a band member for our date and he would be solo. The night before the show, Dave called me at home and said the conflict had been resolved and asked if he could bring the band. Of course, the answer was yes, although I explained tickets had been sold billing the evening as an acoustic show. Dave heard that and he did something I don't think he's done before or since: He performed the first set solo acoustic and after the break brought the band out for the second set. What a night!

As for "July, You're a Woman": He and I had never discussed the (my) faux pas after the Maennerchor debacle. But in the sound check on that November evening, without comment, he and the band ran through a perfect version of the song. Dave ended by saying to an empty ballroom (other than Mitch and me), "That was for you, Alec."

The "theme" didn't end there. When Dave and Jimmie Dale Gilmore recorded their album, *Downey to Lubbock*, they included the song on the record. When they came to Natalie's on the tour to promote the record, Dave said he put it on the record for me. Having said that, Dave and Jimmie didn't include the song in their set that night, nor did they the following year when they came back and did the last Zeppelin show at Valley Dale. Apparently, there was a mandolin on the recording they thought was integral and no one in the band could do it.

The "July" story has a happy ending, however. When Dave came to Natalie's in 2019 to reprise my favorite of his albums, *King of California*, he returned to the stage to play what had been a consistent two-song encore on this very limited tour. After those two songs, Dave gave me a very warm, personal shout-out. He said Columbus was lucky to have me, calling me a "rare bird." And then Dave played a solo acoustic version of "July, You're a Woman," dedicating it to me.

That concert in and of itself was indicative of the friendship Dave and I have developed. In addition to bringing him to Columbus and hanging out many times, I've seen him at the Bottom Line in New York; the Ram's Head in Annapolis; and at SXSW. At the latter, he sought me out in a packed crowd after the show and dragged me away for a conversation designed, at least in part I am sure, to discourage others. I've also seen Dave in some very unusual places. One holiday season, the family was in Los Angeles and I saw that Dave was playing a gig at a little art gallery downtown, supporting an artist or poet friend of his. We packed the crew into the car and made our way to an obscure location in a warehouse district, way off the beaten path. Sure enough, there was Dave with his acoustic guitar, working his magic for thirty or forty people.

One of my favorite Dave "shows" was in Washington, D.C. I was there on business, picked up the morning paper, and read he was going to be at the national headquarters of the AFL-CIO at noon. I didn't have lunch plans, so I walked over to the location and ran into Dave smoking on the front steps. It turns out his dad had been a union organizer for copper miners in four Western states as well as for steel workers in California and Colorado (oh, so that's how he got that tough-guy exterior). Maintaining his support of union causes over the years, Dave told me, "I'm pretty proud of my old man for showing me the harsh economic ropes of life at a young age." At noon, he stood before a microphone in the lobby of the building and entertained hundreds of union members and staffers with one great labor song after another. Talk about magic.

Yes, Dave and I are friends. I suggested him for the roster for the Rock & Roll Hall of Fame's Annual Music Masters tribute to Chuck Berry, a show that Dave opened—with Chuck sitting seventy-five feet away. That was a special moment for Dave and for the rest of us. Our friendship has resulted in my getting the opportunity to present Dave to the Music Fans in a variety of formats and venues that would otherwise be impossible, including on a reunion tour with his brother Phil and two shows with Jimmie Dale, one acoustic at Natalie's and the second with the Guilty Ones at Valley Dale.

Perhaps the best indication of the friendship came in 2019. Early in the year, Dave and I exchanged e-mails and he offered up that he was going to re-release *King of California* to celebrate its twenty-fifth anniversary. He would be doing a small tour in the summer reprising the record. I immediately called Brad Madison, Dave's agent with whom I have worked for years, and told him what Dave had said. I asked him if we could secure a Columbus date. Brad said, "No way, Alec. He is only going to do a handful of dates and all in major markets and bigger venues than yours."

I said I understood. About a week later he called back and asked, "What date do you want?" Dave came for two nights, putting on two shows as strong as any we have done. At the end of the second night, when I thanked him for coming and for doing "July, You're a Woman," he looked me in the eye and said, "You know I'll always do anything for you."

On reflection, Dave and Kieran Kane, both strong branches of the Zeppelin tree, are an interesting contrast. Dave grew up in Downey, California, near Los Angeles; Kieran grew up in Queens, New York City. Kieran went to college in Boston; Dave, after forming the Blasters, attended Long Beach State University, where he studied poetry (later acknowledging his writing professors as influential on his work as a songwriter). Dave is Southern California through and through. After college, Kieran spent time in L.A. as a studio musician, but it didn't take. Dave spent a little time in Nashville in the eighties and it almost drove him out of the business. Kieran moved there about the same time and never left.

I gave Kieran a call as Tammy Rogers had suggested. As I've done so many times, I said, "I'm a corporate lawyer in Columbus, Ohio, with a passion for music." The pitch. "I rent a hall, sell tickets off a mailing list, and try not to lose too much money." When I was done, Kieran asked incredulously, "You want me to do *what?*" He couldn't really get his mind around what I was doing. Keep in mind that at this point, Kieran was just ten years or so from riding the top of the country music charts as a member of the O'Kanes. Persistent, I called him a second time. Maybe a third. No luck. But then, circumstances changed.

I called Kieran in very late 2001 or early 2002, gave him the pitch one more time, and he said, "I've just bought a cabin in the Adirondacks and I need to go check on it. I looked at a map, and Columbus is exactly halfway between there and Nashville." He wanted to do the show and asked if I minded if he brought along his friend Kevin Welch.

And he did. On February 22, 2002, on a freezing cold, snowy night in Columbus, Kieran and Kevin debuted at the Columbus Music Hall. Some Music Fans knew the O'Kanes' music. A few knew Kevin's music. The hard-core Fans knew that Kieran, Kevin, Tammy, and a couple of other Nashville musicians had formed one of the first independent labels in the business, Dead Reckoning Records, and they'd all put out some great, somewhat obscure albums. But truth is, like most Zeppelin shows in those days, the Music Fans came out because I endorsed the music and I hadn't really missed yet. (Well, maybe one, but that's for another chapter.)

That 2002 show was like no other in the Zeppelin annals. Kieran had told me over the phone that the show would "go a little better" with a bottle of Jameson. Armed with that knowledge, Kathy made a run to the liquor store. Kieran and Kevin were appreciative when they came out of the cold for the sound check at the old Music Hall and, especially, when they retreated to the greenroom upstairs before the show. The bottle was waiting and opened for a little pre-show libation. When they hit the stage, they brought the bottle with them and placed it, with two glasses, on a small table between their chairs. Anyone who was there that night remembers "Mr. Bottle," which became an integral part of the act. The Artistes were excellent, as they always were, but let's just say the show was . . . loose. By the end of whatever number of well-earned encores, Mr. Bottle had been drained, to live in infamy among the Music Fans for years to come.

That night began an annual run of Kieran and Kevin shows: February 2003, February 2004, and February 2005, when for the first time they included another Dead Reckoner, musical virtuoso Fats Kaplin, who really brought things full circle—Fats had been a member of the Tom Russell Band throughout the eighties and very early nineties. I had actually met him at the Dell. Yes, it is a scary small world.

The 2005 show will always hold a special place in my heart because that night, we all retreated to our relatively new home in German Village, where Kathy and I had moved the prior February. While Fats regaled the rest of us in the kitchen with stories about the days with Tom and the band, especially in Norway, Kieran and my mother engaged in a long one-on-one discussion in another room about the meaning of life. When it was time to take the Artistes back to the hotel, Kieran looked at Mom and said, in all seriousness, "Will you adopt me?"

My mother died suddenly that fall of 2005. October 20 to be exact. And when Kieran, Kevin, and Fats returned the following February (of course), this time to the Columbus Maennerchor, where the concerts had moved, Kieran ended the show with a dedication to Mom, singing a song he had cowritten and sung to his own mother when she was dying—"When We're Gone, Long Gone." I stood stage left with tears streaming down my face. He's done that to me a few times since 2006; it always breaks me up and it is always appreciated.

The boys' shows got better and better. They came back in February of 2007 and 2008. One of those nights was our introduction to Fats' wife, Kristi Rose, who has a larger-than-life voice and a stage presence that is almost Gothic in demeanor. That night, she and Fats opened the second set as a duo for one song, and years later I had them both at Natalie's for a performance of their own.

We all became great friends and remain so to this day. It was after that 2008 show, the seventh year in a row of coming to Ohio in the coldest and snowiest month of the year, that they finally asked, almost pleading, *"Why do we always have to come in February?"* So the annual date moved to the spring, and through 2012, they collectively came to the Maennerchor and, ultimately, the Grand Valley Ballroom every year. Life's changes happen.

Kevin moved to Wimberley, Texas, after years in Nashville. He was a little closer to his native Oklahoma and, I suppose, his musical roots. He has remained something of a regular on the Zeppelin scene, doing solo shows at Natalie's, staying at our house, and hanging out with me at SXSW from time to time. In fact, Kevin was with us in Columbus in the fall of 2017 as part of the Backroad Boys when his new Australian wife gave birth to their son on the other side of the world, a baby Kevin christened "Shark Tooth" for reasons I can't explain.

Fats, on the other hand, stayed put in Nashville, where those musical virtuoso skills are in high demand all across the musical spectrum. He was not only a regular member of John Prine's band, but for a while he was on the road with Jack White's very rock & roll band. On January 30, 2015, Fats called me from Madison Square Garden, where he was about to go onstage with Jack. They were to be in Columbus the next night at the sold-out Schottenstein Arena and asked if we were going. Although I was slightly familiar with Jack's music (we did see the White Stripes open for the Rolling Stones at Nationwide Arena a number of years earlier), I didn't know it well—other than when 100,000-plus people chanted the riff of "Seven Nation Army" at the Ohio State football games—and we weren't planning to go. He asked if we wanted to go, I said sure, and we agreed to meet for lunch the next day.

After Fats and the band rode the tour bus all night from New York City, I picked him up early on Saturday afternoon at the loading dock at the "Schott" and we went to lunch in Grandview, a suburb on the immediate west side of Columbus. We exchanged stories about the old days, had some chuckles, and as I dropped him off, he said there would be tickets waiting for us at will call that evening. A couple hours later, Fats called and said there had been a change of plans. We were to ask for somebody at the Schott's offices and they would get us our "all access" passes and help us find our way onto the floor, to the head security person, and . . . backstage.

All went according to plan. We arrived at the Schott, made the requisite connections, and were led down to the floor and the backstage entrance next to the stage. We walked behind the stage to the band's dressing room. (The privacy sign indicated Jack's was next door.) Fats greeted us, introduced us to his band mates, and invited us to partake of the substantial spread of food and drink. Then, much to my surprise, he took us to the side of the stage. The opening band, a Latin group from L.A., was playing. Fats introduced Kathy and me to his guitar tech, who tuned his instruments and ran them out to him during the show. Fats told him we were his friends, that we'd be sitting onstage throughout the show, and he should take care of us.

The opener finished up, there was a break, and suddenly Jack and his band, including Fats, sprinted right by us and onto the stage. Twenty thousand people saw a stage with Jack and his band; a few techs; and Kathy and me sitting cross-legged fifteen feet from the action. At one point, Fat's tech urged us to move to the other side of the stage, where our view wouldn't be blocked by the drum riser. We walked around behind the stage, climbed up, and resumed our cross-legged position.

When the show ended, two and a half hours later, we had re-established our position on the entrance/exit side for the band. Fats came over, threw his arms around us, and said, "Give us ten and come back to the dressing room." When we entered, the band was buzzed in that wired high resulting from a fantastic performance before a sold-out house. (Heck, my singer-songwriter friends get that way after a great show for a hundred people, let alone twenty thousand.)

We talked with Fats and the band, then Fats entered Jack's now-open dressing room and returned with him in tow. Fats introduced Kathy and me as good friends and told Jack I was chair of the board of the Rock & Roll Hall of Fame, which I was at the time, and which I think made an impression. Jack's first move was to look at Kathy and tell her how much he liked her coat. We then talked for ten or fifteen minutes. He was a great guy. Tall. Good looking. Really seemed like a regular guy. The whole evening was a complete thrill.

And then there's Kieran, who also remained a close friend throughout. He is smart. So talented. A great songwriter, a fine singer, and, we sometimes fail to appreciate, a marvelous instrumentalist. But life has its challenges. At one point, Kieran seemed to lose the muse. He wasn't writing. When the trio quit performing together (Kevin off to Texas and Fats doing his thing), Kieran wasn't performing. I kept talking him into doing one show a year as he went back and forth to his cabin, but he wasn't doing much else. He seemed totally into painting, and on one of his visits, he told me he was going to give up the music thing and concentrate on his art.

Ah, but the world works in strange ways. Until the past year or two, Kane Welch Kaplin continued to reconvene at Hardly Strictly Bluegrass in San Francisco in October, where they were favorites of the festival's patron, the late Warren Hellman. A couple of years ago, a somewhat younger fiddler from North Carolina, Rayna Gellert, introduced herself to Kieran and said they needed to make music together. They have. In Nashville. In the Adirondacks. Now, a couple of CDs. And at Zeppelin Productions shows at Natalie's. She, too, is a really nice person, a great musician, and has Kieran back in the music game.

SIX

Wine, Women, & Songwriters

'VE BEEN BLESSED WITH A SERIES OF WONDERFUL VENUES throughout the Zeppelin Productions experience, each different from the others, but all with their own benefits and charms.

The first, the Columbus Music Hall, was a late-nineteenth-century firehouse at the northeast corner of Parsons and Oak on the near east side of downtown Columbus. The front of the building consisted of two large garage doors through which they backed in the horse-drawn fire engines in the original days. The doors provided a wonderful backdrop behind the stage. The inside of the old firehouse was very cool, having been renovated completely by proprietor Becky Ogden. The interior walls were exposed brick, and she'd installed woodworking reclaimed from a barn in Kentucky and hung gorgeous chandeliers. The Music Hall had two open, adjoining rooms on the ground floor, and early in my ten-year run of shows, Becky obtained a liquor license and built a bar in the back of the second room. (The initial Zeppelin shows were BYO.) The Hall had folding chairs we set out in rows with a center aisle, and a 150- or 175-person "capacity" was regularly exceeded as we crammed two hundred or more into the two rooms.

The Zeppelin Productions' marketing strategy was minimalist right from the start. Just as we built the roster of Artistes by word of mouth, we also built the audience of Music Fans. As one Artiste recommended the gig to others, the same held true for the Music Fans. Though I never ran an advertisement, we enjoyed great press along the way and lots of support from WCBE-FM. I've simply sold tickets from a mailing list—hard mail for many years and then finally converted to e-mail. In the old days, I mailed out sales-pitch memoranda about upcoming shows, and when Fans sent in a check, I'd mail them the tickets. Heck, I'd mail out the tickets if somebody just said they wanted to come to the show, hoping the check would subsequently show up in the mail or at the door. Tom Russell, who taught me a lot about the promotion business, told me I would increase the chance of someone actually coming to the show if I got a ticket into his or her hands. One of my better ideas was creating an annual "Holiday Package," selling bulk tickets for the first group of shows the following year at a nominal discount. It became a great stocking stuffer for the Music Fans and assured good crowds going into the new year.

Zeppelin Productions as a Wightman family affair had made it really special right from the start. Kathy (who calls herself "the groupie's groupie") continuously worked the door alongside my mother. We'd named Jim "Director of Operations," and his wife, Lisa, happily sold artist merch. A crucial member of the Zeppelin family, Mitch the Soundman has handled the sound for every show from John Stewart until today, subject only to the rare conflict or a couple of serious family illnesses along the way. Jay the security guard—a Columbus policeman and the husband of a coworker—also became a regular part of the Zeppelin crew after an inebriated street person (not a Music Fan) walked in off the street in the middle of a Rosie Flores show, plopped himself into an empty seat up front, and began heckling her. She handled it well, but the episode confirmed my suspicion that on-site security was a good idea. Jay's presence was invaluable some shows later when a Music Fan had a heart attack in the restroom and Jay was able to quarterback a 911 call and the ensuing ambulance arrival and departure.

Soon, Zeppelin concertgoers evolved from friends and family to Central Ohio residents—and some who traveled quite a ways—with a true love for music. Some of the Music Fans were already familiar with the Artistes I brought to town, but candidly, many just came because I gained their confidence with my musical taste. Over time, the list of Music Fans grew from dozens to more than a thousand. And the concerts themselves became something of events as the regulars built their own friendships before and after the shows and during the break between sets.

After our first few years of regularly appearing Artistes at the Music Hall, we sprinkled in others, including Michael Fracasso and Greg Trooper; both became friends and continued to perform off and on for the next three decades, through multiple venues. Lots more came and went. A one-time visitor, Darden Smith, at six foot seven, bumped his head on a chandelier when jumping off the stage in a moment of exuberance near the end of his show. The supersweet Texan Terri Hendrix was later limited as a touring artist by epilepsy. She arrived in Columbus with legendary Lubbock-born guitarist Lloyd Maines, whose daughter, Natalie, is lead singer of the Dixie Chicks (now the Chicks). Lloyd really is a big deal in Austin. Many years later, I had the pleasure of attending a Robert Earl Keen taping for the *Austin City Limits* television show and my host, *ACL's* longtime producer Terry Lickona, was visibly impressed when I received a big hug from Lloyd, who was playing in Keen's band.

One of the best of the early shows was a double-bill with Ray Wylie Hubbard, a grizzled veteran even then, and a very young Slaid Cleaves. I really don't remember how I reached out to them or put them together; I recall they came to Columbus to do a one-off show. Ray was just re-emerging in the business, certainly on a national basis, and he was a great guy. I think he was recent into his sobriety, although I could be wrong; I also believe he was relatively recent into carrying a show solo with his own guitar work. But he was wonderful, and his wife, Judy, also his agent, wrote me a thank-you note for taking such good care of him.

Slaid, at that point, had just released his debut album, and I predicted (incorrectly) major commercial success for him. A superlative songwriter with a distinctive voice, he looks like he stepped out of *GQ*. He didn't return for another Zeppelin show, although he has performed in town over the years. The last time I saw him was in a private lounge backstage at a Columbus Bruce Springsteen concert. We were there thanks to Jon Landau. Slaid was hanging out with a friend, singer-songwriter Rod Picott, who had a buddy in Bruce's lighting crew.

A couple of other Zeppelin one-timers are memorable. In 2003, I stumbled upon an album by Joy Lynn White, a Nashville singer-songwriter with two commercially unsuccessful records on major labels in the nineties. She had self-released a fantastic album of demos of her compositions. Smitten, I somehow reached out to Joy and talked her into coming to Columbus to do a show in January 2004. She brought along a guitar player whose name I forget, and they were stunning. As I drove them to the hotel from Flatiron, playing a new Steve Earle CD and raving about the guitar playing, the guy said quietly, "That's me."

There was one "miss." Paul Burch. I was a fan of the records he'd recorded with an old timey–sounding band. I somehow reached him by phone at his job at Vanderbilt and talked him into doing a solo show at the Music Hall in February 2001. He is very talented, and he's continued to play and record with critical acclaim, but that night he just didn't click with the crowd. I learned a lesson from this "miss," which I have only rarely ignored—don't book an artist unless I have seen the person live or received a very strong recommendation from a trusted someone who has.

I did bring a number of other Artistes to the Music Hall who became regulars over the ensuing years, including the afore-mentioned Michael Fracasso and Greg Trooper, as well as Eliza Gilkyson, Lynn Miles, and near the end of our Music Hall run, Gretchen Peters.

MICHAEL FRACASSO IS AN ENIGMA, at least in terms of his com-mercial success, or lack thereof. Dave Marsh once wrote a lengthy piece about him that struggled with Michael's lack of an "audi-ence." Among other things, Marsh said, "No one can quite explain why he's a secret. Fracasso can do everything a fine musician needs to do. He writes strongly melodic songs with lyrics that offer narra-tive, characterization, and aphorisms. He plays a mean guitar. He can carry a solo show fine, and he's a first-rate bandleader."

I was already a fan of Michael's first two albums when I saw him for the first time at Stache's. Knowing nothing about him per-sonally, I was surprised to see one of my law partners in the very small crowd. It turned out Michael, who is from the Steubenville, Ohio, area, was a 1975 graduate of Ohio State and had roomed with my partner. But even with those Ohio connections, Michael has never been able to build a big audience in Columbus. I've brought him solo. With a band. With a guitarist. I've paired him with Greg Trooper, David Olney (in a match of musical styles that didn't really work), and Chuck Prophet. Later, I brought him with John Fullbright and ultimately as part of the Backroad Boys with John, Kevin Welch, and Dustin Welch. But it's frustrating; I just can't generate the crowd Michael deserves.

That didn't keep us from becoming good friends. I once helped him finance a new CD at a level that entitled me to a homemade Italian meal, which Michael prepared at our house the night after a Columbus show. Accompanying Michael to Fresh Market that afternoon was like visiting the Louvre with an art historian. He is a master chef, and the meal was delicious.

As with Michael, I knew Greg Trooper's music before I ever thought about bringing him to Columbus. I loved his 1992 album *Everywhere*, and when I first met Tom Russell and we explored our musical tastes, I mentioned it and was surprised to learn that Tom and Greg were not only friends, but they had co-taught a songwriting class in Brooklyn. Perhaps more than most Zeppelin artists, Greg moved in heady circles from time to time. But similar to other Artistes, such connections didn't translate into meaningful commercial success. Greg had a great band in New York in the eighties featuring guitarist Larry Campbell, who went on to play with Bob Dylan for years. (How is this for a coincidence? Michael's great friend and sometime band mate and producer, Charlie Sexton, succeeded Campbell in Dylan's band.) Greg had songs cut by the likes of Steve Earle. He moved to Nashville and became friends with Garry W. Tallent from the E Street Band, who produced records for him. But outside of some geographic pockets (especially Houston), he never quite made it commercially.

That 1997 Fracasso-Trooper duo show at the Music Hall was good, but it didn't have the magic of the shows Tom and Andy, or Katy, had been doing. Among other things, Greg was . . . sloppy. He kept messing up songs and forgetting the lyrics. In retrospect, he might have been out of practice. Or maybe he was just relaxed and enjoying himself in this new, intimate venue. But truth be known, I didn't bring him back to town for many years.

Greg still came to Columbus once in a while, however. Six String Concerts booked him at least once, and I remember sitting in the darkened venue (the Music Hall itself) when Greg asked for requests and I shouted out, "So Far Away" from *Everywhere*. Greg stopped, was quiet, and then asked out loud, "Alec, is that you?" Greg also came to town as an opener for John Prine at an outdoor summer concert at the Columbus Zoo. Kathy and I attended, and after Greg's set, I found him signing CDs at the merch table. He sat with us for Prine's show.

Many years later, I finally brought Greg back to Columbus a couple of times, now at Natalie's. We had a nice time hanging out and he put on fine performances. The last time, I accompanied him before the gig while he did a three-song video at a local barbershop taping live music for the internet. Greg stayed at our house that night, and we sat up late talking in the courtyard, where he confided in me about a variety of issues, including his dad's health. This jump-started a friendship that continued with the occasional written or telephonic communication through his diagnosis of and treatment for pancreatic cancer. We had shows in the works during that time, but his health wouldn't permit it. I saved a message from him saying it had been a "wild ride" and that he would give me the details when next we met. Unfortunately, I never saw him again, and a few months later, on January 15, 2017, he died at the age of sixty-one.

ELIZA GILKYSON'S FIRST ZEPPELIN SHOW was in June 2001. She was touring behind a wonderful record, *Hard Times in Babylon*, which opened with a powerful cut, "Beauty Way." She wrote the song at least in part about her brother, Tony, a hotshot guitarist in L.A. who'd played with X and Lone Justice. Eliza and Tony clearly came from a musical gene pool, as their father, Terry, was the songwriter behind such classics as "Memories Are Made of This," a hit for Dean Martin, and "Bare Necessities," from Disney's *Jungle Book*, for which he was nominated for an Academy Award.

Eliza was routed my way via Tom Russell, for whom she sang backup vocals on *Borderland*. After her first solo appearance at the Music Hall in June 2001, she returned in October 2002 with Tom and Andrew, doing an opening set and then singing with Tom as he introduced songs from the new record. She's also appeared on a co-bill with Lynn Miles at the Columbus Maennerchor and solo many years later at Natalie's. Eliza has a strong feminist streak and numerous female fans. Many of her songs and patter were not, shall we say, complimentary of the male species. She told a story about a young woman approaching her after a show and applauding her for "hating men." Eliza explained that the problem was actually the exact opposite.

I reached out directly to book Lynn Miles, a wonderful Ottawa-based singer-songwriter. Her 1996 album, *Slightly Haunted*, remains a classic of the Americana genre. Lynn played the Music Hall four times starting in May 2000 (one of which was the very last Zeppelin show at the Hall, on June 17, 2005), and then three times at the Maennerchor, including the co-bill with Eliza. She either performed solo or with the fine guitarist Keith Glass, a member of the successful Canadian band Prairie Oyster.

Lynn was always a strong live performer, but one occasion stands out. The Maennerchor had a piano, usually located in the back of the hall. On this night it sat next to the stage and Lynn must have asked Mitch the Soundman to mic it during sound check. For her encore, she left the stage, sat at the piano with her back to the audience, and performed Tom Waits' "Grapefruit Moon." The only time she ever played piano at a Zeppelin gig, it was deeply moving.

Lynn became a friend of the family. She and my mother bonded, and Jim and Lisa hosted the two of them for dinner at their house. Lynn stayed at our home a couple of times after Kathy and I moved to German Village, and one hot Sunday morning the three of us walked over to the art fair at the Columbus College of Art and Design. Lynn picked out a beautiful red ceramic bowl for us, telling us to place it by the door to bring good luck. Within days, we unexpectedly received a fairly significant income tax refund from the State of New York.

Unfortunately, Lynn's run as a Zeppelin Artiste came to an end after 2010, following the double-bill with Eliza. Because the Maennerchor and Grand Valley Dale Ballroom were larger spaces than the Music Hall, requiring more people to feel full, we couldn't draw a big enough crowd—which is why I tried the double-bill. (By the way, I am not sure Lynn and Eliza had ever played together before, but they not only did their own sets, but also played a number of songs together—brilliant.) Once we moved our concerts to Natalie's, which would have been a perfect venue for her, the immigration process became more difficult and expensive, and Lynn hasn't played south of the Canadian border in years.

TOM RUSSELL CONTINUED TO ADD to the Zeppelin Artiste tree when he urged me to book Nashville songwriter Gretchen Peters. Born in New York, Gretchen moved with her mother to Boulder, Colorado, as a teen after her parents' divorce. She sang in clubs and ski resorts until the late eighties, when she relocated to Nashville. There, Gretchen quickly established herself as a songwriter, penning hits for George Strait, Pam Tillis, Patty Loveless, Faith Hill, and Martina McBride, for whom she wrote the smash "Independence Day"—named the Country Music Association's Song of the Year and nominated for Best Country Song by the Recording Academy. She also became a very successful songwriting partner of pop star Bryan Adams. Gretchen released a couple of little-known solo records in the late nineties, and when Tom mentioned her to me, she had just seriously embarked on her own singing career with a major-label album, *Halcyon*.

On April 8, 2005, Gretchen played the next-to-last Zeppelin show at the Music Hall, accompanied by Barry Walsh on keyboards and the occasional accordion. Not only does Gretchen write masterful songs, she is also a remarkable vocalist. She and Barry quickly became great friends of our family, and four months later they returned with Tom and Andy to initiate the Columbus Maennerchor as the new Zeppelin venue. That first Maennerchor concert was a thrill. Gretchen and Barry opened with their own set and then joined Tom and Andy as part of the "band" for the second. Gretchen and Barry went on to perform captivating shows at the Maennerchor for all but the last of our seven-year run there.

Our friendship also grew, thanks in no small measure to wonderful post-show Flatiron evenings and, ultimately, hanging out with them at Tom and Nadine's 2008 wedding in Gstaad, Switzerland.

Gretchen's last appearance at the Maennerchor was as special as her first. On February 6, 2010, she joined her friends Matraca Berg and Suzy Bogguss on the Maennerchor stage for an act they appropriately called "Wine, Women, & Song." It was an evening to remember. An extraordinarily successful country songwriter, Matraca grew up in Nashville and wrote her first number one hit at nineteen. Her songs subsequently reached the top of the charts via artists ranging from Reba McEntire to Trisha Yearwood to Patty Loveless. Matraca's cowrite (with Gary Harrison) of Deana Carter's recording of "Strawberry Wine" won the CMA's Song of the Year in 1997, and like Gretchen, she is an inductee into the Nashville Songwriter's Hall of Fame.

Suzy, on the other hand, is primarily known as a singer, not a songwriter. Born and raised in southern Illinois, she moved to Nashville in 1985, and after a stint performing at Dolly Parton's first theme park (pre-dating Dollywood), she returned to Nashville and released her debut, *Somewhere Between*, in 1989. That started a string of chart-topping albums and singles over the next six or seven years, finally sidetracked by time off devoted to her family and diminished commercial success. Since then, she has released numerous records on independent labels, but never replicated the chart success of the early years. Having said that, when the "Women" hit the stage and Suzy sang her first song of the evening, I turned to my brother and said, "I now understand the difference between the voice of a true singing star and the—wonderful—voices of the typical Zeppelin Artistes," most of whom are primarily songwriters. Suzy just sounded . . . different.

The entire Wine, Women, & Song evening was a Zeppelin highlight. As the Women took turns performing their own songs, with the others in support, they captivated the packed house. The couple of bottles of fine red wine I supplied made the show . . . loose. (Think a slightly milder version of "Mr. Bottle" from that first Kieran Kane/Kevin Welch show.) And the post-show trip to Flatiron was equally memorable, with lots of stories and laughs.

Both Suzy and Matraca each returned once to the Maennerchor stage—Suzy somewhat spontaneously. She called me in September 2010 and said she was on the road and had suffered a cancellation. She asked if I could fill in the routing hole. I said yes, but I expressed concern about the late notice, the quick return visit, and my ability to sell tickets. Nonetheless, she insisted on a pretty hefty guaranty and I succumbed to her advocacy. It was a lesson to be learned. The show was fine—the crowd and economics not so much.

Matraca returned the following spring at my request and in support of her first solo album in nearly fifteen years. Her two excellent albums in the mid-nineties barely grazed the charts, despite her exquisite songwriting and vocals. Her lack of commercial success as a performer is another of those music business mysteries. Heck, the truth is, in some ways, Matraca had stolen the trio show a year earlier.

On May 14, 2011, Matraca appeared solo at the Maennerchor. I picked her up at the airport that afternoon, and we shared an early dinner at Lindey's (the restaurant diagonally across from our house). I think it was the first time she had appeared solo in many years and she conceded she was nervous. The nerves didn't appear when she played and sang, however—she was wonderful.

I stayed in touch with Matraca, and in the spring of 2019, I finally persuaded her to return for a show in the intimate environs of Natalie's. Over the years, I urged her to bring her husband, Jeff Hanna, a founding member of the Nitty Gritty Dirt Band, but his busy schedule made it impossible. This time Matraca, clearly more comfortable not playing solo, enlisted fellow Nashville singer-songwriters Marshall Chapman and Tommy Womack. Matraca and Marshall stayed at our house, we walked the streets of German Village (where Marshall had visited when her sister lived here in the early 1970s), and they put on a fun show, with Matraca once again at the top of her game.

The Wine, Women, & Song show also led to future good times, beginning with Gretchen and Barry's Nashville wedding on October 2, 2011, to which Kathy and I were honored to be invited. Actually, the highlight for me came the evening before at a Green's Grocery gathering in Leipers Fork. Tom and Nadine Russell, as well as our new friends Matraca and Suzy, were all there. Tom and Suzy met for the first time that night—even though she'd had a major country hit with his "Outbound Plane" many years earlier. At one point, the two of them hopped onstage (the former grocery is now an event venue) and performed the song. Icing on the cake was meeting Rodney Crowell, who figures prominently in the "music in my life." Emmylou Harris albums introduced me to his brilliant songwriting in the 1970s, and I had mentioned to the Women that he would be a dream Zeppelin act. That night, the three of them dragged me over to Rodney (who officiated the wedding the next day), made the introduction, and got in his face, telling him he had to do my gig in Columbus. (It was reminiscent of Katy and Rosie with Dave Alvin many years earlier.) A few minutes into their harangue, I heard him say, "Okay, I'll do it." They didn't hear him and continued to advocate vociferously until he almost yelled, "*I said, I'll do it!*"

Then, in June 2014, while in my second year as chair of the board of the Rock & Roll Hall of Fame, we held our annual board retreat in Nashville. On Thursday evening, we "closed" the famous Bluebird Cafe for a private board party and, with my assistance, secured the services of the Women to entertain the board after dinner in that intimate setting. Jeff Hanna accompanied the ladies, Barry being otherwise occupied with his own recording session. Once again fabulous, they gave me a warm welcome, and the "official" portion of the evening ended with Gretchen asking if I had a request, accommodating me with a killer version of her "On a Bus to St. Cloud" (a truly great song, especially the version by Jimmy LaFave). After the bus (not the one to St. Cloud) took the board members back to the hotel, I stayed behind, along with a few others—Greg Harris, the Rock Hall CEO; Caprice Bragg, the vice president of development and external relations; and Lauren Onkey, the vice president of education and public programs.

More wine was poured and Gretchen, Matraca, and Suzy, with Jeff accompanying on guitar and sometimes singing, began an extemporaneous "concert" of what seemed like every song they jointly knew, many of which we requested. They just sat there experimenting with tunes and tunings, trying to recall words and singing songs ranging from the Everly Brothers to "Lodi." It was a night I will never forget.

SEVEN

Zeppelin's New Home

I N EARLY 2005, BECKY OGDEN, THE PROPRIETOR OF THE MUSIC Hall through her nonprofit entity, told me she planned to turn the Hall into a full-time jazz club and that my days of promoting shows at that wonderful venue would soon be over. I told her, as did others, she was making a mistake and that Columbus, Ohio, wouldn't support a single-genre jazz club five or six nights a week, but she was determined. Sadly, but predictably, she was out of business within months and the Music Hall was forever silenced as a live music venue.

Ah, but there are silver linings in most clouds, and Becky's decision caused the Zeppelin team (brother Jim, Mitch the Soundman, Kathy, and me) to begin the search for a new venue. Now living in German Village (a residential area immediately south of downtown), Kathy and I discovered on the edge of the neighborhood of (mostly) renovated nineteenth-century homes an iconic German social club, the Columbus Maennerchor. The Maennerchor (which means "men's chorus" in German) purports to be the longest continually active German social club in the United States. Founded in 1848, with the corresponding Damen-chor founded in 1931, its motto is "Harmony—in song and in life—holds us together." Could there be a better place to host the ongoing Zeppelin shows?

The Maennerchor consisted of a house, built in 1921; a large, very traditional rathskeller located in the basement; and in the back, a ballroom with a separate bar area. The layout was not dissimilar from the Music Hall, but significantly bigger. And the ambience, although much different from the Music Hall, was appropriately quirky—low ceilings, chandeliers, a stage at one end, and dozens of pictures reflecting the history of the club and its German heritage. On YouTube you can see Dave Alvin doing "Fourth of July" at the Maennerchor—just the stage, the bare wall behind it, and the very low ceiling. An online comment says, "It looks like Holiday Inn ballroom." From that angle, it did.

After a decade at the Music Hall, the Maennerchor served as an excellent successor for Zeppelin concerts, this time for seven years. With a larger capacity—a 275 fire-code limit in the ballroom that could stretch to three hundred plus using the back bar area— we could produce shows that wouldn't work in the old firehouse. To kick off the Maennerchor in August 2005, Tom Russell put on an extraordinary show, accompanied by Andrew Hardin, Gretchen Peters, and Barry Walsh. In rare form, on stage and off, they played to a packed house.

It marked our only Maennerchor event that year, but throughout 2006, we settled into the comfort of bringing our Music Hall regulars to the new venue: Katy Moffatt with Pat McLaughlin, whom Kathy and I had met at the Bluebird the previous year and whose songs Katy frequently recorded; Kieran, Kevin, and Fats; Dave Alvin; Tom and Andy, for what would be their last Columbus show together; Gretchen and Barry; and Lynn Miles.

We began 2007 with a new Zeppelin artist and a show to remember: Dan Penn, a true legend in the music world. He wrote or cowrote classics ranging from "I'm Your Puppet," a 1966 smash for James and Bobby Purify, to "Cry Like a Baby," a 1968 hit for the

Box Tops. Heck, he produced the first Box Tops album, featuring their chart topper, "The Letter," and is credited with coaching a teenage Alex Chilton to sing it just like . . . Dan. That night Dan performed those classics and a slew of others, including songs recorded by Percy Sledge, Clarence Carter, Otis Redding, and Wilson Pickett—great Memphis soul songs. He also sang country hits written for Ronnie Milsap and Hank Williams Jr.

The highlight of the evening for me was hearing Dan sing and discuss two of his greatest compositions, beginning with "Do Right Woman, Do Right Man." Aretha Franklin intended to cut her first Atlantic album, including that song, at FAME Studios in Muscle Shoals, Alabama, backed by its renowned session players. Aretha's then husband and manager got into a fight with a horn player and studio owner Rick Hall, and they left, taking the unfinished instrumental tracks to New York to finish the recording there with producer Jerry Wexler (who'd originally set up the FAME sessions). Wexler summoned Dan to New York to complete the song lyrics while Aretha and the band waited in the studio. Dan holed up in a closet trying to concentrate, he related, while Aretha kept opening the door, pressuring him to finish, and hollering suggestions at him, until she finally came up with something that triggered his muse. The song was completed, and as Dan later put it, the result is "still one of the best records I've ever heard by anybody—not 'cause it's my song, but just that record."

The other Penn masterpiece, "Dark End of the Street," is one of my favorite songs. I first heard the Flying Burrito Brothers' version on their 1969 debut, *The Gilded Palace of Sin* (which also includes a killer take on "Do Right Woman"), and it has been covered by dozens of artists, most notably Linda Ronstadt on *Heart Like a Wheel*. James Carr's 1967 original "Dark End of the Street" is a singularly powerful recording. That night at the Maennerchor, Dan talked about Carr and the song, saying that people frequently ask him which version of "Dark End of the Street" he prefers, to which he replies, "Did anyone do it besides James Carr?" Sad to say, Carr, a great soul singer, suffered from debilitating mental illness and never capitalized on his tremendous voice, ultimately dying of lung cancer at a relatively young age.

As wonderful as Dan was onstage, in many ways my favorite parts of the evening were before and after the show. One of the nicest people in the world, Dan is completely unassuming, right down to the overalls he wears onstage and off. Dan and his wife and I spoke on the phone for two years before we successfully brought him to Columbus. I envisioned booking Dan together with his longtime friend, cowriter, and musical partner, Spooner Oldham. But Spooner played in Neil Young's band at the time (when Neil wasn't out with Crazy Horse), so was always "on hold" for a Neil tour—which probably happened a fraction of the times they were contemplated.

When Dan and I spoke in late 2006, he finally suggested performing with another keyboardist, Bobby Emmons, whose name I didn't recognize. They arrived on a January night in 2007 for the Maennerchor sound check. Mitch, Jim, and I watched in the ballroom as Dan and Bobby checked their way through a handful of Dan's classics. Suddenly, Dan turned and said, in his thick Southern drawl, "Bobby, let's do one you wrote." With that, Bobby slid into "Luckenbach, Texas." I had no idea—talk about an "oh my" moment. Although Bobby wrote a number of classics, he earned legendary status playing keyboards on American Recordings studio sessions in Memphis. That's Bobby you hear on Elvis' "Suspicious Minds" and "In the Ghetto"; Dusty Springfield's "Son of a Preacher Man"; and, get this, Neil Diamond's "Sweet Caroline"—all cut there (which is also where Dan produced the Box Tops).

After the show, Dan and Bobby joined the family at Flatiron for a late-night dinner. They spun story after story about the Nashville and Memphis music scenes—two hours of pure magic. At one point, they swapped a series of tales about "John" doing this and "John" doing that. Finally, my brother asked the question we all wondered: "Who is John?" They looked at him incredulously and said in unison, "Cash." *Of course.*

I saw Dan again after that show, at Spooner's 2009 induction into the Rock & Roll Hall of Fame as a "sideman" (the category now labeled "musical excellence"). Kathy and I spent time with Dan and his wife that evening, including riding with them on a shuttle to the event itself. He was so appreciative of the hospitality we'd provided a couple of years earlier. Sadly, we lost Bobby Emmons in 2015.

ALTHOUGH NEIL YOUNG MAY BE my favorite artist of all time, when I am pushed to identify my favorite type of music, I have been known to say, "Music from Austin, Texas." German immigrants helped settle Austin and the surrounding beautiful Hill Country, so it's appropriate I introduced some wonderful Austin singer-songwriters to the Maennerchor in the heart of German Village.

I'd been a fan of Bruce Robison and his wife, Kelly Willis, for many years before I brought them to Columbus—and long before I'd even realized they were married.

Bruce was the first of the two to hit the Zeppelin stage, appearing before a big crowd, most of whom had never heard of him, on March 3, 2007. Of course, many had heard Bruce's songs, albeit by other folks, since he'd written a number of hits, including "Wrapped" and "Desperately" for George Strait; "Angry All the Time" for Tim McGraw and Faith Hill; and "Travelin' Soldier" for the Dixie Chicks, one of whom was then married to Bruce's brother, Charlie. Bruce says the latter song took the biggest plunge of any number one in country music history after Natalie Maines denounced President Bush (and the Iraq War) onstage in London, when every country radio station in America dropped the Dixie Chicks, and Bruce's song, from their rotation.

Bruce appeared solo twice at the Maennerchor, returning a second time in June 2009. Actually, he was "solo" (meaning not with Kelly), but accompanied by a crackerjack band that included Eleanor Whitmore, a fiddler who would later form the Mastersons with her husband, Chris Masterson. Together, they become a regular part of Steve Earle's band. Bruce is a fine singer and excellent guitarist; obviously, he's a primo songwriter; and he has great stage presence, all six feet seven inches of him. The epitome of what we look for in a Zeppelin artist, Bruce not only makes great music (meaning I love it), but he's also one of the nicest guys in the world. Not many Artistes slid into the Zeppelin routine quite as smoothly as Bruce. We closed up the Flatiron on both of his solo visits, comparing notes on life and the Austin music scene. Bruce also credited Jerry Jeff Walker's *Viva Terlingua!* as a game-changing album, some forty-five years after its release. Bruce ultimately hosted Jerry Jeff on one of his first "Next Waltz" social media programs.

As much as I liked Bruce and his shows, I harbored a special desire to get Kelly to Columbus. When I would tiptoe into that subject with Bruce and his agent, they made it clear that Kelly rarely toured outside of Texas, neither solo nor, certainly, with Bruce. They had four young kids, and somebody had to stay home and keep order in the household.

I have been a Kelly Willis fan since her very first record in 1990. She was signed to MCA and had the full major label publicity machine behind her. She released excellent albums and also acted in several movies. Though the critics loved her from the beginning, she never achieved meaningful chart success.

In my years of promoting shows and seeing and hearing such great music, I stick by my rule of not trying to explain why some artists "make it" commercially and others don't. I sometimes compare musicians to professional tennis players or golfers. The difference between the very best local musicians and the artists I book for Zeppelin shows—most of whom struggle to get by unless scoring as a songwriter—is like the difference between the very best country club tennis player or golfer and the athletes just scratching to survive on the professional satellite tour. It is light years—no comparison. The touring "pros" are just that much better than the local amateur. But as I point out, with tennis or golf there is an objective standard for success. If you can beat the opponent, you win. There is no such standard in the arts, including music.

I have only breached my rule with respect to a couple of Zeppelin Artistes, posing the question of "Why X and not Y?" One is Chuck Prophet. More on him later, but my question there is "Why Tom Petty and not Chuck Prophet?" (Not to disparage the late Mr. Petty, by any means. But in my book, Chuck should enjoy similar commercial success.) The other is Kelly, about whom I've been known to ask, "Why Faith Hill and not Kelly Willis?" I asked that question for years, even before I'd met Kelly and seen her perform. (I have seen Faith live a couple of times, and after seeing Kelly, it only strengthened the rhetorical—to me—nature of my question.) The irony of it all was really brought home when I learned both women were nominated for the Academy of Country Music's Best New Female Vocalist Award in 1993, and sure enough, Faith won. *Sigh.* I once posited the "why/why not" question to a friend with lots of music industry experience, including in both Nashville and New York. I gave him my musician–tennis player/golfer analogy, and then specifically raised the Faith/Kelly question. He had his own answer. He said that while Kelly was in Austin raising four kids under the age of five, Faith "would have run over her grandmother with a truck to be a star."

Imagine my thrill when Bruce and Kelly succumbed to my pleas and agreed to come to Columbus together. One of the few times Kelly had performed outside of Texas in years, it was certainly the first time they had done so together in ages. To be clear, at that point their oldest was ten and the youngest was five, and they didn't simply leave them "alone." On June 11, 2011, Zeppelin

Productions promoted a Kelly Willis/Bruce Robison show at the Maennerchor. For this special concert evening, a huge crowd turned out—not only the Zeppelin regulars (who had seen Bruce twice), but also members of a pretty big cult following that Kelly had developed over the prior two decades. Kelly, by the way, was absolutely as nice as Bruce, from the moment of our first introduction at sound check, when she sported her bespectacled librarian look, to her first step on the Maennerchor stage, where she looked like the glamorous country star I think she should be.

Not only was the show special, but so was the evening for both Kelly and Bruce, who was celebrating his forty-fifth birthday that day. He was energized by the concert and ready to roll to Flatiron and party. Kelly, however, on the way to the restaurant, said, "Drop me off at the hotel," to take advantage of her first chance to be alone, take a hot bath, and relax in years. She sent Bruce off with the rest of us, and we sat outside on a beautiful summer evening, enjoying a late-night dinner, a drink or three, and great fun. Both Bruce and Kelly celebrated Bruce's birthday, but in their own ways.

A couple of years later, Bruce and Kelly finally released their first album together, *Cheater's Game*, and I enticed them back to Columbus as part of a broader tour in support of the record. In April 2013, Bruce, Kelly, and the band hit the stage of our new venue, the Grand Valley Dale Ballroom. They put on another fantastic show, and they were as dazzled by the ballroom as the crowd was by them.

Bruce and I stayed in touch. One year when Moose and I attended SXSW, Bruce invited us to a small room upstairs at the Continental Club to see Kelly and him do a private show with their band. They were trying out new material for *Cheater's Game*, including a creative version of Dave Alvin's "Border Radio." Another night I joined 20,000 of my closest personal friends to see Tim McGraw and Faith Hill at Nationwide Arena in Columbus, and they did "Angry All the Time." I messaged Bruce from the arena and told him to head to the mailbox to pick up the royalty check. He quickly replied, expressing surprise they were still including the song in their set.

I also contributed a few dollars to support the production of Bruce's 2017 release, *Bruce Robison & the Back Porch Band*. My contribution entitled me to a set of longhand lyrics to the song of my choice, and I picked one of my favorites, "When It Rains," the lyrics of which are now framed and hanging in my home office. Bruce subsequently teased me that I picked his song with the most lyrics.

Although they are royalty in their hometown (the "King and Queen" of Austin music), the couple's lack of any real commercial recording success, not to mention those four kids at home, resulted in neither artist touring much outside of Texas for years. Finally, in 2017, we booked Bruce, touring behind *Back Porch Band*, for our new, intimate venue, Natalie's. Not to be. A month before the concert date, Bruce contracted typhus, a rare and potentially life-threatening infectious disease that, in the words of his sister's Facebook post, "caused pretty severe complications to his liver, kidneys, and immune system." He was hospitalized for quite a while, including an extended stay in intensive care, and his tour and everything else in his life were put on hold for months.

As a result, and unexpectedly, the first of the couple to play Natalie's was Kelly, who released her first record in more than fifteen years with 2018's *Back Being Blue* and hit the road in support of the album. In June 2018, I had the pleasure of introducing Kelly to a hundred or so Music Fans rather than the thousands Faith Hill was probably playing to somewhere that evening. I can guarantee you, I know who was . . . best. We did finally get Bruce back to Columbus and his Natalie's debut when he and Kelly appeared on November 1, 2019. The show exceeded even my expectations. I've heard Music Fans say it many times over the years as they leave a show, but this night many said, *"Best show ever!"*

———

IN MANY WAYS, THE EPITOME of the "Austin sound" comes from three guys who grew up in Lubbock, Texas—Joe Ely, Jimmie Dale Gilmore, and Butch Hancock. The story has been told so many times, there is no point in repeating it in much detail here, but suffice to say, Joe, Jimmie Dale, and Butch returned to their hometown in the late 1960s after personal sojourns elsewhere. As roommates, they played music together and, with various backup musicians, formed the Flatlanders in 1970. Their respective musical backgrounds made for a mix that would characterize their sound, collectively and individually, for decades to come—Jimmie, a "well of country music," as Joe would describe him; Butch, a folkie and a poet; and Joe, a rock & roller. After a handful of local gigs and an appearance at the 1972 Kerrville (Texas) Folk Festival, the band headed to Memphis to record their first album. The promotional single from the record, Jimmie's now classic "Dallas," was a commercial bust, and the "album" was only released as an eight-track tape. It quickly slid into truck-stop oblivion, finally being re-released as a CD to much fanfare in 1990 under the appropriate title *More a Legend Than a Band*.

A legend is exactly what the Flatlanders became as each of the principals built sterling reputations and, at least to some degree, commercially successful careers as singers and/or songwriters on their own. Joe's career blossomed first and strongest. From his self-titled debut in 1977 and for decades to come, he has been a leader not only of the Austin music scene, but also something of an icon in that world where rock & roll mixes with country music. In 1978 he and his crackerjack band (which included drummer Davis McLarty, now a friend through his role as booking agent for Kelly and Bruce, among others) played London, where they became tight with the Clash, and ultimately opened for them on a U.S. tour a couple of years later. (That's reportedly Joe in the background on the Clash's single "Should I Stay or Should I Go.") Soon, Joe and his band were headlining major shows in Texas and elsewhere. He continued to make one excellent record after another, out front as a great singer, songwriter, and guitarist, carrying on the legacy of Lubbock native Buddy Holly. He recorded, played live, and became pals with Bruce Springsteen. On his acoustic tours, including song swaps with the likes of Guy Clark, Lyle Lovett, and John Hiatt, he moves smoothly into the Tex-Mex sound and performs what Tom Russell says is the definitive version of Tom's "Gallo del Cielo."

Butch, on the other hand, stayed mostly under the radar screen, recording and performing as a solo act when not in the company of one or more of his fellow Flatlanders. He releases the occasional studio album (going back to the late seventies), but his reputation primarily derives from his songwriting, with his compositions recorded by Jerry Jeff Walker, the Sir Douglas Quintet, Emmylou Harris, the Texas Tornados, Rosie Flores (a killer version of his "Boxcars"), and of course, both Joe and Jimmie Dale.

Jimmie Dale's career has meandered more circuitously than the other two. As a kid, he heard his father's records—Jimmie Rodgers, Hank Williams, and honky-tonk music—all influences on his unique, high-lonesome vocal style. After the Flatlanders dissolved in the early seventies, he lived in a Colorado ashram studying metaphysics with an Indian guru—a lifetime influence on what is clearly a gentle soul. Jimmie finally made his way to Austin, where Joe and Butch had already set up camp, and released his first solo album in 1988. Since that time, Jimmie has made one great record after another, albeit infrequently. At the top of my list is 1993's *Spinning Around the Sun*, which includes two Butch classics. And in one of the great "will the circle be unbroken" moments of the Zeppelin world, Jimmie teamed with Dave Alvin, an unexpected pairing if there ever was one, to release 2018's *Downey to Lubbock*. (Jimmie is probably best known to the masses for his performance as Smokey in the 1998 movie *The Big Lebowski*, where he is threatened by the Dude's sidekick Walter, played by a pistol-waving John Goodman.)

Jimmie Dale was the first of the Flats I saw live, in 1988 or 1989, when Kathy and I stood against the bar at Stache's and were blown away by Jimmie's absolutely distinctive voice and his fabulous band. Another night, at Ludlow's, a bar in Columbus' Brewery District, Jimmie appeared with a then-unknown opener, Patty Griffin, who went on to her own successful Austin-based career.

I also saw Joe at least once before bringing the Flats to Columbus. Our daughter Emily spent a summer in Boston during her college years, and Kathy and I visited her for a long weekend. Joe was playing at Club Passim, a folk club in Cambridge, and Kathy and I, along with Emily and a friend or two, went. Afterward, I introduced myself, invoked the names of some common friends (Tom Russell, for sure), and told him about the Zeppelin shows. Polite and interested, he gave me the name of the agent who opened the door to getting the Flatlanders to Columbus, individually and collectively.

Jimmie came first. In October 2008, he played his first Zeppelin show at the packed Maennerchor—ticket sales never being an issue for Jimmie, Joe, or the Flatlanders because of their significant following in Central Ohio. Jimmie put on a great show, had a nice time with the family afterward, and, according to their agent, advocated for getting the rest of his compadres to Columbus. And get them to Columbus we did, on multiple occasions, beginning on November 22, 2009. Earlier that year, the Flatlanders released their third album since reuniting in the late nineties, and they were touring in full promotion of the record. They arrived at the Maennerchor in a luxury touring bus and set up camp in the parking lot on an unusually warm afternoon; Joe detached his bicycle from the back of the bus and pedaled around German Village.

The Flats had a full band featuring the superb guitarist Robbie Gjersoe. A magnificent show, Joe, Jimmie, and Butch played all the classics as well as songs from the new record. Every once in a while, one of them—usually Butch—would call an audible that would have the others scratching their heads. Yes, that night was memorable from start to finish.

For starters, literally, the Flats arrived with an unannounced opening act, Ryan Bingham, a young singer-songwriter whom Joe had befriended. A little rough around the edges, Ryan cut his musical teeth in the clubs and bars of the Southwest while trying to make it as a bull rider on the rodeo circuit. He'd released a couple of albums, but he was unknown to the crowd. That wouldn't last. Earlier that year, Ryan had worked with T Bone Burnett on the soundtrack of *Crazy Heart*, a movie (starring Jeff Bridges) released about the time he hit Columbus. Among other songs, Ryan wrote and performed the film's theme song, "The Weary Kind," and within months it won "Best Song" awards at both the Golden Globes and Oscars. I paid him something like $100 as an unannounced (even to me) performer that night.

The finish to the night was also memorable. It was Sunday and Flatiron was closed, so we flocked to Gresso's, a bar/pizza place across the street from the Maennerchor. We closed it down several hours after the show—"we" meaning the Flats; the family; the then-CEO of the Rock Hall, Terry Stewart; and the recently hired vice president of development, Greg Harris, who went on to succeed Terry as CEO and become one of my closest friends. Let's just say the Flatlanders enjoy their after-parties. Jimmie—whose onstage storytelling is known for his . . . digressions—told story after story. Joe kept up with him. Lots of wine was consumed—and spilled. Ryan never left the bar, deep in meaningful conversation, I'm sure, with a young woman from Columbus.

The Flats are all great guys, but in many respects, Butch is the most down-to-earth. He and Kathy conversed that night for what seemed like hours. At one point, he talked her into going on one of the rafting trips he guides down the Rio Grande. (Yes, he really does those.) I think I was to be included, but I'm not sure. A number of years later at SXSW, Moose and I set up camp one afternoon in a small venue near Threadgill's with a roster of great musicians, including Kevin Welch. At one point, a nice lady sat down next to me, and after she made knowledgeable comments, I asked who she was. She said she was Adrienne Hancock, Butch's wife. In a moment of questionable judgment, I introduced myself, explained that I promoted shows in Columbus, and related the tale about that infamous evening. I told her that in all the years of promoting shows, I had never seen Kathy so smitten by one of the artists. Adrienne looked at me, smirked, and said, "All the married women like Butch."

One other memorable aspect of that first Flatlanders show, and the subsequent ones as well, was their road manager. The Zeppelin team has been challenged by a difficult road manager or two along the way, but this guy was in a class of his own. Apparently, our Flatlanders contract required me to provide a stage crew to load the band in and out. I've never provided that service, other than Mitch, Jim, and me (mostly Mitch and Jim) helping carry equipment to and from the vehicle. On this night the Artistes wanted to roll across the street with us as soon as the show ended, leaving the road manager and backup musicians to break down the fairly substantial setup and load the bus. When the road manager finally arrived at Gresso's, he was livid. He chewed me out, telling me over and over again that I was disrespecting Joe, Jimmie, and Butch because they were "legends"—all the while ignoring the fact that the "legends" were having the time of their lives at Gresso's.

Thankfully, the road manager wasn't also the booking agent, and within the year, Joe played a wonderful show at the Maennerchor in June 2010. Then, on my birthday in 2011 (January 23), the Flatlanders returned. Also on a Sunday night, the show once again ended at Gresso's. The group was a little more sedate this time as we retreated to a private room in the back and enjoyed pizza and drinks with Joe, Jimmie Dale, Butch, and a rather expanded Zeppelin family.

We brought the Flatlanders back to Columbus one more time, to the Grand Valley Dale Ballroom in June 2012. They stayed in Columbus an extra night and I took them all out to dinner the day after the show, where we enjoyed a relaxing conversation. Afterward, Joe even e-mailed me the manuscript of a book he was writing. Great guys all around, each one is quite different from the others. Joe also performed solo one time at Valley Dale in June 2014 (with guitarist Jeff Plankenhorn, who returned to Columbus to play Natalie's in early 2020), but after being regulars for a few years, none of the Flats made it back to Columbus again until Jimmie Dale performed twice with Dave Alvin, once at Natalie's and then at the final Zeppelin Productions concert at Valley Dale.

INEXPLICABLY, I "MISSED" THE FIRST twenty-plus years of Chuck Prophet's career—the fault, and the loss, all mine. Among other things, a young lawyer in our firm's Los Angeles office, knowing my taste in music, had told me since the mid-nineties I would love Chuck. But I never took the bait, and it wasn't until 2008 at SXSW that I finally learned what I'd been missing.

Born and raised in Whittier, California, Chuck attended college in San Francisco but quickly dropped out, and in 1985 he joined a "cosmic country rock" band from Arizona, Green on Red, for eight years. I missed that band, too, though lots of folks in the music world did not. Chuck made a handful of really good solo albums on independent labels between 1990 and 2000, before being signed by New West Records in 2002. Somewhere along that path, he suffered from serious substance issues, including crack cocaine, which, an "authorized" biography on his website says, "brought him to his knees." He cleaned up, got sober, and cut two strong records for New West, *No Other Love* and *Age of Miracles*. He also caught the attention of Lucinda Williams, who took him on the road as an opener, which, according to Chuck, was the turning point in his career—a career that has actually always percolated nicely within the bounds of the industry itself. He's written with the likes of Dan Penn and Nashville songwriter Kim Richey. He's played guitar with Warren Zevon, Cake, and Jonathan Richman. He's written and recorded with Kelly Willis and produced her 2007 album, *Translated From Love*. (Dan Penn and Kelly Willis—notice how those Zeppelin circles seem to be unbroken?)

His songs show up in cool places. Heart covered "No Other Love," Chuck's version of which appears prominently in the movie *P.S. I Love You.* Along the way, his songs were featured in TV shows like *True Blood, Californication,* and *Sons of Anarchy.* Later, he cowrote all the songs and produced what I believe is Alejandro Escovedo's finest record, *Real Animal.*

Nevertheless, notwithstanding his "percolating," New West dropped him after those two strong albums. In 2007, Chuck signed with North Carolina indie label Yep Roc, releasing the wonderful *Soap and Water.*

That's when I belatedly "discovered" Chuck at SXSW in 2008. John and Lori Collins (yes, there had been a pair of "Mooses" since 1980), Kathy, and I headed to Austin that March, with Kathy recovering from back surgery. What a trooper—especially the first night, when at the end of a long day, the four of us headed to a basement bar on Sixth Street to see this artist I had heard about for years. More than 150 people packed a room designed to hold 75. And as hot as the temp was inside, Chuck and his band, the Mission Express, were even hotter: Chuck, of course, on vocals and lead guitar; his wife, Stephanie Finch, on keyboards; a tight rhythm section; and James DePrato, a great guitarist still with the band to this day. They did songs off the new record, finishing up with a veritable anthem, "Let's Do Something Wrong," which had the crowd singing at the top of its lungs—"*Let's do something wrong, let's do something stupid, something we'll regret tonight.*" We were blown away.

That set off three days of stalking Chuck and the Mission Express wherever they played. Late on Friday afternoon, while the ladies escaped the sun, Moose and I saw them under a tent at a downtown Austin parking lot. The next day, on a sweltering Saturday afternoon, we struggled through the mob behind Yard Dog art gallery on South Congress, inching our way to the front of the low, almost nonexistent stage, where I stood thirty-six inches from Chuck's face throughout the entire set. I thought every song at every performance was fantastic.

Coincidences don't exist. On Saturday, the last night of the festival, the Mooses, Kathy, and I went to the Continental Club for its blowout finale. The crowd was SRO, literally, with nearly everyone standing. I moved past the riser protecting the soundman and board, and as I came around the structure's corner, who should be there? None other than Chuck and Stephanie. I reached out my hand and introduced myself. Chuck said he recognized me from Yard Dog. I gave him my "I'm a corporate lawyer from Columbus, Ohio, with a passion for music" speech, told him about Zeppelin Productions, and said, "I would love to bring you to Columbus." With a sly smile on his face, he said, "Sure, but you better save your pennies."

Save my pennies I did. Actually, getting Chuck to Columbus wasn't all that difficult or, relatively speaking, expensive. I quickly discovered Chuck's agent was Mongrel Music, which represents Dave Alvin, and I already had a credible working relationship with Brad Madison, who handles Mongrel bookings east of the Mississippi. The real issue was that Chuck and the band had been on the road for months promoting *Soap and Water*, and he had no tours planned after the summer of 2008. The economics of dragging the whole band across the country for a one-off show, or even just a few dates, didn't work. And I couldn't pay too much because I was concerned how well Chuck would draw in Central Ohio since, to my knowledge, he'd never played there. I suggested to Brad, "How about a solo acoustic show?" Although Chuck's SXSW gigs had been high-energy, full-band rock & roll shows, something about his music (including his albums I'd now purchased) convinced me he would also be great solo. Brad didn't dismiss it out of hand. However, when he raised the idea with Chuck, he wasn't convinced. Apparently, Chuck hadn't played live without the band in quite a few years and he was uneasy about doing so.

Somehow we persuaded Chuck to take the plunge, and on Saturday, January 17, 2009, he appeared at the Maennerchor, wrapping up a little three-date tour (including Beachland Ballroom in Cleveland and Club Cafe in Pittsburgh) as part of a double-bill with Michael Fracasso opening, another of my brainstorms—hoping to generate a crowd. Not to worry. My enthusiasm for Chuck, emanating from SXSW the year earlier, translated into strong ticket sales, and we had a nice crowd on a cold January night. Chuck wowed the Music Fans with his material, guitar work, and vocals, including the creative use of a "Bullet mic"—a staple of his show. Chuck later confessed he was nervous and uncomfortable onstage without the band, but then thanked me for the encouragement. Ten years later, solo tours are now a regular part of his performing and economic life.

When we brought Chuck back to the Maennerchor a second time, on Saturday, July 31, 2010, he sprung out of his rental car upon arrival, warmly shook my hand, and exclaimed, "I have been looking forward to this show since I walked off the stage a year ago." That night, Chuck, again solo, put on a superb show. He was on fire: loose, comfortable, sounding fantastic. A perfect set list, and the patter brought it all together. Chuck was pleased as punch. To this day, Kathy says it's her favorite Zeppelin show ever.

Chuck missed Columbus the next couple of years, but then he truly became a Zeppelin regular. He and the Mission Express played Natalie's in May 2013 (that is the night we had 110 people in the venue, way too crowded) and then came back to the Grand Valley Dale Ballroom in November the following year. It was another show to remember, one for which Mitch the Soundman made a soundboard recording that would have made a great live album. Since 2015, Chuck has performed at Natalie's Worthington many times, sometimes solo, sometimes with the band, and once in a unique duo show with Stephanie. Most recently, solo, he played the second-ever Zeppelin show at Natalie's Grandview in January 2020.

One of my favorite "Chuck moments"—and there are many—occurred in August 2017, when he and the Mission Express appeared at Natalie's on the day Kathy had her fourth chemotherapy treatment for ovarian cancer. As I sat with Chuck and Stephanie after sound check, I told them about Kathy's ordeal, that Chuck was her favorite Zeppelin Artiste, and although I had my doubts, she was committed to attending that evening. I also warned them that if she made it, her "hair" wouldn't really be . . . her hair. Kathy made it, still a trooper, especially where Chuck is concerned, and we sat at our usual table in the back of the room in front of Mitch and the soundboard. Chuck and the band put on another remarkable show, earned their encore, and as soon as they hit the last note of the evening, Chuck jumped down from the stage and walked right up the aisle to Kathy, looked her in the eye, and said, "Your wig looks better than Ronnie Wood's." A classic.

Like a number of the Artistes, Chuck has become a good friend, staying at the house when he is solo (or as a duo with Steph). We've also hung out together around the country. In addition to seeing him at SXSW and at Slim's, I spent a fun Sunday afternoon with Chuck in a coffee shop in the Castro District of San Francisco in November 2019. We talked about a variety of things, including a musical he's been working on based on his wonderful album about San Francisco, *Temple Beautiful*, and my own interest in the Broadway musical world.

CHUCK WASN'T MY ONLY SXSW "discovery." In 2009, Kathy, the Mooses, and I were sitting outside at Threadgill's on a sunny afternoon to see Kevin Welch and his Scandinavian band. At some point during Kevin's set, a woman sitting in front of us turned around and said, "If you like this kind of music, you need to go hear Sarah Borges." That was a new name to us, but we looked her up and discovered she was playing that evening at a restaurant on the edge of town. We decided to check her out.

On a beautiful March night, Sarah Borges and the Broken Singles, performing on the outside deck of a restaurant, were truly entertaining. Electric guitar in hand, she fronted the band like the pro she is, with terrific songs, mostly originals and some well-chosen covers. With an excellent voice, striking looks, and a charismatic stage presence, Sarah came across as smart and very funny. Her music was, and still is, hard to categorize. Making that point, her own website bio says she's been called punk, country, and Americana. Sarah herself says, "Can we just call it rock & roll, for crying out loud?"

Yes, we can, and do. Although Sarah and the band were a little more "rock & roll" than my typical Zeppelin offerings, I wanted to introduce her to Central Ohio. Funny how the world works: I quickly learned that Mongrel Music also booked her. On September 19, 2009, Sarah Borges and the Broken Singles made their Columbus debut at the Maennerchor, kicking off a ten-year run when, except for a brief hiatus, she became the most frequent visitor to the Zeppelin Music Fans. That first show was like catching lightning in a bottle. Sarah and the band blazed, bringing not only their cross-genre music, but also their wonderful, high-energy stage performance. And "their" really means Sarah. At either her first or her second show, just four months later in January 2010 (violating my "not more than once a year" rule, which I've violated a number of times for Sarah), she had the Music Fans—average age at least twenty-five years older than Sarah—standing on their chairs, singing along, and dancing to "Open Up Your Back Door." Sarah has always been an absolute pleasure to promote. From the moment she hits town until she's back on the road, she has a smile on her face and appreciates all we do to make her experience a good one.

When Sarah first came to town, she'd bring product to sell that included not only her CDs, but also hand-stenciled T-shirts and other personalized paraphernalia. Sarah had a blast helping Lisa set up the display and, again, appreciated her efforts to move the merch (as contrasted with an artist or two who turned the product sales into a detailed inventory-control process).

Sarah also appreciated the benefits of dealing with a promoter not in it for the money. Through those years at the Music Hall, the Maennerchor, and then the Grand Valley Dale Ballroom, essentially all the concerts were promoted on a straight guaranty basis. The Artiste (or the agent) and I agreed on a dollar amount for the show, and I paid that amount if 250 Music Fans showed up or twenty-five. (We have *never* had a show when only twenty-five showed up.) If the gate proceeds exceeded the guaranty, after paying Mitch the Soundman, facility rental, security, and other out-of-pocket expenses, I generally gave most or all of the overage (and sometimes then some) to the performer. That's what I did the first night with Sarah. She obviously wasn't expecting it, and maybe it hadn't happened before. When I gave Sarah substantially more than the guaranty after one of those Maennerchor shows, she broke down and cried.

SARAH HAD A BABY, THE Broken Singles broke up, and we didn't see her again in Columbus until 2014, when she came twice to Natalie's (July and November, breaking that rule again) in the company of an excellent band, Girls, Guns & Glory, now known as Ward Hayden & the Outliers. Each time, the band did a strong first set and then backed Sarah for her set. In July 2015, Sarah double-billed a Natalie's concert with Amy Black, a Boston businesswoman-turned-musician. Interestingly, both were backed by a band of Berklee music school students as their summer internship project, kind of a cool approach. Candidly, though, her 2014 and 2015 performances weren't quite up to par. There might have been a reason. I am pleased to report Sarah has been sober since August 9, 2015.

In March 2016, Sarah was a late addition (by the agent) to the bill when Dave and Phil Alvin appeared at the Grand Valley Dale Ballroom. Solo acoustic in a fairly large venue, she blew the crowd away. She returned to Natalie's just a month later (talk about breaking the rule) for a previously scheduled solo gig and returned in the same mode the following March. She stayed at our house both times, and we had long conversations about . . . life. In 2016, Sarah returned to the studio for the first time since 2013, recording an excellent EP produced by Eric Ambel, the original guitarist for Joan Jett and the Blackhearts, who later played with Steve Earle. Sarah re-formed the Broken Singles, and she returned to Natalie's in November 2017 (with Eric on guitar), June 2018, and again March 2019. (That calendar rule is totally out the window with Sarah.) It was a pleasure to see her each time, because she and the band just keep getting better. Then on December 10, 2019, Sarah was the first Zeppelin Artiste to perform at the new Natalie's Grandview. A red-hot band with Eric on lead guitar and the Bottle Rockets rhythm section accompanying her, it was the best she's ever sounded.

My father, John, before emigrating from Scotland at the age of nine. Some of my earliest musical memories are of him singing along to his beloved Scottish tenor, Kenneth McKellar. It was clear my lack of singing ability was genetic.

I was raised in a house my grandparents bought in the thirties. My parents purchased it from them in 1949, and my mother, Betty, lived there until she died in 2005.

The burgeoning rock & roller with a passion for Dion is seated front row, third from the left. "The Wanderer"?!

*My parents got me a
Webcor Music Man,
just like this one, for
Christmas 1961. For
most of the next decade,
the sounds of Dion,
the British Invasion,
and psychedelia passed
through those detach-
able speakers.*

*I hung out and bought dozens of albums at the Music Grotto in downtown
Cleveland and Record Rendezvous at Richmond Mall, the latter depicted here in
an artist's sketch.* (Photo courtesy of Special Collections, Michael Schwartz Library,
Cleveland State University.)

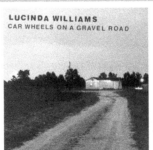
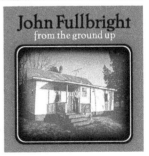

If I were stranded on a desert island with my Webcor Music Man, I'd want these albums with me—and Moondance *and* Blood on the Tracks *and* Pet Sounds *and. . . .*

On the tennis court in the fall of 1967. I played serious tennis for another fifty years (albeit without the Wilson Kramer wood racquet), until sidelined by knee miseries. That's when I started working on this book.

High school graduation photo, 1968.

I purchased the first issues of Rolling Stone at the Music Grotto in the fall of 1967. My mother bought me a subscription for Christmas that year and I continue to subscribe to this day. Who would have thought that, fifty years later, I would serve on the board of the Rock & Roll Hall of Fame Foundation, chaired by Rolling Stone cofounder Jann Wenner?

The Dukies ran James Cotton off the stage, chanting "We want Janis." The Moose (John Collins) and I chased him backstage to apologize. My first "brush" with stardom—literally, as Janis went by me.

With the Moose on the day of our college graduation, May 1972. We each had a haircut for the occasion. Moose's had been over his shoulders. He remembers a girl we knew did the honors. He doesn't think there was a bowl involved, but you couldn't prove it from this picture.

Kathy and I saw Neil Young on one of our first dates—at Mershon Auditorium on the Ohio State campus in November 1973. He didn't take the stage until around midnight, performing songs from Tonight's the Night, two years before the LP was released. (Photo courtesy of the OSU Libraries University Archives.)

159

An action photo as Kathy and I leave the church, with rice flying, on June 19, 1976. Three nights later we were seeing Jerry Jeff Walker (with Katy Moffatt opening) on our honeymoon in Cincinnati.

At the wedding of my friend Ace (Dick Clark), November 1976. Kathy had ditched the wedding perm by this point. Mine was . . . permanent, until it wasn't.

ZEPPELIN PRODUCTIONS, INC. presents.....

TOM RUSSELL
and Guitarist
ANDY HARDIN
w/ special guest
KATY MOFFATT

FRIDAY, MAY 24, 1996
8 p.m. doors open at 7:30 p.m.

Columbus Music Hall
734 Oak Street (corner of parsons and oak)
Phone: (614) 464-0044

tickets
$10 advance
$15 at the door   call (462)-2636

An early effort to expand the Music Fans beyond just friends and family. I hung posters in local record, book, and music stores.

After each show, the Zeppelin "family" would head to Flatiron for a late-night dinner and celebration. This night, it was (left to right): Mom, brother Jim, sister-in-law Lisa, Tammy Rogers, Kathy, me, Rosie Flores, and Mitch the Soundman. If those walls could speak. . . .

Rosie (left) *asked before her September 9, 1999 gig at the Columbus Music Hall: "Do you mind if I bring a friend?" It was Tammy, Nashville fiddler and founding member of the Grammy-winning SteelDrivers.*

Rosie and Mom at the end of the evening. A great picture, if I do say so.

December 31, 1999. Y2K. The world could have come to an end. What better way to go out than with a party at our house and special guest, Katy Moffatt?

There weren't a lot of warm and fuzzies offstage, but it was an honor to produce a Guy Clark show at the Music Hall in April 2004. (Photo courtesy of Scott Lavelle.)

After ten years at the Music Hall, Zeppelin Productions moved to the Columbus Maennerchor in 2005. An old German social club, it provided another wonderful, quirky venue.

Katy Moffatt onstage at the Maennerchor in 2006. (Photo courtesy of Ed and Kathy Summers.)

On Kieran Kane's first visit to Columbus, he asked if he could bring his friend Kevin Welch (left) along. That started a string of annual shows, later with Fats Kaplin. This one is at the Maennerchor in 2006. (Photo courtesy of Ed and Kathy Summers.)

Tom and Nadine Russell married in a small church in Gstaad, Switzerland, in June 2008. Gretchen Peters sat in the front of the church and sang Tom's song "Guadalupe." He joined in on harmony. Oh my!

Many great songwriters have graced the Zeppelin stages, but maybe none better than Jimmy Webb. July 2009.

Wine, Women, and Song. There were plenty of all three onstage at the Maennerchor in February 2010. Left to right: Matraca Berg, Gretchen Peters, and Suzy Bogguss. (Photo courtesy of Ed and Kathy Summers.)

Daughter Emily was my companion for the 2010 Rock & Roll Hall of Fame Inductions at the Waldorf Astoria. At the after-party, she met Billie Joe Armstrong from Green Day. Her boyfriend (now husband), Cameron O'Reilly, said, "At least you didn't settle for the drummer."

Tom and Nadine Russell, with me, at the Gretchen Peters–Barry Walsh wedding in October 2010.

Rodney Crowell officiates the service for Gretchen and Barry.

Gretchen, Matraca, Tom, and Suzy onstage at the reception, doing Suzy's hit "Out-bound Plane," a song Tom co-wrote with Nanci Griffith.

The Flatlanders visited the Maennerchor on my birthday, January 23, 2011. Daughters Emily (left) and Nora with Jimmie Dale Gilmore.

It was Sunday, Flatiron was closed,
and we headed across the street to
Gresso's. Here I am with Joe Ely,
in 2011.

Jimmie Dale and Butch Hancock.
Kathy was smitten by Butch. His
wife later told me, "All the married
women like Butch."

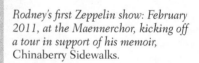

Rodney's first Zeppelin show: February
2011, at the Maennerchor, kicking off
a tour in support of his memoir,
Chinaberry Sidewalks.

We did our first show at the Grand Valley Dale Ballroom on September 29, 2011.
Built in 1918, it continued a string of wonderful, quirky Zeppelin venues.

Bruce Springsteen gave the keynote address at SXSW, March 2012. At one point he asked for a guitar and sang "We Gotta Get Out of This Place," saying, "That's every song I've ever written." (Photo by Brian Birzer.)

The October 2012 Rock Hall Music Masters tribute to Chuck Berry had a decidedly "Zeppelin" flavor. I hosted a dinner the night before at Johnny's Bar on Cleveland's west side. From left: Brad Madison of Mongrel Music; me; Dave Alvin; Greg Johnson, owner of the Blue Door in Oklahoma City and John Fullbright's manager; John's friend; John; Chuck Prophet; Dan Kennedy, Chuck's manager; Cindy Barber, owner of Beachland Ballroom in Cleveland; Chris Faville of Mongrel Music; my now-son-in-law Cameron O'Reilly; my sister-in-law, Lisa; Kimiko Tokita, Rosie Flores' manager; and our friends Bob and Lucinda Kirk. Obscured, out of the picture, taking the photo, or otherwise indisposed were Kathy; my brother, Jim; daughter Emily; and Rosie. (Rock Hall CEO Greg Harris was a late arrival.)

Chuck and Mrs. Berry during a quiet moment at the Ritz-Carlton. I was told Mrs. Berry's appearance at the event was a rare occurrence.

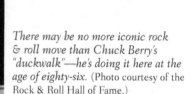

There may be no more iconic rock & roll move than Chuck Berry's "duckwalk"—he's doing it here at the age of eighty-six. (Photo courtesy of the Rock & Roll Hall of Fame.)

There was only one performer with the . . . guts . . . to do the duckwalk with the master sitting a hundred feet away. Rosie! (Photo courtesy of the Rock & Roll Hall of Fame.)

The late Jesse Winchester performing one of his last shows—Valley Dale, May 2013. He was gentle, almost fragile, but strong of voice and spirit. (Photo courtesy of Scott Lavelle.)

December 12, 2013. A once-in-a-lifetime experience. I stood on the stage and introduced Hall of Fame inductee Art Garfunkel. When we met before the show, he said, "Nice smile."

Many Artistes have done in-studio sessions at WCBE-FM, including John Fullbright in January 2014. Veteran Music Director Maggie Brennan was uncharacteristically tongue-tied in his presence.

169

Gretchen Peters, Matraca Berg, and Suzy Bogguss entertained the Rock Hall board at the Bluebird Cafe in June 2014. A few of us stayed for a late-night songfest. The women insisted I join in, at least for a picture.

Phil Alvin and Dave Alvin at Valley Dale in March 2015. (Photo courtesy of Christopher Limle.)

The inductions returned to Cleveland in 2012. I couldn't resist having my picture taken the night before with 2011 inductee Darlene Love.

Dave Grohl stopped by at the 2015 inductions to say hello to Greg Harris and me. I introduced him to our table and he exclaimed, "You brought the whole fucking family?!"

Caprice Bragg was vice president of development and external affairs at the Rock Hall during my tenure as chair of the board and through Phase 1 of our capital campaign, which I co-chair. She made my jobs easier though her skills, professionalism, and friendship.

Other Artistes urged me to bring Ramblin' Jack Elliott to town for years, but I didn't do so until August 2015. He entertained Jim and me after the show with wonderful stories, including how he first heard "Me and Bobby McGee." 171

Mary Wilson ended up with family and friends at the after-party for the Music Masters tribute to Smokey Robinson in 2015.

I have witnesses. Sheryl Crow walked up to me after a tour of the James Cancer Hospital in 2015 and said, "I know you from somewhere."

A Rock Hall board reception the night before the Everly Brothers tribute in October 2015. Here's Graham Nash with Greg Harris and me.

172

Don Everly insisted he wouldn't perform, but the finale found him stepping to the microphone to take a verse of "Bye Bye Love." From the left: Vince Gill, Dawn McCarthy, Alison Krauss, Allison Moorer, Lydia Rogers of the Secret Sisters, Shelby Lynne, Peter Asher, Rodney Crowell (with Ledisi and Keb' Mo' behind him), Emmylou Harris, Don, Graham Nash (with J.D. Souther behind him), and Emmett Kelly. (Photo courtesy of the Rock & Roll Hall of Fame.)

Don backstage with three-time Grammy award–winning singer, songwriter, and guitarist Keb' Mo'. (Photo courtesy of the Rock & Roll Hall of Fame.)

Those smiles say it all. Emmylou and Rodney revel in the success of the evening. (Photo courtesy of the Rock & Roll Hall of Fame.)

Jed Hilly, executive director of the Americana Music Association, helped smooth the way for the Rock Hall to gain the support of both Don Everly and Patti Everly, Phil's widow, for the Music Masters tribute. Jed, left, with Don and Greg Harris. (Photo courtesy of the Rock & Roll Hall of Fame.)

Talk about reveling in the success of the evening! The Everly Brothers tribute was the result of great teamwork led by Lauren Onkey, Rock Hall vice president of education and public programs; Greg Harris; and Jason Hanley, then director of education and subsequently Lauren's successor. (Photo courtesy of the Rock & Roll Hall of Fame.)

Graham was almost part of the Wightman contingent for the weekend, here with Jim, Lisa, and me at the after-party.

At the end of the Everly evening, Rodney and I shared a quiet moment. He told me how proud he was of the show. Me too.

Barry Walsh and Gretchen Peters have played the Music Hall, the Maennerchor, Valley Dale, and, here, Natalie's in February 2016. (Photo courtesy of Ed and Kathy Summers.)

Lori and John Collins: The Mooses. The Moose has been a part of the music in my life since we met the first week at Duke in 1968. After attending multiple Rock Hall events, he said, "I didn't know how expensive it would be to be your friend."

175

Bishop Al Green, pastor and founder of the Full Gospel Tabernacle Church in Memphis. Seeing him preach in September 2016 was indeed a religious experience.

Nora picked up our VIP tickets for Desert Trip in October 2016 and ran into someone she recognized as a Grateful Dead fan, Bill Walton.

The family arrives at the second night of Desert Trip—Neil Young and Paul McCartney. From left: son-in-law Matt Gilstrap, Nora, me, Kathy, Emily, and Cameron.

Greg Harris looks on as Jann Wenner, cofounder of Rolling Stone *and longtime chair of the Rock & Roll Hall of Fame Foundation, cuts the ribbon opening the* Rolling Stone: 50 Years *exhibit. May 2017.*

August 2017. I told Chuck Prophet that Kathy was having chemotherapy and had lost her hair. After the show, he walked up to her and said, "Your wig looks better than Ronnie Wood's." Perfect.

The Backroad Boys (from left: Dustin Welch, Kevin Welch, Michael Fracasso, and John Fullbright) did two nights at Natalie's in October 2017. Great fun.

March 2018. Paul Simon (fourth from left) spoke to students and faculty at Ohio State. Afterward, he met with me; Kathy; OSU president (and Rock Hall board member) Michael Drake; Brenda Drake; Beth Gerber; Professor Timothy Gerber; Cathy Ballenger; Bill Ballenger, director of the Ohio State School of Music; and Alan Michaels, dean of the Moritz College of Law.

Jon Landau was kind enough to provide access to two front-and-center seats for January 11, 2018.

Dave Alvin in action at the last Zeppelin show at Valley Dale, with Jimmie Dale Gilmore. June 2018.

I interviewed Jorma Kaukonen about his memoir, Been So Long, *at Gramercy Books in November 2018.*

At the Gramercy interview, Jorma teased that I'd never promoted a Hot Tuna show. Four months later, he and Jack Casady did two shows at Natalie's, in March 2019.

New York inductions have become a long-weekend tradition for Kathy and me, the Mooses, and Jim and Lisa. Dinner at Del Posto in 2019.

Matraca Berg's long-awaited return to the Zeppelin stage. Natalie's in May 2019.

Tom Russell started me in the promotion business in March 1995. He is still going strong. Here, at Natalie's in June 2019.

Me introducing Dave on the second night of his King of California shows, July 2019. He ended the show telling the crowd I was a "rare bird" and that Columbus was "lucky to have" me, finishing with "July, You're a Woman," a mutual favorite.

Left: Rock & Roll Hall of Fame inductee Richie Furay did two shows each at Natalie's in August 2018 and 2019. He sounded as good as he did with Buffalo Springfield and Poco many decades earlier.

Below: Kieran Kane was contemplating giving up music and concentrating on his art. Rayna Gellert got him back in the game. Here they are at Natalie's in October 2019.

For many years, Bruce Robison and Kelly Willis couldn't tour together because someone had to stay at home with the four kids. The little ones grew older and the duo came to Columbus a couple of times, including at Natalie's in November 2019.

Natalie's Grandview opened the night before Thanksgiving 2019, with owner Charlie Jackson giving a heartfelt welcome.

Sarah Borges has been a Zeppelin regular for ten years. She did the first Zeppelin show at Natalie's Grandview in December 2019.

January 2020. The last Zeppelin show at Grandview before the pandemic. Chuck Prophet, solo, previewing songs from a yet-to-be-released Land That Time Forgot.

I was ten years old when I first heard "The Wanderer" on my transistor radio. Almost sixty years later, Dion pulled up a chair and sat next to me for a reading of the musical based on his life. February 28, 2020.

EIGHT

Songwriting Masters

THOUGH I RESPECT GREAT SINGERS, GUITARISTS, AND LIVE performers, what truly moves me is the songwriting. I would give my left . . . arm . . . to write really good songs. Not surprising, with limited exceptions, every Zeppelin artist I've brought to town is a wonderful songwriter. Certainly, that's true of the original "regulars": Tom Russell, Katy Moffatt, Rosie Flores, and Dave Alvin. For some, songwriting gave them an entrée into the Nashville music scene: Kieran Kane, Kevin Welch, and Gretchen Peters. The guys from Austin all write excellent songs: Bruce Robison, of course, and each of the Flatlanders—Joe Ely, Jimmie Dale Gilmore, and especially Butch Hancock. So does Kelly Willis, for that matter. And songwriting remains a strong suit of later additions to the Zeppelin roster, including Chuck Prophet and relative newcomer John Fullbright.

I've also had the pleasure and honor of introducing some songwriting legends to the Music Fans: John Stewart early on and, also at the Music Hall, Guy Clark. At the Maennerchor, Dan Penn. At the Grand Valley Dale Ballroom, Jesse Winchester and, later, Rodney Crowell. But arguably the finest songwriter to ever grace a Zeppelin stage was Jimmy Webb. He wrote such hits as "Up, Up and Away," "By the Time I Get to Phoenix," "The Worst That Could Happen," "MacArthur Park," "Wichita Lineman," "Galveston," and "Highwayman"—a song so powerful that the Highwaymen (Johnny Cash, Waylon Jennings, Kris Kristofferson, and Willie Nelson) named themselves for the song after recording it.

Think of the singers who did his songs: Glen Campbell, for sure; Frank Sinatra recorded "Didn't We"; Art Garfunkel sang "All I Know"; and "The Moon Is a Harsh Mistress" was a hit for both Joe Cocker and Judy Collins, singers at the opposite ends of the vocalist spectrum.

Some of my own Jimmy Webb favorites are a bit more obscure: "If You See Me Getting Smaller," which I first heard by Waylon Jennings; "Postcard From Paris," which I knew from John Denver; and Nanci Griffith introduced me to "If These Old Walls Could Speak."

As I got to know Jimmy and dug into his history, I discovered new favorites, like "Adios" and the wonderful recitation of his visit to the home of his contemporary songwriting hero, "P.F. Sloan." (The Rock Hall board once held a retreat in New York City, where an unstable P.F. Sloan, seated at our conference table, regaled us with a conspiracy theory about how he could have, should have, and would have been bigger than the Beatles if not for. . . .)

The son of an Oklahoma minister, Jimmy relocated with his family to Southern California as a teenager. When his dad moved the clan back to Oklahoma, Jimmy, already having delved into the music business, stayed behind. In no time at all, and while still a teen, he penned some of those above-mentioned hits.

In 2017, Jimmy published a memoir of his early years, *The Cake and the Rain*. I read that book and Bruce Springsteen's book, *Born to Run*, back to back, and I remember my immediate reaction. With Bruce, the narrative didn't always tell me exactly "what" he did, but I knew "why." There is deep insight into Bruce's psyche and motivations, both positive and negative. With Jimmy, I learned in great detail what he did, some of it not too flattering, but I never really knew *why*. Maybe it was simply that success came too fast for a young man to handle. In many ways, it wasn't a particularly pretty picture. I am pleased to say, however, that Jimmy is now more than twenty years sober and has been happily married for a long time to Laura Savini, a New York City public television personality.

As is the case with a number of artists, I can't recall how I reached out to Jimmy to do a Zeppelin show. I eventually dealt over the phone with an older woman in New York City who acted as both Jimmy's manager and agent. Whatever her official role, she was nice, but very protective of him. Jimmy wasn't doing many live shows in those days, but we somehow coordinated a little two-night Ohio run with Jimmy appearing at the Beachland Ballroom in Cleveland on Friday and at the Maennerchor on Saturday. (In retrospect, it is possible Cindy Barber at Beachland booked Jimmy first and then routed him to me, which was the way Cindy and I coordinated many times over the years.)

Regardless, the deal was Jimmy would fly into Cleveland Hopkins Airport from New York and I would meet him at the end of the concourse, carrying a sign with his name on it just like the chauffeur I would be for the next forty-eight hours. I'd drive Jimmy to a hotel for a few hours, pick him up and take him to sound check, return him to the hotel for a bit more rest, and then get him back to Beachland for the show. After the show, I would drive him to Columbus, where we would slide into the more familiar Zeppelin routine. It all worked great, including the airport scene, where I was petrified I would meet one of my law partners getting off Jimmy's plane. I had stepped down from a law firm leadership position just about twelve months earlier, and I was sure one of my partners would see me and think it had come to this. My sign worked, Jimmy and I met up, and we headed into downtown Cleveland. As his "protector" had suggested, Jimmy was keeping it close to the vest. She might have even described him as something of a recluse.

His show at Beachland was good, but he clearly was nervous, bordering on stage fright from what I could tell. When he calmed down, the patter became more relaxed and, most assuredly, the songs were wonderful. By the end of the show, I felt comfortable about what was in store for us the next night in Columbus. After Jimmy took care of the usual post-show obligations, including signing old LP covers, hobnobbing with fans, and getting paid, we slid into my car with Jimmy riding shotgun. (My chauffeuring responsibilities didn't extend to wearing a cap or Jimmy riding in the backseat.) He was clearly relieved the show was behind him and he may have even confessed to his jitters. But he remained quiet—until about the time we hit the Cleveland airport, fifteen minutes south of downtown.

For some reason, he determined I was safe. We talked nonstop the entire two hours back to Columbus. By this point, I had become very comfortable with artists, having learned that they are just people who happen to have music as a job. Although many enjoy talking about music—theirs or that of others—most often they'd just as soon have a respite from their job and discuss other things. Certainly, most musicians don't want to be asked the same silly questions journalists have asked them for years. So no, I didn't ask Jimmy what that cake was doing out in the rain. That isn't to say we didn't also talk some music over the drive. I remember getting pretty deep insight into a variety of folks, including Linda Ronstadt and Carly Simon, about whom Jimmy had very different feelings. We also discussed songwriting generally. He told me that although songs are often rooted in real life, you shouldn't take them literally. Once after a show, he recounted, a fan disdainfully challenged the timeline in "By the Time I Get to Phoenix," arguing there was no way he could be in Albuquerque by lunchtime, or some such thing. Jimmy said he just looked at the guy and said, "It's only a song."

Jimmy's show at the Maennerchor on Saturday, June 11, 2009, was one to remember. We had a well-tuned piano (a requirement of the contract) onstage and Jimmy "attacked" it from the start. His piano playing was, shall we say, aggressive. The set list was magnificent. (How could it be otherwise?) He told great stories about Glen Campbell, Sinatra, Elvis. And although no one will ever accuse Jimmy of being Pavarotti, his singing was just fine, especially as he settled in and the night wore on. After the show, Jimmy enthusiastically came back to our house, where a small group of friends and family joined us for a postmortem. Much of the evening was spent listening to Jimmy, who was vice-chair of the American Society of Composers, Authors, and Publishers, talk about legal issues associated with songwriter royalties in the then-developing digital age. He was still going strong a number of hours later when we finally wrapped things up and I took him back to the hotel.

The next day, Jimmy and I had lunch at Max & Erma's in German Village before I took him to the airport. He spent much of the time trying to expand my musical horizons beyond the singer-songwriter world and, in particular, into classical music. Days later, he sent me a primer list to get me started, and although I bought a few CDs off that list, classical music never really "took" with me beyond the occasional quiet Sunday morning. I don't have a lot of regrets arising out of the "music in my life," but one of them is that, like a few other "legends" I've met (Dan Penn and, later, Art Garfunkel come to mind), I didn't stay in touch with Jimmy. I absolutely should have. We clicked on a personal level over those forty-eight hours. But—I didn't.

ALTHOUGH THE ALBUM *VIVA TERLINGUA!* changed my musical life and certainly opened the door to that "Austin sound," the truth is, I had an ear for the confluence of rock & roll with country music right from the start. And the "start" may well have been the Byrds' 1968 album *Sweetheart of the Rodeo.* The band's least commercially successful release to that point in time, it became a hugely influential record, if for no other reason than it introduced the world to Gram Parsons.

Parsons actually had been around for a little while. A trust fund kid from Winter Haven, Florida (and Waycross, Georgia), he endured a troubled childhood, spent time as a teenager in the Greenwich Village folk scene, and enrolled for a semester at Harvard in the fall of 1965. In Boston, he formed the International Submarine Band, which relocated to Los Angeles, where they recorded their one and only album, *Safe at Home*, released in 1968 after the band had broken up. Parsons' tenure with the Byrds was short and tumultuous, but his influence was unmistakable on the sole album he made with the band. *Sweetheart of the Rodeo* is pretty much the full immersion of a rock & roll band into traditional country music. Though Parsons originally sang lead vocals on most of the songs, because of a contract with his prior label, Roger McGuinn replaced Parsons' vocals on all but three songs. (One of those three, however, is Parsons' classic, "Hickory Wind.")

Within weeks of completing the album, Parsons split from the Byrds, either due to his objection to a tour of apartheid South Africa or to his new friendship with the Rolling Stones, Keith Richards in particular. I guess those aren't mutually exclusive. Whatever the case, Parsons hung out at Richards' London home, they developed a close friendship, and Gram is credited with introducing the Stones to country music, which became evident in their albums of the time. Parsons never received any songwriting credits on such Jagger-Richards compositions as "Honky Tonk Women," but they did allow him to record the first version of their "Wild Horses" on the Flying Burrito Brothers' second album.

Ah, the Burrito Brothers. If *Sweetheart of the Rodeo* wasn't the moment of conception of country rock, the honor could go to *The Gilded Palace of Sin*, released by Parsons' new band just a year later. By that point, Chris Hillman had also left the Byrds and formed the Flying Burrito Brothers with Parsons. Their debut has stayed in my heavy rotation for years, with one great song after another delivered masterfully by an excellent band with superb vocals by Hillman and, especially, Parsons. Things went downhill fast, however, in no small part due to Parsons' heavy drug use. The Flying Burrito Brothers toured sporadically, although the Stones included them on the bill for the disastrous Altamont festival. They appeared in the ensuing movie, doing a version of the C&W classic "Six Days on the Road." Their second and final album with Parsons, *Burrito Deluxe*, was a mixed bag at best, although it includes that first appearance of "Wild Horses."

By 1971, Parsons was back hanging out with the Stones while they recorded *Exile on Main Street*. After a failed attempt at recording a solo album, Parsons' life took a turn for the better, at least musically, when Chris Hillman urged him to stop by a Washington, D.C., folk club and hear a young singer who'd caught Hillman's ear. The rest is history. In January 1973, Gram's first solo album, *GP*, was released—"solo" with what was really a duet partner, that young vocalist from Washington, Emmylou Harris, and the backing of Elvis Presley's band, including the legendary guitarist James Burton. (I had the honor of meeting James at a Rock Hall tribute to Les Paul, whom I also met, many years later.) That album spoke to me at the time like few records have, perhaps in part because the pain and anguish in Parsons' distinctive voice struck a chord with a very unhappy first-year law student. And so did his second album, *Grievous Angel*, although life was much better for me when it was released in January 1974, four months after Parsons' death. That album, like the first, included impeccable songs, a mix of Parsons' originals and inspired covers, all offered up by a vocal duet for the ages.

Speaking of "for the ages," the circumstances surrounding Parsons' death have been told many times, but in summary, just after finishing his second album, he overdosed on morphine and tequila at the Joshua Tree Inn. Afterward, and consistent with what he claimed were Parsons' wishes, his longtime compadre Phil Kaufman and a friend stole Parsons' body from the airport (it was being flown to New Orleans for burial), drove it back to Joshua Tree National Park, and burned it there.

While Gram Parsons' legacy was established in a tragically short life, Emmylou Harris' legacy has been built over fifty years of recording, touring, and providing leadership in the country music community. Although Emmylou has written songs over her career, her principal talent as a performer (other than her own beautiful, distinctive voice) is her ear for exceptional songwriters. And one of the first to benefit from that ear was Rodney Crowell, who would perfect the country-rock sound pioneered by Parsons.

RODNEY IS JUST A FEW months older than me, born in Houston in August 1950. His 2011 memoir, *Chinaberry Sidewalks*, chronicles a childhood that the writer Mary Karr says on the back cover was "not one you'd sign up for." In August 1972, Rodney moved to Nashville, where he fell in with a group of out-of-the-mainstream songwriters like Townes Van Zandt, Steve Earle, Steve Young, and, especially, Rodney's best friend, Guy Clark, and Guy's wife, Susanna. The musical (and substance) landscape is well chronicled in the aforementioned documentary *Heartworn Highways*, filmed at the time but not released until 1981. Moving back and forth between Texas and Nashville, Rodney sat in with Emmylou at Austin's Armadillo World Headquarters in January 1975. She had already recorded his "Bluebird Wine" for her debut, *Pieces of the Sky*, released a month later. She asked Rodney if he'd join her new backup band, appropriately styled "the Hot Band," as a rhythm guitarist and vocalist. He agreed and left the next day for Los Angeles. With that move, Rodney's career was on a trajectory for success, first as a songwriter and then as a recording artist.

As a songwriter, his success was immediate (having worked at the craft for a number of years, he might argue with "immediate"). His compositions soon provided hits for Waylon Jennings, with "Ain't Living Long Like This," and the Oak Ridge Boys, with "Leaving Louisiana in the Broad Daylight." The Nitty Gritty Dirt Band scored with "Voilà, an American Dream," always a favorite of mine. In the early eighties, Crystal Gayle hit number one on the country charts with "'Til I Gain Control Again," and Bob Seger reached number two on the pop charts with "Shame on the Moon." By that time, Rodney was married to Rosanne Cash, producing her albums and writing songs for her, including "No Memories Hangin' Round" and "I Don't Know Why You Don't Want Me," a cowrite with Rosanne.

Rodney's recording career took a little time to take off. Continually reading those album covers and liner notes, I focused on songwriter credits, so I grabbed his debut album, *Ain't Living Long Like This*, upon its 1978 release. Though a wonderful record, it flopped, as did the follow-ups—all filled with excellent songwriting. Rodney did make the charts with *Stars on the Water* in 1981, but it wasn't until 1988 that he struck the commercial mother lode as a recording artist with *Diamonds & Dirt*. That album spawned five number one hits over the next two years (the first album in country music history to do so), including the 1990 Grammy winner for Best Country Song, "After All This Time." For the moment, Rodney was a country music star.

Unfortunately, commercial success and Rodney weren't compatible. He and Rosanne divorced after thirteen years of marriage and three kids, and his chart success came to a screeching halt. He left Columbia Records after the 1992 album *Life Is Messy* (a not-so-subtle title), released two more records for MCA, and then went into recording hibernation. The royalty checks kept rolling in as a result of hits for folks like Alan Jackson ("Song for the Life"), Lee Ann Womack ("Ashes by Now"), and Tim McGraw (one of my favorite Rodney songs, "Please Remember Me"), but Rodney didn't record again until he made a stunning artistic comeback: *The Houston Kid*, released in February 2001, is simply a great record. Autobiographical in no small measure, it is stripped down and light years from the big-production, ready-for-arena sounds of his major-label records a decade earlier. Just eleven years after that Grammy, Rodney was recording for Sugar Hill Records, an independent (but very high quality) label headquartered in my one-time stomping grounds, Durham, North Carolina.

Interestingly, I've come to know Barry Poss, the founder of Sugar Hill, as we both serve on the advisory board of Duke Performances. Poss is a Canadian who did give up the day job, walking away from his Duke PhD dissertation in sociology to follow his passion for music. He founded Sugar Hill in 1978, and by the time he sold his label to Rounder Records in 2015, he'd released albums by Rodney, Guy Clark, Robert Earl Keen, New Grass Revival, Doc Watson, and Dolly Parton, among many others.

Rodney's very strong releases over the next ten years were quite personal in nature. He told me once he really didn't like the sound of his own voice at the peak of his commercial success, but he had now found a vocal groove with which he was comfortable.

On February 26, 2011, Zeppelin Productions presented Rodney Crowell at the Maennerchor. This was the biggest deal in the sixteen-year history of my production business. And to think I was getting him to Columbus because Gretchen, Matraca, and Suzy had harangued him at Gretchen and Barry's wedding. I was nervous about the magnitude of the event, but the evening couldn't have gone better. Rodney arrived in a luxury motor home, driven by his longtime sidekick and sound engineer, Donivan Cowart. It was the first night of a book tour for *Chinaberry Sidewalks*, and Rodney traveled with his own stage set—a veritable living room motif with a chair, end table, and lamp. Rodney's publisher had arranged for the Book Loft, an independent bookstore in German Village, to sell books at the show. Let's just say the product table looked a little different than at other Zeppelin concerts.

Rodney loved the quirky venue and the adoring crowd. He was totally solo, just Rodney and a guitar. He sang a few of the hits, both his and those done by others, but much of the very powerful show was composed of songs from the semiautobiographical albums of the past decade, interspersed with appropriate readings from the book. At one point late in the show, he asked the crowd for requests. Someone hollered out, "Please Remember Me." He paused, said he didn't think his voice was up to it, and went on to another song or two. Then, he simply sang it. *Wow.*

Afterward, Rodney sat in the back of the Maennerchor and signed tons of books for a long time. When he was done, we hopped in my car and headed to Flatiron while Donivan, who had helped Mitch run the soundboard, broke down the stage (more furniture than music equipment) and then drove the motor home to meet us. It was another evening of great stories, chuckles, and getting to know a new Artiste friend.

By Rodney's next visit to Columbus, we had moved from the Maennerchor to the Grand Valley Dale Ballroom, where Rodney did two very special shows. The first, in October 2012, came on the heels of Rodney's release of *Kin: Songs by Rodney Crowell and Mary Karr*, an inspired collaboration between a songwriter and a poet/writer best known for her memoir, *The Liar's Club*. They connected after Rodney did a shout-out to her in one of his songs, and they met and wrote material for the new album, much of which was performed on the record by others. This night, Rodney was accompanied onstage by a young Australian guitarist, Jedd Hughes, and Columbus' own Molly Pauken on bass, who'd toured with them in the past. In anticipation of the show, Rodney reached out to her, and the usual duo on this tour turned into a trio for one night. That alone made the evening special. They did a handful of songs off the new album, including my favorite, "Anything but Tame." But they also played some old favorites like the one Rodney sang at Gretchen and Barry's wedding ceremony, "Love Is All You Need." The crowd was slayed. So was Rodney—by the whole experience.

The next day he posted on Facebook:

Grand Valley Dale Ballroom: Somewhere on a side road in Columbus, Ohio, there sits a throwback structure called the Grand Valley Dale Ballroom, which was built in 1918 and is on the National Historic Registry. Count Basie, Woody Herman, Billie Holiday, Artie Shaw, and Frank Sinatra played there as did Tonya (their wording not mine) Tucker, the Buckinghams, the Kingsmen, and Tommy James AND the Shondells. From where I stood, it was the best acoustic set that Jedd, Molly, and I ever played. Thank you, Alec Wightman.

That 2012 night was also special because accompanying Rodney was his longtime friend Joanne Gardner, who served as road manager, product saleswoman, and obvious confidante. Joanne is the former senior vice president of video production for Sony Music, where she oversaw video production for hundreds of artists, especially in Nashville, and has won numerous Country Music Association and Academy of Country Music Awards. She retired, moved to Montana, and occasionally comes out on the road with Rodney just to help keep the train on the track. Joanne and I hung out—she enjoyed the whole experience, too—and we stayed in touch. (A few years later, she played an important role coaching me on the front end of putting together an event that marked one of the great weekends of my life, musical or otherwise, when the Rock Hall honored the Everly Brothers with its Annual Music Masters tribute.)

Rodney returned to Valley Dale one more time—oh my, an unforgettable night, topping even the 2012 show. On May 14, 2014, guitarist Steuart Smith, who's played with the Eagles for years, joined him. The show also featured singer-songwriter Shannon McNally as the opener who then joined Rodney on backup vocals, accompanied for a few songs by Joanne herself. They started with an in-studio at WCBE-FM, which has provided so much support for Zeppelin shows. I met Rodney, Shannon, and Joanne in the station parking lot. It was a hot day and they looked a little travel-worn. Shannon wore shorts and Joanne commented, "Great, Shannon is wearing her legs today. No one will notice the rest of us."

That may have been the case in the afternoon, but everyone noticed Rodney that night. In superb form, he clearly was having the time of his life. He and Steuart totally engaged the packed house, pushing the music to the limits—one spectacular song and performance after another, clearly extending way beyond any pre-planned set list. Standing stage side with me as Rodney led the band into multiple encores, Donivan confirmed we were seeing something that didn't happen very often. Finally, Rodney told the crowd he was going to end with his favorite song. And with that, he closed with a breathtaking version of Townes Van Zandt's "Pancho and Lefty."

Afterward, in the greenroom off the ballroom balcony, Rodney and Steuart sat quietly basking in the glow of a magnificent evening, with Shannon and Joanne standing nearby. It was the final night of the tour, or maybe the last night with Steuart on board. I caught Rodney telling Steuart, with great emotion, how much he meant to him, complimenting him on how he had grown as a guitarist since they first met.

As of this writing, that 2014 show was Rodney's last concert in Columbus, which I hope we will remedy soon. It certainly hasn't been for lack of trying. In 2013 and 2015, Rodney and Emmylou Harris released their first-ever duo albums to much fanfare, critical acclaim, and many awards. Unfortunately, Emmylou's agent booked their tours, and even though Rodney suggested otherwise, a Zeppelin show wasn't in the cards. Further complicating

Rodney's return, medical issues have haunted him from late 2014 to the present. He was ultimately diagnosed with autonomic dysfunction, or dysautonomia. In late 2017, the diagnosis enabled him to tell the world what was causing the "wacky symptoms" that had kept him off the road for an extended period.

Rodney reached out in late 2018 to tell me his longtime manager, Lisa Jenkins Oltz of Vector Management, was moving to Columbus and that we should get together. Her husband was "some kind of researcher," according to Rodney, and had taken a job at Ohio State. It turns out that Dr. Eugene Oltz is now chair of the Department of Microbial Infection and Immunity at OSU, a pretty important position as I write this chapter in the middle of the COVID-19 pandemic. We connected and quickly became friends. In April 2019, Rodney, on the mend, came through Columbus (with Joanne) en route to a gig in Ann Arbor; he stayed with Lisa and Gene, and the whole group joined us for drinks at our home and dinner at Lindey's. Rodney, never wanting to arrive as a guest without a gift, brought us a box of Franzia wine, duly autographed, which holds a place of honor in our wine cellar.

A few weeks later in New York, Kathy and I got to see Rodney at the now-closed City Winery on Varick Street. We'd told him over dinner in Columbus we would be there, and when we arrived at the door, the hostess had full-access badges ready for us. Rodney had turned his New York weekend into a family affair and his wife, Claudia, sold his merch. She alerted us that Rodney requested our presence in the greenroom after the show. It was another fantastic performance, made even better by the personal rush of visiting afterward with Rodney, all by himself in his dressing room, for a nice conversation. As is the case with so many of the Artistes, if you had told me when I bought that first Rodney Crowell album in 1978 . . .

————

IN THE SPRING OF 2011, the board of the financially strapped Columbus Maennerchor made the difficult decision to sell its principal building to the Columbus Board of Education. Not only was the social club itself struggling, but the maintenance and required repairs to the building were financially prohibitive. Among other things, for the prior few years any rain during a show resulted in water leaking through the ballroom roof, especially into the greenroom, where the performers set up camp. After the closing of the transaction, the school board moved quickly and demolished the ballroom. So ended a wonderful six-year run of Zeppelin Production shows at the Maennerchor. The shows in 2011 alone were memorable: the Flatlanders, Rodney Crowell, Kane Welch Kaplin, Matraca Berg, and Kelly Willis and Bruce Robison—five big-time shows by veterans of the Americana music world. And we ended with a bang by introducing a newcomer to the Music Fans, John Fullbright.

I had continued to build the Zeppelin tree by asking each Artiste after the show to recommend another performer who would be a good fit for the Music Fans. In 2011, one after another, particularly those from Austin, gave me the same name—John Fullbright. Kevin Welch said, "Trust me." I knew my music, but I'd never heard of him, so I did a little research. John was twenty-three, born and raised in Woody Guthrie's birthplace of Okemah, Oklahoma. (Woody Guthrie, Jimmy Webb, and John Fullbright? There must be something in that Oklahoma red dirt.) He had a limited-release live CD recorded at the famed Blue Door in Oklahoma City (the owner of which, Greg Johnson, was managing his career), and in another spin of the small Zeppelin world, his agent was Gigi Benno, Andrew Hardin's girlfriend. So I booked John for the last show at the Maennerchor, and, concerned about how he might draw when nobody in Columbus had ever heard of him, I fell back to one of those Michael Fracasso pairings, hoping we'd get a decent crowd for the two of them.

July 30, 2011, was a steamy Saturday. I was to pick up John at the airport at 6:00 p.m. and we'd sound check at 6:30, with the show, as always, starting at 8:00. At 5:30 or so, my home phone rang and it was John. It was the first time I'd ever talked to him. I asked where he was, and he replied, "Dulles Airport." He had overslept, missed his flight from Oklahoma that morning, been re-routed through Washington, D.C., and was now booked on a flight scheduled to land in Columbus at 7:45. This wasn't good—but not a disaster. I told John to simply take a taxi from the airport and get there as soon as he could. I thought perhaps Michael, the head-liner, could open the show, but not surprisingly, he didn't want to do so as the more veteran performer.

So a few minutes after 8:00, I took the stage in a timely fashion, as I always do, only this time to explain a slight delay—which I've only done twice in twenty-five years. But the crowd was nice, folks ordered up another drink, and we waited. At 8:15, a cab pulled up in front of the Maennerchor, with brother Jim and Music Fan Mark Sutter waiting outside. John hopped out with his guitar in hand, they escorted him inside, he shook my hand, and he jumped onstage. Just like that. No warm-up. No sound check. In an inter-view with the *Columbus Dispatch* a few years later, John told the story and said he didn't even know what the room looked like until the show was over. It didn't matter. He started to sing. And play. Guitar, harmonica. At some point, he moved to the piano next to the stage. Within minutes, he had the crowd in the palm of his hand. Words can't do justice to the impact of hearing this young man for the first time (and, I might add, every time thereafter).

Michael followed John after he wrapped up his set. His own performance was enhanced dramatically when John sat down at the piano, watched Michael's hands on the guitar, listened to his vo-cals, and accompanied him by ear on songs he'd never heard. That night began a special friendship with John, not just for me, but the Music Fans generally. I have introduced them to many unfamiliar artists, but with limited exceptions, they were veteran performers, though not well known to the general public. With John, they discovered someone at the very beginning of his career. And you know how much I like to be on the cutting edge of finding new talent.

I brought John back to Columbus within months, now to our new home at the Grand Valley Dale Ballroom. Having learned my lesson, I sprung for two nights in the hotel and urged him to arrive the day before the show. It was worth it for multiple reasons. Not only did I sleep better, but when I picked John up at the airport, he proudly pulled out the master disc from a brand-new album he had finished recording the day before. John had not yet heard the finished product outside the studio. We slipped it into the high-end CD player in my Lexus, cranked up the volume, and drove around German Village and the south end of Columbus, listening to it over and over again. It was as breathtaking as his live performance.

The next night, January 7, 2012, John took the stage at Valley Dale. Based solely on the buzz from that first show, the crowd had grown from 100 or so at the Maennerchor to 200 or 250. John, still only twenty-three, again captivated the audience from the first note. His songs, many of which we'd heard in July, were stunning. In less than six months, his voice sounded even more powerful, and it has continued to grow over the years. His musicianship—on guitar, keyboards, accordion, harmonica—was brilliant. I'm not sure he even reads music, having basically learned to play by ear. Kathy called him a "savant" right from the beginning. It's hard to argue.

The record we listened to that cold January night, *From the Ground Up*, was released in May on an indie label with no real publicity behind it. Nevertheless, by the time John came back to Columbus, he had been nominated for a Grammy for Best Americana Album, ultimately losing to Bonnie Raitt.

When John returned to Valley Dale a second time, the following January, he brought a full band. Remember my telling you there were two times in my twenty-five years of promotion I had to go onstage and explain a delay? Well . . . John and the band got to Columbus early afternoon on the day of the show, January 11, 2013. We'd arranged a WCBE in-studio performance at 2:00 p.m. that afternoon, at least as much to help John promote the record as to sell tickets to the show. Now on his third visit to town, we already knew we would have a huge crowd at Valley Dale that evening.

John was accompanied in the studio by Terry "Buffalo" Ware, a great guitarist who has played with most everyone on the Austin scene, especially long stints with Ray Wylie Hubbard and Jimmy LaFave. The rest of the band hung out in the halls or the van until they finished the three-song set and interview. I then went home and the boys made their way to the Hyatt on Capitol Square where, in those days, I usually put up the artists. It was agreed I would swing by around 6:00 and lead them to Valley Dale for the sound check and 8:00 p.m. show. Déjà vu. John called at 5:30—this time to tell me they accidentally parked the van outside the hotel in a "no parking from 4:00 to 6:00 p.m." spot. And you guessed it—the van had been towed, with all their equipment in it. The van—and their equipment—was now ensconced at 2700 Impound Lot Road, on the south end of Columbus, the opposite direction from Valley Dale.

So began a night to remember. I swung by the hotel and everyone piled into my Lexus, Buffalo riding shotgun, and we headed to the impound lot. Nothing is easy. John didn't have the registration for the van, which had Oklahoma plates, so the Columbus police refused to release it, not to mention the instruments and equipment. John worked his magic. It took a while, but he managed to establish ownership of the van to the satisfaction of Columbus' finest. Off we went to Valley Dale, where three hundred or so people were waiting for a show. John did not want me to explain the delay or why we were setting up the stage and doing a sound check on the fly while the crowd mingled. Instead, he took charge, and like his prior shows, he knocked the crowd over from the first note. After a handful of songs into the first set, John fessed up and told the crowd what had happened.

In those days (at the Music Hall, Maennerchor, and Valley Dale), most Zeppelin shows consisted of two sets with a break. It gave the crowd a chance to stretch their legs and hit the facilities, and although Zeppelin never received revenue from the drinks, it did enhance the venue's take when folks re-upped at the bar. That night, the break took a different spin. After John and the band retreated to the upstairs greenroom, my friend Sally Curley passed the hat among the Music Fans to take up a collection to pay the towing fee and fine. She handed me the substantial collection, and I took it upstairs to John. Deeply moved, he couldn't believe it. He insisted he couldn't take the money and asked me to return it. That couldn't happen—there was no way to tell who gave what amount. So he reluctantly but gratefully accepted it, thanked the crowd profusely during the second set, and has told that story from the stage in Columbus and elsewhere for years.

John has continued to be a good friend and a part of my life, albeit sporadically. I don't see or hear from him often, but when I do, it's always fun and warm. We've hung out at SXSW, and the family has made short treks to see him at both the Lancaster Covered Bridge series and the Nelsonville Music Festival in southeastern Ohio. We also introduced John into the Rock Hall world in June 2012, when he and his band entertained our board at its annual retreat, held in Austin that year. Like John's first Columbus show the prior year, no one in the room had heard him before, and although some didn't stick around to listen, those who did were blown away. John also participated in the Rock Hall's Annual Music Masters tribute to Chuck Berry in October 2012. And on his Cleveland visits from time to time, he has become good friends with—and a houseguest of—our Rock Hall CEO, Greg Harris. In fact, Greg's son, Jack, cites John as the inspiration for his own aspiring singer-songwriter career.

Now a regular on the Zeppelin roster, John returned for another solo show at Valley Dale in January 2014, again arriving with the master of a new CD. We reprised our evening of two years earlier, driving around listening to the soon-to-be new record. He returned to WCBE for a solo performance and interview with Maggie Brennan, the station's music director and early afternoon on-air host. I watched as John's music and intense presence took hold of her. She had trouble talking. She confessed later she'd been hosting in-studio sessions for many years and that had never quite happened. The next night, John told the crowd the story from 2012 and said he hoped the "reprise" would bring him the same good luck this time around. The new CD, *Songs*, was released in May to strong critical reviews, but no second Grammy nomination.

John played his last show at Valley Dale in May 2015, a show scheduled before the longtime operator of the venue went under in February. Thankfully, I knew the building's owners, and notwithstanding the absence of any operating support, we went ahead with a booked Dave Alvin and Phil Alvin concert in March and this one in May. I hired a caterer to provide drinks, we bought our own toilet paper for the restrooms, and both shows went on.

When John visited Columbus in July 2016, he played the smaller Natalie's, where we packed the place, though we charged an unusually high ticket price. Afterward, John stayed at our house, and we spoke at length about the challenges of the business, especially for struggling singer-songwriters. John had become good friends with Michael Fracasso and Kevin Welch, neither of whom had drawn significant crowds in recent visits to Natalie's. We agreed to try a two-night stand with John, the two of them, and Kevin's son Dustin, with whom John was close. Those shows, on October 16 and 17, 2017, were a complete success, economically and artistically. The Backroad Boys, as they were billed, had a blast. Both nights sold out, once again at a hefty ticket price, in no small measure due to John's presence. The "Boys" sat onstage together, taking turns doing material from their respective and extensive repertoires.

It took until June 2019 for John to return with his own band for a two-night stand. He was as good as ever, but there'd been no new album in more than five years and, with an exception or two, no new songs. After the show John and I had a serious one-on-one discussion downstairs at Natalie's. He was obviously cognizant of his rapid success as a young man, but said he was happy with the slower pace of his life. He wasn't performing much and he certainly wasn't writing. I later read an interview in which John was asked if he feels the pressure of creating new material while meeting the standard set by his earlier work. He said, "I'd be lying if I said I didn't." He concluded by saying, "It wanes and waxes back and forth between being terrified and overconfident."

OVER THE YEARS, I'VE DREAMED of being a songwriter. I envy the creativity. The skill. Mostly, the ability to connect with others, and with the universal emotions we all share, through lyrics and melody. But that ability can also be a burden. The creativity and the skill come from hard work. Oh, on occasion, the song might "write itself," but I would guess the master songwriters will tell you it takes discipline, effort, time, and energy. It certainly takes education. Maybe not in school, but in the "classroom" of the singles and albums and barrooms and arenas—listening to the work of the masters that came before.

It also takes staying power to sustain that creativity and skill over years and decades. I concede there are those who seem to be born with "it," whatever "it" might mean. The savants. Those few who write unbelievably great songs as kids. As teenagers. Songs that connect us with emotions most of us didn't even know we had at that age, at least not until we heard those songs. How did Jackson Browne write "Looking Into You" or "These Days" as a . . . kid? The early hits by Dion, for that matter. Perhaps equally mystifying, how do they sustain it?

At one end of the spectrum, there is Willis Alan Ramsey, a cult figure if ever there was one, who made a legendary album in 1972 (almost all of the songs have been recorded by others, some as major hits) and has *never* recorded since. Or Paul Siebel, one of my favorites, who made two of the finest singer-songwriter records ever in 1970 and 1971 (which include much-covered classics like "Louise" and "Any Day Woman") and completely dropped out of sight, working for the parks department on the Eastern Shore of Maryland, never to make another record.

At the other end of the spectrum: Rodney Crowell; his longtime compadre, the late Guy Clark; Tom Russell, for that matter; or even Dion, who released a powerful new record, *Blues With Friends* (including guests ranging from Bruce Springsteen to Paul Simon to Van Morrison) in June 2020, a month before his eightieth birthday. These guys have continued to turn out beautiful, meaningful—sometimes edgy—lyrics and melodies for decades.

I envy them to some degree, but I will say: It sure is fun, and a lot easier, to simply push the button and have them speak to, and often for, me. They do it so well.

NINE

A Once-in-a-Lifetime Opportunity

WHEN THE MAENNERCHOR WAS SOLD IN 2011, I WAS
once again in the market for a new venue. The shows
had been increasingly successful with bigger crowds.
We were attracting more "known" artists. Most important, I was
having too much fun to quit. So Mitch the Soundman, brother
Jim, and I explored alternatives. We had criteria: certainly, excellent acoustics. Good sightlines to the stage. Parking. But there
were two other criteria on which I insisted: a liquor license (many
of the Music Fans like to have a drink when listening to live music) and—"quirky." The quirkiness of both the Music Hall and the
Maennerchor not only contributed to the ambience for the crowd,
but the Artistes loved both venues, and it gave our shows a unique
appeal in the competition for bookings.

The team looked at venues ranging from BalletMet's new rehearsal space to a Brewery District winery called Via Vecchia.
We considered the large and small theaters in the Riffe Center, a
downtown tower filled with state government offices. We visited a
couple of new performance spaces on the north end of town, the

McConnell Arts Center in Worthington and the Northland Performing Arts Center on the site of an old shopping mall on Morse Road. None of them were quite right. Even when the other criteria were satisfied, they weren't . . . quirky enough.

Then we hit a home run—the Grand Valley Dale Ballroom located on Sunbury Road on the east side of Columbus, not far from the airport. It was built in 1918, soon damaged by fire, and reconstructed in 1922. It had played host to all the great jazz and big band stars of the thirties and forties. Frank Sinatra sang there. So did Billie Holiday. Glenn Miller, Tommy Dorsey, and Harry James brought their bands to Valley Dale. So did Duke Ellington. At one time, both CBS and NBC did coast-to-coast live radio broadcasts from the ballroom, and their signs still hung on either side of the stage. Not surprising with that history, Valley Dale is on the National Register of Historic Places. In the 1960s, Valley Dale became a rock & roll venue. A series of plaques on the balcony wall list all the performers who graced the stage over the years, and the names take your breath away: the Dave Clark Five, Otis Redding. One of the most valuable bootlegs on the market is from a 1966 Valley Dale show by the Velvet Underground & Nico as part of Andy Warhol's Exploding Plastic Inevitable tour.

Once I started doing concerts at Valley Dale, dozens of Music Fans told me they had been there during their high school and college years. Yes, there were the national acts, but local legends like the Dantes regularly performed. And the ballroom hosted proms and weddings and receptions. In fact, my only previous visit to Valley Dale had been for a huge party hosted by a number of friends to celebrate their sixtieth birthdays.

Valley Dale had been owned, in whole or in part, by a local family for decades. After its glory years, it fell into serious disrepair until another local family (who, it turned out, I knew well) invested money in the property and took a silent ownership interest. Their investment funded much-needed maintenance and repairs, and they signed a long-term management agreement with a third-party operator.

Mitch, Jim, and I were immediately smitten when we first visited the property. All the criteria were satisfied. Great acoustics. Wonderful sightlines. Lots of parking. A liquor license. And it was quirky to the max. The only cause for pause was size. Valley Dale is big, with a U-shaped balcony around the slightly raised hardwood dance floor that fronts the stage. If you used all that space, the place could hold up to a thousand people, standing. On the other hand, with folding chairs in rows, the dance floor had a seating capacity of three hundred, just about the same size as the Maennerchor. The only difference, which we learned over time, is that with its high ceiling and that U-shaped balcony, the place felt cavernous unless you had at least two hundred or more on the floor.

Actually, there was one other cause for pause: On my first visit, I learned the third-party operator was a guy I knew from his prior business dealings with one of my clients. Let's just say those dealings hadn't ended well and I had played a principal role in terminating his relationship with my client. I had no idea he and his wife managed Valley Dale, but he was quick to stress that bygones were bygones as far as he was concerned. Since my dealings would primarily be with his wife, it didn't seem like an issue. Nevertheless, based on prior experience, my antennae were always up.

The Zeppelin team transitioned well to the new environment. I continued to print and sell tickets off an e-mail list, sending them out by hand. Kathy took the tickets and cash at the front door on the balcony level. Lisa set up the merch table on the side of the main floor. Jim smoothly handled the more demanding "operational" aspects of the larger venue. Mitch masterfully delivered sound in the bigger room and even purchased a stage lighting system he set up from the balcony. We also closed curtains under the balcony and around the dance floor, which made for a more intimate setting.

On the other hand, the economics of the venue were more challenging than the Music Hall or the Maennerchor. The ballroom booked up well in advance on weekends for weddings, receptions, and corporate events. So, with the exception of the dead of winter, the rent for a Friday or Saturday evening was prohibitive. As it turned out, other nights meant less competition for the entertainment dollar, the Artistes were happy to get a well-paying weeknight gig, and the Music Fans didn't care. Shifting primarily to weeknight concerts turned out fine, but the rent was still higher than at the Maennerchor or the Music Hall.

Our first show at Valley Dale was in late September 2011, with Tom Russell again debuting a new Zeppelin venue. The next year we filled the place nicely with the regulars—John Fullbright, Kane Welch Kaplin, Gretchen Peters. An attempt to introduce a new artist to the Zeppelin fold was a lesson learned when Kim Richey, a talented Nashville songwriter, didn't draw more than 125 or so, despite her Ohio roots. That crowd would have looked fine in the Music Hall and been acceptable at the Maennerchor (where we'd set out the right number of chairs and spaced them so the room looked full), but Valley Dale was cavernous.

Just a couple of months later, Charlie Jackson's new, more intimate venue, Natalie's, opened and the days of "stretching" with a performer at Valley Dale were over. We still hosted our regulars, like Dave Alvin, the Flatlanders, Rodney Crowell, Kelly Willis and Bruce Robison, and Chuck Prophet at Valley Dale. And we introduced new artists like the legendary Jesse Winchester. But I used Natalie's for smaller draws, where the venue even handled the logistics of ticket sales and concert staging.

The Valley Dale experience ended ignominiously in 2015 when the operators went under—dramatically and unexpectedly. After seventeen years of operating the ballroom, they closed the doors on February 5 with bills unpaid and dozens of event contracts unfulfilled. Radio, television, and newspapers were replete with stories of wedding couples left at the altar, or without an altar, as it were. The operators were gone and the otherwise passive owners took possession, albeit unequipped to fulfill their operators' obligations. Since I knew the owners, they provided access to the venue, so indeed my Dave and Phil Alvin and John Fullbright shows went on.

By 2016, the owners of Valley Dale had a new operator, and I did two more shows, a return visit by Dave and Phil that spring and one with Dave and Jimmie Dale Gilmore in 2018. The venue was spiffier than ever, plumbing issues that had plagued the restrooms were resolved, and the concerts were great. But by then, I was doing shows regularly at Natalie's and was completely spoiled by the experience. Going back to personally selling the tickets and taking on the responsibility of putting on the actual shows, let alone the pressure of trying to fill the larger venue, was no longer in the cards.

I can't deny it, however, that Valley Dale provided another great Zeppelin run. The Artistes loved it, especially the history. They would walk the balcony before the show and look at the plaques and pictures commemorating the venue's historic past. Dave Alvin used to talk about the ghosts he felt in the room. We put on amazing concerts at Valley Dale—but one stands out among them all.

IN OCTOBER 2013, I RECEIVED a call from Jules Belkin, who'd been friends since the 1960s with Mort Lewis, Art Garfunkel's manager and one-time manager for Simon and Garfunkel. Mort had phoned Jules to see if he knew of a safe three-hundred-seat venue where Art, who'd been off the road for a few years with throat issues, could test a new format. Accompanied only by a guitarist, Art would sing, read poetry, tell stories, and do a Q&A with the audience. Jules thought of my shows at the Grand Valley Dale Ballroom. I told Jules I didn't know if I was more honored at the prospect of promoting an Art Garfunkel show or that Jules, who with his brother had dominated rock & roll promotion in the Midwest for four decades, would call me for help promoting a show. The truth is . . . it was the latter.

Jules put me in touch with Mort and the "negotiations" began. Although I had now been promoting shows for eighteen years and had dealt with many agents and managers, Mort had been doing this for more than fifty years. Heck, he started in the jazz world with Dave Brubeck. We had absolutely nothing in common, and yet we got along famously from the first conversation. We both chuckled as I tried to explain exactly how I did what I do—and why. He asked, "You are a corporate lawyer?" "You've never run an ad?" "You aren't in this for the money?" All foreign to him.

On the other hand, my credibility was high, mostly due to Jules, I am sure. My being chair of the board of the Rock & Roll Hall of Fame didn't hurt. And I later realized he and Art had researched me. At one point, Mort asked me about the venue, clearly not the typical theater or arena he was familiar with. I described Valley Dale: a 1918 ballroom, on the National Register of Historic Places. The stage. Folding chairs on a hardwood dance floor. The chandeliers. All of this sounded right to him. But then I talked about the balcony and the high ceiling. Mort questioned, "Isn't it a real low ceiling with skylights?" I had no idea what he was talking about. Later I surmised he was picturing the Maennerchor and that Art must have spoken to his good friend Jimmy Webb.

Mort and I made a deal. It wasn't the economics of a typical Zeppelin show. For nearly two decades, I had operated solely on a guaranty basis. Tell me how much the artist wants, and I will pay it no matter how many tickets are sold. If I sell more than expected, I'll give the performer more money. My "accounting" system (or lack of same) simply didn't allow for the traditional "percentage of the gate" arrangement. Mort didn't work that way. He wanted to get Art a guaranty and a percentage of the gate, after my out-of-pocket expenses. I said okay. A mistake.

With that, we were off to the races. The show was booked for Thursday, December 12, just a few weeks away. I got my tickets printed at Kinko's like I always did, I sent out my e-mail to the Music Fans, and just as expected, I was inundated with checks. Like shooting fish in a barrel—no follow-up e-mail this time. And certainly not the dreaded (by me, though the Music Fans love it) groveling e-mail when sales are slow.

By Saturday December 7, we had sold three hundred plus. The floor of Valley Dale would be full. The pressure was off. Little did I know about pressure. The next day I awoke, got my morning cup of coffee, and opened up the Sunday *Columbus Dispatch*. Imagine my surprise when I turned to the arts and entertainment section and above the fold on the front page was a picture of Art, accompanying an interview. A sidebar gave ticket information, listing my law office phone number. I had no idea this was coming. No one had told me.

The phone began to ring. Messages were left. When I got to the office on Monday, it was one call after another. I mailed out tickets left and right, hoping people would either send the checks or bring them to the door. At some point I just started telling people to show up and pay when they got there. There was no letup Tuesday morning. We were now well over four hundred "sold," I was sure. For the first time, we would be putting seats on the balcony—and under the balcony. We needed more chairs. There wasn't enough parking on site. We needed additional security. When I updated the operator on the status, he smelled blood and wanted more rent, especially when I told him that Art insisted people not leave their seats during the show, including to buy drinks (the venue's principal source of revenue). On Tuesday afternoon, I shut down ticket sales, having no idea how many people were planning to come.

By the way, not getting out of your seat during the show was the least of Art's requirements. Mort warned me that if anyone did as much as check their e-mail during the show, let alone take pictures or record anything, Art would walk off the stage. It wasn't hard to confirm that one on the internet, with multiple incidents of Art doing just that. I e-mailed all the Music Fans a stern admonition.

The day of the show arrived. So did Art's "team": The guitar player. Art's traveling soundman with a résumé a mile long. And a young "handler." They were pleasant enough and worked well with Mitch to set things up. But the requirements continued. I wish I could remember them all, but there are a few highlights.

First, we were told Art insisted no one see him until he appeared onstage. That meant he had to appear from the back of the stage, rather than the side, where every other Artiste had taken the stage for a Zeppelin show. Unfortunately, the only way to get onto the stage from the rear was through a room that hadn't been accessed in years and was filled with junk. We had to clean it out, fast. Furthermore, the greenroom, where he would await his entrance, was upstairs on the balcony, and people might see him exit the room. So Jim and Mitch were forced to "curtain" off the door and the brief walk to the steps with tablecloths and microphone stands.

Finally, speaking of Mitch: For the only time in his soundman career, he did laundry. Well, he ironed Art's shirt. Art needed to be in a crisp white shirt onstage and it had to be ironed right before the show. Mitch's wife, Susan, came to the rescue and delivered her iron to the venue, and sure enough, Mitch ironed the shirt. We learned all of that before Art even arrived for the sound check.

Art arrived through the back door and was suddenly onstage in his jeans and a Philadelphia Phillies ball cap. I now had read enough about him to be wary. I walked from the rear of the ballroom to stage left, went up the three or four steps, stuck out my hand, and introduced myself: "I'm Alec Wightman." Art looked at me and simply said, "What a great smile." I'm sure I breathed an audible sigh of relief. Art couldn't have been nicer.

As showtime approached, Valley Dale filled to the brim, at

least by Zeppelin standards. The seats on the dance floor quickly filled. And then those chairs under the balcony and in the balcony, where Mort sat with Jules and Fran Belkin. Reports from the outside suggested a parking overflow onto the grass (not a good idea because it poured during the show and cars got stuck in the mud) and neighboring properties. Thankfully, we had beefed up security for help with traffic control before and after the show.

Art was to go on at 8:00 p.m. At 7:50, his soundman looked me in the eye and gave me the warning about cell phones, leaving seats, and whatever. He told me if I didn't deliver that warning to the crowd, he would get onstage and do so himself. I did just as I was told. I then made the introduction: *"Rock & Roll Hall of Fame Inductee Art Garfunkel"*—the first time I had ever used those words to a Zeppelin Productions crowd.

The show was magical. Oh, the voice maybe wasn't as strong as it used to be—he said he couldn't hit the high notes. (He didn't do "Bridge Over Troubled Water" for that reason.) But he did the hits, both Simon and Garfunkel's and his own. I could close my eyes, hear that familiar voice, and think, "I brought Art Garfunkel to Columbus." Art's format succeeded for the most part. He told some great stories and read his poetry off what looked to be the back of envelopes. The Q&A was the only suspect part of the show, but that had more to do with the quality of the questions. One Music Fan in the balcony asked what Art thought of the performers I brought to Columbus, especially Tom Russell. That didn't get a meaningful response.

After the show, Art was ecstatic. I couldn't resist and told him about the family tradition. Kathy, Jim, Lisa, and I were going to Flatiron for a post-show dinner and I asked if he would like to join us. I was pleasantly surprised that he agreed. (When I met with Mort the next day at his hotel, he told me he had been with Art since the mid-sixties and he could count on one hand the number of times Art had done something like that.)

Dinner at Flatiron created its own memories. It was only the five of us at a table enjoying a delicious meal and conversation. Art was relaxed. Nice. Funny. He was still wearing his ball cap, and at one point I mentioned that the great Phillies pitcher Roy Halladay had just announced his retirement due to injury. I asked Art how close he had come to retiring with his throat issues. Art became very serious. He thought for a moment and started to talk about the fear that he would never sing again. He was just getting started, almost emotional, when suddenly a woman walked up to the table, interrupted, and almost shrieked, "Mr. Garfunkel, you were wonderful tonight!" Art was visibly shaken and moved away from the table, not returning until after the "interrupter" had departed.

The next day, I met with Mort to "settle up," and my mistake in agreeing to a percentage of the gate came home to roost. I worked diligently that morning in an attempt to construct the economics of the prior evening. Art was entitled to a percentage of the gate above the guaranty after deduction of my expenses. I had given Mort an estimate of both when we had negotiated weeks earlier, but now I really didn't have a handle on either. First, there was revenue. I knew how much I had taken in, but I had to admit, there seemed to be more people in the house than that dollar amount reflected. As to expenses, sigh . . . I had spent more on security than I'd expected, and the operator had extracted more rent since he couldn't sell drinks during the show. We had to rent more chairs. I'm sure there were other expenses for which I didn't have a handle.

I gave Mort a "bottom line" number. He was cordial, but visibly displeased. I'm not sure how we left it. Maybe I gave him a check? I'm not sure, but as I was driving home, I got a call from Jules. He was even nicer than Mort, but clearly Mort had expressed his displeasure, and Jules wanted to walk through my math. I felt awful. I wasn't in this for the money. I'd been given that once-in-a-lifetime opportunity (trust me, I was now convinced it was "once"), and I didn't want a bad taste in anyone's mouth, including mine.

I disengaged from the conversation, drove to my office, wrote a check to Mort for a big round number that was materially higher than my attempt at a bottom line, and mailed it with a letter of thanks and explanation. It was the most money I had ever paid an Artiste by a multiple, and the most money I had ever "lost" on a show by a multiple, but it was worth every dime. But, just once. . . .

Ten days later, I received a longhand letter in the mail. It is framed and hangs on the wall in my home office. It reads:

Dear Alec,

Now it's more than a week since we both shared a truly grand experience putting on a show together, and elevating four hundred people to that place beyond the mundane where Art lives. You were just great to work and hang with, Alec—a class act and a fellow child at play. Deep thanks.

Art Garfunkel

I didn't reply. This was Art Garfunkel, for goodness' sake. I knew how private he was, and I just . . . didn't reply.

The next summer, I was at a Cleveland Indians game with Greg Harris and a couple of the top executives for Sony Music. Somehow, we got to talking about Simon and Garfunkel, who had recorded for Sony (and its predecessor, Columbia) from day one. I told (some of) my Art Garfunkel story, including about the letter. I also told them I had never replied. They were stunned, both by the letter and my lack of response. They confirmed what a private person Art is, and said that was clearly a personal letter and that I should follow up, even on such a tardy basis.

A few days later, I wrote Art a letter. His return address was on his envelope, and I dropped mine in the mail to his home on the Upper East Side. I told him Kathy and I would be in New York in a few weeks on our way to Europe and asked if he wanted to get together. I really didn't expect to hear from him. Within the week, my office phone rang. The caller ID said "Garfunkel." Sure enough, it was Art. We had a nice conversation and agreed to meet for lunch, with our wives, on the day Kathy and I were in town. Art originally suggested lunch at the Mark Hotel, but when he discovered it was closed for renovations, he made reservations for us at the original Smith and Wollensky at Third Avenue and 49th Street.

Just the four of us met for lunch. Kathy and I were going to Istanbul, where Art had recently returned from, and he drew us a map of the city on a napkin and indicated the location of his favorite restaurants. The Garfunkels were on their way to the Poconos for a long weekend with their young son and would be picking up a rental car for the trip since they had no need to own an automobile in the city. It was a wonderful lunch, but just like Dan Penn and Jimmy Webb, I'm sorry to say I didn't stay in touch.

IN EARLY 2012, MY FRIEND Charlie Jackson asked if I would consider investing in a project he had in mind—a restaurant designed for live music. Charlie had always wanted a music venue where he could book acts. His daughter, Natalie, was returning from New York and was enthused about bringing coal-fired pizza to Central Ohio. Why not combine the two?

I had known Charlie for a number of years. When I first started going to Flatiron in the early nineties, it had the finest jukebox I had ever heard. Whoever was stocking it shared my musical tastes, at least within the context of a broad, eclectic mix. Roger McLane, the manager of Flatiron, told me the "whoever" was Charlie Jackson, the owner of Aardvark Video in the Short North area of Columbus. When I started taking Artistes to Flatiron after shows, they were as impressed by the jukebox as I was. Many a dollar was spent playing music you just didn't hear every day in those settings. It quickly became routine for our performers to leave their own

CDs behind, and sure enough, next time I stopped by for lunch or a drink after work, Charlie had them in the machine.

As the list of Music Fans expanded, a disproportionate number of folks hailed from south of Columbus. It's unclear if Charlie, who lived in Circleville, was the motivating force for that interest or just part of the mix, but he certainly became a regular at Zeppelin shows. His distinctive long, gray ponytail stood out among what was originally a crowd of mostly lawyers and businesspeople. Within just a few years, the Music Fans had transitioned to true music lovers, and Charlie was front and center among them. It was obvious he really knew his music.

At some point around 2005, as Becky Ogden struggled to make a go of the Columbus Music Hall as a purely event-rental property, Roger McLane from Flatiron inquired as to whether I was interested in joining Charlie and him in exploring the purchase of the venue. Their thought was to turn it into a restaurant to be managed by Roger, with live music booked primarily by Charlie. We briefly explored the concept, but I was in no position to risk the substantial capital required to renovate the old firehouse. After all, I had spent the first two decades of my legal career advising clients not to invest in food-service establishments.

So here we were, just seven or eight years later, and this time I bit. My financial condition was a little more secure, with college tuitions behind me, much fewer dollars were involved, and Charlie's proposal contemplated a first-class music venue at which I could promote shows on favorable economic terms. I was just a year into the Valley Dale experience, but the thought of a smaller venue for Zeppelin Artistes who couldn't come close to filling the cavernous ballroom definitely had appeal.

One other little twist also inspired my interest. I had two "dream acts" for Valley Dale—Nick Lowe and Richard Thompson, both represented by the same agent. When I inquired about Nick or Richard, I couldn't get to first base. As I heard it, those types of acts only spend limited time on the road, and the agent was inclined to give those dates to venues that could handle the rest of his roster. He said, "You want to talk about Nick Lowe and Richard Thompson, let's talk about Todd Snider." I didn't want to talk about Todd Snider. I wanted to talk about Nick Lowe and Richard Thompson. By then, I was only doing a handful of shows a year in a venue for which I needed to sell lots of tickets, so that didn't really work. However, I understood the business realities from the agent's perspective. Now, I thought, maybe having a smaller venue open six nights a week for live music would complement the larger venue. Feeling ambitious, I could accommodate an agent's broader roster at Natalie's and thereby increase my chance of getting bigger acts for Valley Dale.

Natalie's Coal Fired Pizza and Live Music, located on High Street in Worthington just across the Columbus city line, opened in early August 2012. The food was first-rate right from the start, especially that coal-fired pizza. So was the staff, headed by Natalie and composed of nice, smart young people, many of whom were musicians. As a music venue, the place was everything I hoped for. It had good acoustics, which improved to excellent with tweaking over time, especially by Mitch the Soundman. Mitch not only runs sound for the Zeppelin shows at Natalie's, but he has also done so for other national acts booked by Charlie. As a result, he worked with Natalie's regular soundman and outside technicians to perfect the acoustics. With table seating for sixty-five and room for another thirty or so as "general admission" (bar stools, window seats, and standing room), Natalie's creates a warm, intimate environment. Yes, there is food and drink service during the shows, but it is a "listening room" once the music begins. The music is front and center, not background noise. Think Nashville's Bluebird Cafe.

Charlie, as the "talent buyer," made a smart decision coming out of the blocks. He knew Columbus wouldn't support live music of a single genre six nights a week. So he booked jazz, bluegrass, rock & roll, country, folk, blues, gospel, and, yes, "national act singer-songwriters." As a result, the music at Natalie's has been a sustained success.

Succumbing to the ambition to expand my own bookings, the first three Zeppelin Productions shows at Natalie's ignored my then-seventeen-year operating philosophy. That is, first and most important, only promote artists who satisfy my two criteria—"great music" (defined as "I love it") and "nice people." Second, only promote performers who I know satisfy those criteria because I have seen them live or have a referral from someone I absolutely trust. And third—don't forget I am only in this for fun. Instead, my first three shows were acts I had not only never seen, but I had never even really heard of them. The results were . . . mixed.

The first show was a winner. At the recommendation of Brad Madison at Mongrel Music, I introduced Eilen Jewell to Columbus on September 14, 2012. The Music Fans still trusted me, although I'm sure the curiosity engendered by a brand-new venue didn't hurt. Whatever the reason, we had a big crowd despite the fact that no one knew her music. Of course, there was a new definition of "big," given the seating capacity of sixty-five. Eilen hit a home run, satisfying both "criteria." The music was great and she is really nice. Eight years later, she and her band, which includes guitar virtuoso Jerry Miller, are Zeppelin regulars and have built a solid fan base in Central Ohio. The other two shows . . . not so much.

About ten days later, we brought another new artist, Zoe Muth, to town. Again, neither I nor anyone else in Central Ohio was familiar with her music. In an attempt to sell tickets, I arranged for an in-studio at WCBE the morning of the show. She had committed to the engagement, so imagine my surprise when she e-mailed me the night before and said she wouldn't be there. She was in Washington, D.C., and a friend had invited her to stay an extra night and take a tour of the White House. She would arrive late afternoon in time for the sound check. Really? She was just blowing off the radio spot? You can also imagine how pleased I was the next morning to call the host at WCBE and tell him he had a half-hour hole in his program in about two hours. I wasn't any happier when she and her band showed up for sound check with little remorse. We had a small crowd for the show, and I did "tell on her" to her agent the next day. I don't know what became of Zoe after that. I can say, the cover page of her website still promotes the release of her "latest" album and an upcoming appearance at the Americana Music Festival, both dated 2014.

The third of my debut shows at Natalie's was an Austin-based singer-songwriter named Guy Forsyth. He had been part of the Asylum Street Spankers, a favorite band of one of my Washington law partners who always urged me to bring them to Columbus. The *All Music Guide* describes Guy's live performances as "loud, raw, and raucous." I probably should have read it before booking him. He was all of that and more, at one point walking around shirtless on the floor of Natalie's, even going behind the bar, singing at the top of his lungs. Shall we say, not exactly the sensitive singer-songwriter type? Certainly, not a typical Zeppelin artist. I do see Guy is still out there doing his thing. His website says his most recent project is a band called the Hot Nut Riveters. I have to admit that sometimes his songs come up on my iTunes random shuffle and they catch my ear. But I never reached out to bring him back to Columbus, or vice versa.

So much for my booking ambitions. I didn't need to ruin my reputation with the Music Fans by bringing in acts that didn't satisfy the "criteria." And it wasn't fun. Instead, I went back to the "regulars." The intimate environs of Natalie's provided a perfect venue for Artistes for whom Valley Dale was just too big. I could host old friends like Katy Moffatt, Rosie Flores, Greg Trooper, and Andrew Hardin, who all generated nice crowds that "filled" the place. Some of them hadn't been to Columbus in a number of years. It was wonderful—and fun.

Inspired by a visit to SXSW in March 2014, I took one more run at an ambitious approach to Zeppelin bookings at Natalie's. That summer and fall, I brought in a number of performers I had seen in Austin: the Iguanas, Parker Millsap, and Dayna Kurtz. They were all good in their own way, but it was a struggle. No personal connections. Not as much fun.

One thing is for sure—I love the Natalie's venue. It is so easy to promote shows there. All I have to do is book the artist and send my sales-pitch e-mails to the Music Fans. Natalie's does all the work, not only selling the tickets online, but actually running ads and doing publicity like a real business. Promoting shows at Natalie's is actually easier for the whole Zeppelin team. Kathy isn't at the door taking tickets or making change. Lisa isn't selling merch since the Natalie's host does it from the front counter. Jim still shepherds performers to and from the greenroom, which is downstairs in this location, and he tends to their needs onstage. But he doesn't have to deal with lighting and facilities management. The four of us just sit at what has become the family table, right in front of Mitch and the soundboard. And even Mitch has it easier, no longer having to lug as much equipment in and out of the venue.

For me, the real benefit is the economics. There is no rent. No security guard. No Zeppelin expense other than Mitch. It's even better than that. At Natalie's, there's an actual accounting system, and with limited exceptions, the artists are paid a percentage of the gate rather than a guaranty. (Of course, true to the Zeppelin business model, that percentage is often 100 or more.)

As Valley Dale met its demise, the "regulars" slid into a nice rhythm at Natalie's. Tom Russell. Sarah Borges. Chuck Prophet. The Artistes love the venue. They find a real connection with the audience. That isn't to say we haven't introduced some new folks from time to time. We have, but those have been few and far between. What we have done is entice some folks to play Natalie's who ordinarily wouldn't play a venue that small. We increase the ticket prices and get creative. Some, like Jorma Kaukonen, solo or when he is with Jack Casady as Hot Tuna, do two shows a night. Others, like Richie Furay, do a matinee and an evening performance. (By the way, note that I have introduced three Rock & Roll Hall of Famers at Natalie's with just those two billings.) Some, like John Fullbright, do two nights. The economic model is such that the payday is almost as good, if not better, than playing the old Maennerchor or Valley Dale shows, and with a lot less risk to—or pressure on—me.

The success of Natalie's Coal Fired Pizza and Live Music ("Natalie's Worthington") encouraged Charlie and Natalie to consider a second location with a slightly larger capacity for music. After a couple of years exploring alternatives, they settled on a location in the Grandview area, closer to downtown Columbus and the Ohio State campus. Once again, I agreed to invest. Natalie's Music Hall and Kitchen ("Natalie's Grandview") opened in late 2019 in a location that had previously been a sports bar known as the King Avenue Five. A distinguishing feature of this location is that the restaurant is separate from the music venue. Drinks and a light menu are served in the Music Hall, but the layout provides an opportunity to do more on the restaurant side of the business and does not require turning over the dinner crowd each night to make room for the music patrons.

In reality, there were two "openings" for Natalie's Grandview. The game plan was to open the entire operation in late October 2019, but construction and permitting delays got in the way. Charlie had a show booked for October 30, and I had Kelly Willis and Bruce Robison scheduled for November 1 and Hot Tuna for November 5. All of those shows and a number of others had to be moved back to Worthington, which Charlie had the foresight not to otherwise book. The Music Hall didn't host its first show until the night before Thanksgiving, with the restaurant opening a couple of weeks later.

Natalie's Music Hall is fantastic. The acoustics and lighting are perfect, thanks in no small measure to the hard work and investment of Mitch the Soundman. The ambience is spiffy. There is a big, high stage, so the sightlines are impeccable. There is even a real greenroom (not a space behind a curtain in the downstairs kitchen, as is the case in Worthington) with a full-length mirror, something Kelly Willis once said was her only request for the new venue. The hall immediately garnered rave reviews from patrons and performers alike, including Sarah Borges, who did the first Zeppelin Productions show on December 10, 2019.

The restaurant is also top-notch, but the delays not only prohibited an appropriate "opening," they also caused the place to get up and running in the middle of the holiday season. Not good. While the Music Hall was immediately packed every night for live music, the restaurant business started slower. Then, just as things were picking up, everything was shut down by the COVID-19 pandemic.

There are few sectors of the economy that have suffered more than the food service and performing arts businesses, and Natalie's has the challenge of operating two locations that are in both. Thankfully, a loyal customer base has helped them survive through carryout and, finally, a return to limited in-house dining. As for live music, it's the challenge of dramatically less capacity due to social distancing and, now, the grand experiment of live streaming, albeit with local acts since no performers are on the road for the foreseeable future. As I've been known to say, "Hold on to the sled."

TEN

Mixing Business With Pleasure

VEN I HAVE TO SMILE ABOUT THE DICHOTOMY THAT DEVEL-
OPED in my adult life. I was a successful corporate lawyer
with a very substantial client base. I was heavily involved
in law firm management. I've been privileged to hold leadership
positions with a number of important community organizations.
But through it all, I continued to promote national act singer-
songwriter shows. Having said that, I am so thankful I never tried
to combine my legal career with my passion for music. It would
have only ended up hurting both. Given the economics of the
music world, I likely wouldn't have been as successful as an entertainment lawyer as I was as a corporate lawyer. And combining
the two would have taken the fun out of the music. So, to be clear,
not only did I not give up my day job for music, I also didn't try to
combine them.

That isn't to say music wasn't helpful getting through the
trials and tribulations of the law business, or that the law business
wasn't helpful in advancing my engagement with music. Both were
the case.

In the fall of 1973, I was hired as a law clerk by a small Columbus firm. I became an associate and then a partner with my name on the door. My principal mentor there, Jeff Fromson, thoroughly enjoyed music, but I opened his eyes to a whole new world. He was soon a passionate fan of John Stewart, Tom Waits, and other singer-songwriters to whom I introduced him. I don't think my success in that setting had anything to do with music per se, but it certainly was a link to a positive working relationship. We broke up that little firm in 1982 and I joined the Columbus office of BakerHostetler, a national law firm with its biggest and oldest office in Cleveland. That professional move turned out to be fortuitous in many ways, both for my legal career and my passion for music.

When I came to BakerHostetler in September 1982, music again was a connection to numerous workplace friendships. Some of those nights at Stache's or the Newport were in the company of coworkers. I can't count the number of times a group of us sang Jerry Jeff Walker's versions of "Jaded Lover" or "L.A. Freeway" as we barreled down the highway on Myrtle Beach golf outings or rafted down the New River on law firm summer outings.

After spending six or seven years as number two in the management of BakerHostetler's Columbus office (and, at the time, also being the youngest person elected to the firm's policy committee, our "board of directors"), I was named to a firm-wide management position in 1993. As our firm's new legal services partner, I was asked to help break down the geographic barriers that existed in our office-centered management system. I would now facilitate the associate and non-equity partner compensation system on a firm-wide basis, and the heads of our national practice groups would report to me.

For the next ten years, I traveled coast to coast among the firm's offices. My love for music not only became a distinguishing feature for me within the management ranks, but it also created a bond with many of our lawyers, especially the young ones. Whether I visited an office or attended a formal function (partner or practice group retreats, new partner programs, associate academies, or minority attorney conferences), other lawyers sought me out to talk music. And many a night ended with my rounding up a crew and heading to a local venue for live music, whether it was the Continental Club or the Mucky Duck in Houston, the Birchmere outside of Washington, D.C., Jack's Sugar Shack in L.A., Swallow Hill in Denver, or the Beachland Ballroom in Cleveland. Not unlike in the small-firm setting, my enthusiasm for the Artistes was contagious. I once drove Leonard Greenbaum, our national head of litigation, from Columbus to Cleveland, playing and talking about music all the way. By the time we arrived, he had arranged for Katy Moffatt to entertain at a private party in Washington, D.C. (Leonard also hosted Katy and Tom Russell at the Litigation Group Retreat in 1997.)

The real role music played in my legal career was as a distraction. An escape. Maybe a better word would be *therapy*. I was under a lot of pressure, working from 7:00 a.m. to 6:30 p.m. five days a week, and almost always at least a half day on weekends. In the early days, I did much of the law work myself, but that evolved into delegation and the lost sleep that goes with being responsible for work on somebody else's desk. From the very start of my career, I was also fortunate to have client relationship responsibilities, which only increased over time—as did the law firm management responsibilities and the attendant travel.

Music was my outlet—recorded music always. Live music, for sure. But I was also a frustrated disc jockey or, actually, a wishful "songwriter," who relied on other writers for the songs. I created my first mix cassette tape at my brother's apartment in Cleveland in 1980, and I have made dozens of them since: tapes, then CDs, and now streaming playlists. They reflect the mood of the moment, the events of the day, the time of year, and the people around me. Most of them are really good, if I do say so, although Kathy would suggest many are "too sad." Ah, they were therapy.

In 1996, the executive partner of the law firm ran my name up the flagpole as his potential successor. I was young, probably not ready, and although I was in the final batch of three candidates, I didn't get the job. But life wasn't all bad. My law practice was booming. The year before, I had become the lawyer in charge of the firm's relationship with Cardinal Health, one of its largest clients. I was still in the legal services partner position, which I enjoyed immensely. And I continued to buy, listen to, go see, and now promote music.

That law firm executive partner position would be open again at the end of 2003, and this time I was ready and wanted the job. But although I had overwhelming support outside of the firm's Cleveland office, the leadership there didn't want the job to go elsewhere. The policy committee was in a deadlock for the better part of two years. Not a comfortable situation, but even then, music helped get me through. A playlist I made at the time, for driving back and forth to Cleveland for management meetings, opened with the Flaming Lips' "Fight Test" and Nick Lowe's "I Live on a Battlefield" and ended with Joe Ely's "Fightin' for My Life," Neil Young's "Walk On," and Rodney Crowell's "This Too Will Pass." A great playlist for then and now, with contributions from what were still future Zeppelin artists.

In November 2003, I agreed to split the CEO position with one of my Cleveland partners, ultimately proving, as I've often said, why Wharton doesn't teach a two-person leadership model. That management structure lasted until 2008, when the dynamics changed and I stepped down. The experience wasn't the highlight of my career, but one wonderful thing came out of it.

Shortly after the policy committee approved the appointment of two executive partners, the firm engaged the services of a Cleveland public-relations firm to help with the publicity surrounding the management transition. The firm's Cindy Schulz took the lead on the press release, and during our interview she asked what I did with my time when I wasn't working. I said, "I chase my kids around, play tennis three or four times a week, and promote national act singer-songwriter shows." I could see her eyes roll back into her head. A month or two later, Cindy called and asked if I could come to Cleveland and have lunch with some folks from the Rock & Roll Hall of Fame.

In February 2005, I went to lunch at the decidedly non–rock & roll Cleveland Union Club with Terry Stewart, then CEO of the Rock & Roll Hall of Fame, and Bill Summers, then chair of the board of Cleveland Rock & Roll Inc. The Rock Hall's institutional structure is a bit confusing, so a brief overview of the history is illuminating.

The Rock & Roll Hall of Fame Foundation was formed in 1983 by Ahmet Ertegun, cofounder and longtime president of Atlantic Records, along with some music industry moguls, including Jann Wenner, cofounder and editor of *Rolling Stone*; other record company executives like Seymour Stein; and industry movers and shakers like attorney Allen Grubman. In 1986, they held the first induction ceremony in New York City, behind closed doors in the ballroom of the Waldorf Astoria Hotel. The event was black tie (though the dress code wasn't always adhered to), and the tickets were expensive and pretty much invitation only. That's the format that existed until 2009, although the ceremony was held one time each in Cleveland and Los Angeles.

Among the inaugural group of inductees were Elvis Presley, James Brown, Little Richard, Fats Domino, Ray Charles, Chuck Berry, Sam Cooke, the Everly Brothers, Buddy Holly, and Jerry Lee Lewis. If you ever had doubts that the roots of rock & roll came from a big bang collision of country music with rhythm & blues, take a look at that list.

Around 1985, the foundation asked for proposals from cities for a physical site for a Hall of Fame. There have been theories over the years as to why Cleveland prevailed over competition including Philadelphia, Memphis, and New York itself. Was it because the Cleveland disc jockey Alan Freed ostensibly coined the phrase "rock & roll?" Was it because Cleveland's Moondog Coronation Ball purported to be the first major rock & roll concert? Was it just because Cleveland was a great music city, as evidenced by those many shows I'd seen growing up?

No, like most things in life, if you can't answer the question, follow the money. Cleveland, under the leadership of George Voinovich (who transitioned from mayor of Cleveland to governor of Ohio during the selection process), put together a public-private partnership to fund construction of the building. As part of that process, a second entity was formed—a tax-exempt, Ohio non-profit corporation now called Cleveland Rock & Roll Inc. For all intents and purposes, that entity owns and operates the building in Cleveland pursuant to a management and licensing agreement with the foundation. The agreement provides for a third hybrid entity, jointly controlled by the other two, which among other things employs the CEO.

The iconic I.M. Pei–designed Rock & Roll Hall of Fame and Museum opened with a dedication ceremony and concert on September 1, 1995. BakerHostetler, like most major Northeast Ohio businesses, contributed to the construction fund. Given my open and notorious passion for music, Kathy and I were the natural beneficiaries of two concert tickets from the firm that had us positioned front and center, twenty rows from the stage, on the field of Municipal Stadium. The show that night was legendary. It featured everyone from Bob Dylan to Aretha Franklin, and from Al Green to Jerry Lee Lewis. It lasted more than five hours, ending sometime after 1:00 a.m., when an unhappy Chuck Berry, struggling to get on the same page with the backup band headed by Bruce Springsteen, dropped the mic and walked off the stage.

Back to the 2005 lunch. Terry, Bill, and I got along famously. We all shared a passion for music. Terry's knowledge and enthusiasm for the art form put even mine to shame. (By the way, Terry previously served as CEO of Marvel comics, starting a tradition of Rock Hall CEOs coming from pretty cool places.) Continuing in the small world vein, Bill and I had a commonality in that he had gone to high school with one of my best friends in Columbus, the "Dancing Bear," Bob Barnett. Shortly after our lunch, Terry and Bill asked if I would join the board of the Rock Hall—specifically, the board of Cleveland Rock & Roll Inc. Terry told others later he had been knocked out when he asked me about my interest in music, not expecting the CEO of a major national law firm to respond, "I promote concerts." Terry also liked a line I often used when asked how I found time to promote those concerts with a busy legal and law firm management career. My standard response was, "I spend less time and money than most of my partners do playing golf." It was true.

Leaping at the opportunity to join the board, I took the role seriously from the beginning. I attended all of the board meetings and the annual retreats. I sprang for the big bucks and bought a seat at the annual inductions. Kathy and I were at the opening of an ill-fated New York annex. And most important, Terry and I became friends.

A few years into my board tenure, Terry, knowing about my involvement with the James Cancer Hospital (where I had chaired the foundation board for four years, including during a major capital campaign), asked if I would chair the Rock Hall's development committee. I again said yes, perhaps surprising him a little because that position was seen as a thankless job in an environment that was fairly "event" oriented—with expensive events at that.

Truth be known, after putting the money together to construct the building, the Rock Hall had lived exclusively (and sometimes not so well) off its gate receipts and the rent and royalties from its merchandise store. Cleveland Rock & Roll Inc. was a tax-exempt organization, but there wasn't any sustained philanthropic effort. Board members and other patrons felt purchasing those expensive event tickets was a sufficient "contribution."

We accomplished a few things in my run as development committee chair. We reconstituted the committee and began to create more of a "culture of philanthropy" at the board level. We kicked up the annual fundraising a notch or three. Jann Wenner, then chairing the foundation board, put heat on Terry to build a long-anticipated Library and Archives, and that became the principal pillar of a successful $35 million capital campaign. Perhaps the biggest thing we accomplished was identifying the need for a full-time vice president of development and, eventually, persuading Greg Harris to fill that role.

Greg was a perfect candidate for the job. Not only did he have a master's degree in history and museum studies, he had also dropped out of college for a while to start the Philadelphia Record Exchange, a retail operation specializing in rare and used records. Oh, and he also spent time in the eighties road managing singer-songwriter Ben Vaughn and his band.

Greg may have been the perfect candidate, but he wasn't an easy catch. He was happily employed as vice president of development at the Baseball Hall of Fame and his family was living comfortably in bucolic Cooperstown, New York. (From my way of thinking, his previous employer was even cooler than Marvel comics.) Our first run at Greg came up short. But after an unsuccessful alternative hire—a talented development professional who lacked a passion for rock & roll—we were back knocking on Greg's door, this time successfully. Greg came on board in late 2008. I was chairing the board development committee at the time and he was the vice president of development, so we worked closely together from day one. And our relationship quickly grew beyond just the working one. We became great friends and had a blast together, including attending Rock Hall events.

SERVING AS CHAIR OF THE board of the Rock & Roll Hall of Fame was one of the highlights of my life. At some point into my tenure as chair of the development committee, I was asked to join the executive committee of the board. That committee is really where the action takes place, because the board itself is way too big for an "operating" board. If you were designing the organization with a clean slate, you would have a much smaller board and create a separate foundation for those who want to provide financial support and attend events. But like many nonprofits, that's not how this organization developed.

The executive committee gave me a new perspective on the governance issues surrounding the Rock Hall and, in particular, the tension between the "New York" foundation (especially in the person of Jann Wenner, its longtime chair) and "Cleveland." Jann is a different kind of guy. Smart. Visionary. But, let's just say, not lacking in self-confidence. He'd been remarkably successful with *Rolling Stone* and for some period of time was arguably the most influential person in rock & roll. But he can be autocratic, abrasive, and . . . mercurial. In my experience with him, even when I agreed with his positions (which was a high percentage of the time), his style could be very difficult.

I am not sure what all went on between "New York" and "Cleveland" over the first twenty years. By the time I came on the scene, there was a level of distrust coming from New York and a sense of paranoia in Cleveland—definitely *not* a close working relationship. And that was a problem because the management and licensing agreement gave the foundation certain rights with respect to the museum, including hiring the CEO through the "hybrid" entity.

In 2006, the foundation hired Joel Peresman as its president and CEO. Joel was a music industry pro, having served as a talent agent and then as vice president of concerts (handling all the bookings) for Madison Square Garden. We became good friends as he settled into his job and I became more engaged with the Cleveland board, often getting together for drinks when I was in New York and even meeting on the tennis court a few times. With Joel, there was now someone from "New York" involved with "Cleveland" on a regular basis. Joel's presence offered lots of positives as the communication between the organizations became more consistent and constructive. However, Jann now got regular reports from the Cleveland front and didn't always like what he was hearing.

The tension, especially between Jann and Terry, was increasingly palpable. They are two strong personalities with different styles. As the tension mounted, the initial reaction of the Cleveland board leadership was to push back. I surmise that difficult discussions occurred throughout 2009 and early 2010, especially as related to the forthcoming renewal of Terry's contract.

The tenor of the relationship between "New York" and "Cleveland" began to change when Bill Rowley became chair of the Cleveland board in June 2010. Bill had been instrumental in staging a successful 2009 induction at Public Auditorium in Cleveland. He worked well with Joel, who produced the show, and made peace with Jann. At some point, Terry agreed to a contract renewal that provided he would step down as CEO effective at the end of 2012. But even after the terms were finalized, ongoing tension continued between "New York" and "Cleveland." Tension lingered within the board of Cleveland Rock & Roll Inc. too. Terry's larger-than-life personality was much loved by many. He did a great job heightening the profile and credibility of the Rock Hall, both in Cleveland and within the music industry. Some Cleveland board members really didn't like the "New York" pressure seen as leading to the forthcoming CEO transition.

In that dynamic context, three things happened for me. First, Bill Rowley asked if I would serve on the search committee for a new museum CEO. The committee included, among others, Joel and Bill Summers, the former chair who had first invited me to join the board. We hired Heidrick and Struggles, a major search firm, and began to look for what I was sure would be a big-time museum, amusement, or entertainment industry player to succeed Terry. There was one internal candidate, Greg. He was doing a wonderful job as vice president of development, and he threw his hat in the ring for the CEO position. He really wanted the job. I saw my principal assignment as managing his expectations so he would stay when someone else got it.

We conducted a very successful search, interviewing some of those big-time players I originally thought we would hire. But every time the committee reviewed the bidding, we would say, "But he's not as good as Greg." At the end of the day, Greg Harris was our unanimous choice. In November 2012, he was announced as the new CEO, effective January 1, 2013.

The second thing that happened to me was totally unexpected. As I mentioned, Bill Rowley became chair of the board in June 2010, for what was to be a two-year term. After Terry's contract was renewed, with the proviso he would step down as CEO at the end of 2012, Rowley said he needed to stay on for a third year as chair to see through the selection and transition to a new CEO. That threw a monkey wrench into the anticipated chair succession process. Sometime thereafter, Bill Summers reached out to me and asked if I would consider chairing the board beginning in June 2013. I hadn't seen that opportunity coming. I was flattered, but noncommittal. I had tried to "lead" a Cleveland-based entity from 140 miles south once before, albeit in a co-capacity, and it hadn't worked out so well.

Bill Rowley soon made the request with more formality. The opportunity was real. I continued to express concern. Interest, for sure, but also concern. We all remember certain catalytic moments in our lives, and I had one of those in the summer of 2012. I reached out to Jules Belkin, certainly the most experienced person on the Cleveland board from a music industry standpoint. He was also someone who had been very nice to me from my earliest involvement with the board. Among other things, he got a kick out of the fact that this corporate lawyer from Columbus was doing the same thing he had done for forty years—promoting concerts, albeit on a "slightly" smaller scale. Jules met me for lunch on a sunny summer day on the patio at L'Albatros in Cleveland. I told him about the board chair opportunity, and I expressed my concern that I wouldn't be effective as a non–Northeast Ohio resident. He swatted the concern away and urged me to do it. So I did.

In the fall, Cleveland Rock & Roll Inc. announced I would be its next board chair. My good friend Greg Harris became CEO of the Rock Hall on January 1, 2013, and I followed as chair of the board that June. Greg and his team get the credit for the successes of the next three years—they are on the job 24/7—but it was fun to be a part of the ride.

For starters, we initially prioritized improving the economics of the museum by growing attendance, which had been flat for years. I developed a mantra, "turn the turnstiles," and the team did just that. Attendance increased by double digits annually. At the first board executive committee meeting after I stepped down as chair, Chris Connor held up an attendance graph for the prior three years, pointed at the "hockey stick" increase, and said, "This shall forever be known as 'The Wightman Curve.'" Nice.

A big part of the Rock Hall world, events became increasingly successful, both economically and artistically. The inductions, which had returned to Cleveland in 2012, did so again in 2015, setting the stage for an agreement to begin holding them in

Cleveland every two years starting in 2018. Other events such as the annual gala and, especially, the Annual Music Masters tribute shows, reached a new level of artistic excellence.

Most important, I'd like to think I helped Greg, who had no prior CEO experience, quickly grow into being a superb chief executive. He led an excellent strategic planning exercise, built and motivated a strong leadership team, broke down operating silos within the organization, and inspired a high level of performance and morale throughout.

Things were successful at the board level too. In the spring and summer of 2013, I did a "tour" to meet in person or telephonically with nearly all of the eighty or so board members. (Remember, it is a very large board.) I listened to their concerns and interests, looking for new opportunities to get more folks engaged. We energized the board committee structure, including a reconstituted executive committee, providing management with a heightened level of support while increasing board involvement beyond just writing checks and attending events. We also strengthened the board, encouraging the committee on trustees to articulate and enforce "expectations," financial and otherwise. Some board members stepped up and some stepped out, but that gave us an opportunity to add stronger contributors to the fold. In fact, I've said that one of my legacies to the board was the addition of three of the most powerful people in Central Ohio: Nick Akins, the chair and CEO of American Electric Power; George Barrett, the chair and CEO of Cardinal Health; and Michael Drake, the president of the Ohio State University, all extraordinarily successful professionals who just happen to be musicians.

Working closely with Greg and his team (especially Caprice Bragg, the vice president of development and external affairs), the stage was set for a major capital campaign to fund, among other things, a redesign of the museum. That campaign, of which I am proud to serve as a co-chair, kicked off in December 2016 with the moniker "Museum 2.0: Rock Hall Remixed & Remastered." Our initial goal was $55 million, but by June 2018, we had already raised $57 million without going outside our board and the "New York" foundation. A wonderful confluence of events at that point enabled acquisition of the property immediately to the west of the museum, and now phase two of the campaign will fund an expansion of the building.

Finally, I took one important issue off the table early. In August 2013, I had lunch with Chris Connor, the chair and CEO of Sherwin-Williams, at Fat Cats, another favorite restaurant in the Tremont area of Cleveland. We had a good discussion and I asked Chris if he would consider following me as chair. He agreed to do so, but cognizant of his own career plans (an undisclosed intent to retire at the end of 2016), he said I needed to agree to serve for three years, not two. That didn't require much of an arm twist if others were comfortable with it. Greg and the rest of the board leadership supported the idea, so we had an outstanding successor chair in place—a successor who was able to provide a $9 million leadership gift to kick off the campaign.

I had more fun over those three years as chair than I could have ever imagined. It was also a nice boost to my leadership self-confidence that had taken a hit in the law firm environment. I am pleased and proud of what was accomplished during my tenure.

There was a third unexpected development. As Bill Rowley was winding down as chair, he persuaded Jann to add for the first time three members of the Cleveland Rock & Roll Inc. board to the New York foundation board. The three initial selections were Rowley; Bill Summers, who was known and respected by the foundation board, having served two terms as Cleveland board chair (including being called back for a second term when financial performance waned); and me.

Serving on the foundation board has been a fascinating experience, albeit much less time consuming and, given Jann's leadership style, less participatory than other boards. Nevertheless, it is a thrill to be on a board that includes people like Jann, Jon Landau, Irving Azoff (the Eagles' manager), Ron Perelman, Robbie Robertson, and other recognizable names from the music industry, Wall Street, and professional world.

I got along with Jann from the beginning. (Not everyone does.) My relationship with Joel helped. I am sure Jann liked it when I told him I had been a subscriber to *Rolling Stone* since 1967, although he quickly added they didn't have records to prove it. And my credibility may have been heightened through Jann's partner's sister, with whom I serve on the James Foundation board (that small world thing again). It certainly didn't hurt that Greg and his team performed mightily right from the start. But the truth is, I have generally found a way to work with successful people with strong egos, letting them fill the room while finding a way to keep myself in it. I've never thought about it before, but songwriters and performers need to have strong egos just to put themselves out there day after day, night after night. Perhaps my "skill" in working with those egos has contributed to how I forged bonds with so many Artistes.

Greg and I visited Jann for the first time in December 2012, after Greg was named CEO and I was on tap to be the new chair, and we made pilgrimages to his office at the *Rolling Stone* headquarters at least twice a year thereafter. When we first met with Jann, he lectured us on everything from macro issues like the need to create a more exciting experience in the museum (which was at least in part the inspiration for the campaign) to micro personnel issues.

But even as the performance of the museum improved, Jann consistently refused to say positive things. Instead, he would be almost nasty as he searched for areas to criticize. After one of our sessions, I stopped as we walked out of his office and expressed my displeasure about the way he had talked to Greg in the face of his outstanding performance. Jann bristled, saying his job was to always look for areas for improvement. I countered by saying that I'd found you get a lot more out of people by encouraging success rather than always complaining. Jann said, "I guess we just have different leadership styles," to which I replied, "Yes, we do." With that, a visibly uncomfortable Greg and I walked away as Jann yelled down the hall, "*Alec, I get the last word around here!*"

All's well that ends well. By the end of my tenure as chair, when Greg would conclude increasingly positive reports about the performance of the Hall, Jann would smile and say, "I can't find anything to complain about." *The ultimate compliment.*

ELEVEN

My Hall of Fame Greatest Hits

M
Y ROCK HALL INVOLVEMENT HASN'T BEEN ALL ABOUT BOARD
meetings, turning turnstiles, and capital campaigns. There can't be another board in the world as much fun as this one. What other board has an annual celebration like the induction ceremony, let alone unbelievable special events from time to time? There were two of those special Rock Hall events in 2009 alone.

First, there was the concert at the Surf Ballroom in Clear Lake, Iowa, commemorating the fiftieth anniversary of the "day the music died"—the plane crash that killed Buddy Holly, Ritchie Valens, and the Big Bopper. Greg Harris had only been on the job as vice president of development for a few months, but we were already great friends. He, Kathy, and I met in the nearby Mason City airport on the afternoon of February 1. The first thing we did was drive our rental car into the Iowa countryside and walk through a cornfield in minus-ten-degree weather to see a small marker placed at the exact location where the plane went down. That was just the start of a surreal two-day experience.

243

We arrived the day before the show. A handful of Rock Hall trustees attended, and we had access to the rehearsals at the ballroom. Sometimes my introductory "hooks" work and sometimes they don't. A member of the house band was Bobby Keys, the longtime saxophone player for the Rolling Stones, among many others. In the 1980s, I did law work for Western Natural Gas Company, headquartered in La Jolla, California. Their receptionist was an Australian woman named Desley Keys. Learning about my passion for rock & roll, she once told me she had been married to Bobby and had followed him to the United States. I, of course, couldn't resist. I walked up to Bobby at some point during the rehearsals, introduced myself, and told him I knew his ex-wife Desley. He looked at me, surprised and visibly displeased, simply growling, *"There are so many of them."* The conversation went no further.

That night, Sunday, February 1, we all gathered in the bar of the Holiday Inn in Mason City (birthplace of *The Music Man* writer and composer Meredith Wilson) to watch the Super Bowl. "We" meant not only the hard-core contingent from the Rock Hall but also many of the performers who would appear the following night at the Surf Ballroom. Kathy and I sat in a booth next to Graham Nash most of the evening and briefly met Peter Asher (there with his late musical partner, Gordon Waller)—a remarkable coincidence since five years later both Graham and Peter would be my guests at a private dinner the night before the Rock Hall Everly Brothers tribute.

Joe Ely was there with his wife, Sharon, although I hadn't yet met him in the Zeppelin context. I spent a lot of time talking to Dave Mason, once again running down a dead-end road by bringing up my recent experience with his former Traffic band mate Steve Winwood. Hmm . . . maybe they didn't part best of friends? A highlight of the evening was the Super Bowl halftime show. I moved up and sat on the floor in front of the TV, leaning against Wanda Jackson's chair to watch Bruce Springsteen and the E

Street Band. I received a warm greeting from Wanda when I told her I was close to her good friend Rosie Flores.

The show the next night was fun, literally fifty years to the day of the concert that preceded the plane crash. There were 1,800 people crammed into the Surf Ballroom. In addition to the afore-mentioned performers, the five-hour concert featured Delbert McClinton, Los Lobos, and Pat DiNizio from the Smithereens, as well as Buddy Holly contemporaries like Sonny Curtis and the Crickets and Buddy's protégé Bobby Vee. The next morning we rode the car-rental shuttle bus to the terminal with the previous night's emcee, Cousin Brucie, the New York City disc jockey to whom I had listened on my transistor radio five decades before.

ALMOST NINE MONTHS LATER, I had another surreal forty-eight hours, only this time in New York City. Instead of 1,800 people, there were 18,000 crammed into Madison Square Garden for the 25th Anniversary Rock & Roll Hall of Fame Concerts, October 29 and 30, 2009. Arguably, two of the best nights of rock & roll ever.

For me, this time, I was just a fan. No mingling or handshakes with the stars. But we had great seats and two fabulous nights of music. It is all out there on film (HBO broadcast the shows four weeks later), CD, and DVD, but the highlights are worth recalling. Both nights opened with Jerry Lee Lewis. He was followed the first evening by an extended set with Crosby, Stills and Nash, joined at times by Bonnie Raitt, Jackson Browne, and James Taylor. Bonnie called what appeared to be an audible, saying David Crosby had asked her backstage to do one of my favorite songs (especially her version), "Love Has No Pride," which she sang with tears rolling down her cheeks.

Next up: Paul Simon, who performed a handful of his songs. After accompanying Little Anthony and the Imperials for one of theirs, Paul was joined by Art Garfunkel for what turned out to be one of the duo's last joint performances. Stevie Wonder went next, plagued by sound problems (I was told he was the only performer who insisted on using his own sound equipment and crew), with guest appearances by Smokey Robinson, John Legend, B.B. King, Sting, and Jeff Beck. The first night ended very late, as a Bruce Springsteen show should, after Bruce and the E Street Band performed with Sam Moore, Tom Morello, John Fogerty, Darlene Love, and Billy Joel.

And then the second night: Jerry Lee opened again, this time followed by Aretha Franklin, with guests Annie Lennox and Lenny Kravitz. Jeff Beck was up next, a last-minute substitute for Eric Clapton, who had gallstones, playing with Sting, Buddy Guy, and Billy Gibbons from ZZ Top. The volume, already loud, went up materially when Metallica took the stage, offering up a couple of originals and a cover of Bob Seger's "Turn the Page." Then, believe it or not, Metallica served as the band for Lou Reed, Ozzy Osbourne, and finally Ray Davies from the Kinks.

That night ended late again, with U2. Oh, but not just U2. First, U2 with Bruce Springsteen and Patti Smith singing "Because the Night," the only song that had to be repeated over the two nights to get it just right. Then Bruce and U2 did the band's "I Still Haven't Found What I'm Looking For." There was one final sequence: U2 backed Mick Jagger and Fergie (from the Black Eyed Peas) on a steamy "Gimme Shelter" before Mick and Bono wrapped up with U2's "Stuck in a Moment You Can't Get Out Of" and "Beautiful Day."

There are a variety of connections between the Surf Ballroom tribute show and the 25th Anniversary Concerts, but one stands out for me. There were actually four headliners on that fateful mid-winter tour of the Midwest—Buddy Holly, Ritchie Valens, the Big Bopper, and . . . Dion. On that cold, snowy night of February 2, 1959, Buddy said he couldn't take another night on the tour bus and chartered an airplane to fly to the next stop. The plane could hold four people: The pilot and three of the stars. They flipped coins and Dion was a "winner." He would get a seat. But when Buddy told him it would cost $36, Dion balked. That was equivalent to a month's rent for his parents' flat in the Bronx and he couldn't justify the expense. He told Ritchie, who had lost the toss, to take his seat. As a result, one of the highlights of the 25th Anniversary Concerts for me was the opportunity to see Dion join Paul Simon onstage to do "The Wanderer."

WHEN I INTRODUCED ART GARFUNKEL as a "Rock & Roll Hall of Fame" inductee in 2013, I fully appreciated the significance of those words. Having attended every induction ceremony since 2005, I've seen the impact the inductions have on the inductees, the presenters, and the fans. It is a deeply moving experience.

I'd been on the Rock Hall board for just about a year when I attended my first inductions. I knew this whole experience was going to be something special when I made my way to the credentials table at the Waldorf Astoria before the pre-party. Like most such events, the guests were routed to short lines divided alphabetically. Of course, S–Z was at the far end, and as I made my way past A–C, I saw Eric Clapton waiting to pick up his lanyard and seat assignment. Okay, this wasn't going to be like most events.

The 2005 induction ceremony was a tough one to top. I sat in the front row of the ballroom balcony with a table of folks I didn't know, including Henry Juszkiewicz, then the chair and CEO of Gibson Guitars. I saw Clapton, again, onstage with B.B. King inducting and playing with Buddy Guy. Neil Young did the same with the Pretenders, including joining them on a killer version of Chrissie Hynde's ode to her Northeast Ohio home, "My City Was Gone." Bruce Springsteen did the honors for U2. This was all before the after-party, where I sat next to Samuel L. Jackson at the bar, chatted with Dan Aykroyd about his investment in the

House of Blues chain, and of course, met Bruce and his wife, Patti Scialfa.

That year may have been tough to top, but each year has had its highlights for me. In 2006, Jann Wenner read a handwritten fax from the lead singer of the Sex Pistols, not the first inductees to refuse to appear, but perhaps the most . . . "eloquent?" Johnny Rotten had scrawled: *"Next to the SEX-PISTOLS rock and roll and that hall of fame is a piss stain. Your museum. Urine in wine. Were not coming. Were not your monkey and so what?"*

In 2007, I was there with my daughter Nora, and, at the after-party, Lenny Kaye (longtime guitarist for inductee Patti Smith) and his wife walked right over to us because the ladies had on identical dresses from Anthropologie. The Kayes were perfectly wonderful people, making my twenty-three-year-old daughter feel comfortable, notwithstanding being the youngest person in the room.

There has always been controversy about what constitutes rock & roll, and the induction of Leonard Cohen by Lou Reed in 2008 sparked much debate. (You can guess on which side a lover of singer-songwriters like me came down.) But that year's class also included the Dave Clark Five, veterans of the British Invasion, who were inducted by Tom Hanks. One of the fun aspects of the inductions is celebrity watching. That year, Hanks was sitting right in front of me with Meg Ryan.

Cleveland played host to the inductions in 2009, the first time ever the event was open to the public. The ceremony was held in Public Auditorium, that same venue where I had seen so many classic concerts in my youth. Opened in 1922, it was once the largest space of its type in the United States. With its giant floor almost the size of two basketball courts, there's room for 1,200 people seated at tables—many more than at Barclays, where the inductions would be held in Brooklyn. The Auditorium's single-tiered, horseshoe-shaped balcony around the floor seats another five thousand or more. I was chairing the development committee (and, with my table mates, had paid the "big bucks"), and our staff was kind enough to give us a table in the second row on the floor, on the far-left outside aisle as we faced the stage. That table location became a favorite over the years because at least half of the presenters and inductees entered the stage from the steps in front of us, and they often waited right behind me.

With the inductions now open to the public, new energy revitalized the ceremony. Terry Stewart and Bill Rowley get primary credit for the vision and execution, overcoming skeptics like me who thought selling $50,000 tables in Cleveland would be a challenge. No cause to worry that year, or in subsequent years. And talk about energy! When inductees Metallica took the stage, their music's volume was exceeded only by the volume of the crowd. It was the first of two times I would see the band live that year, and I was knocked out both times. They also seemed like stand-up guys, renting the House of Blues in Cleveland the night before the induction to host an invitation-only party for every person who ever worked for them, flying in their roadies, secretaries, and support team to join in the celebration.

The 2010 inductions were back in the ballroom at the Waldorf, and this time I invited my daughter Emily as my guest. At one point, she returned from the ladies' room and said she'd been with a woman sitting at the table next to us, and that all the people were telling her how much they enjoyed her songs. She pointed out Carole King. Oh, and 2010 was the year Emily and Valarie McCall, one of our younger board members, wandered through the after-party and ultimately met a very inebriated Billie Joe Armstrong, the lead singer of Green Day, who had inducted the Stooges earlier in the evening. Val took a picture of Billie Joe draped all over my daughter like he'd known her forever. Emily immediately sent the picture to Cameron, her then boyfriend and now husband, who replied, "At least you didn't settle for the drummer."

The year 2011 was the last year the induction was held without a public crowd. It was a good ceremony at the Waldorf, with inductees ranging from Alice Cooper to Tom Waits, the latter inducted by Neil Young. The night was topped off by a long, rambling acceptance speech by Neil Diamond, who had just disembarked from a flight from Australia, followed by two performances of "Sweet Caroline." But the energy in the room was just not the same without thousands of screaming fans.

With the induction ceremony back at the Public Auditorium in 2012, we had our "special" table near the stage entrance. A visibly nervous Chris Rock paced behind me before inducting the Red Hot Chili Peppers, and Bette Midler stood with her hands on the back of my chair for a long time before ascending to induct Laura Nyro. As always, that year's show was fantastic and the energy in the room convinced everyone that the Waldorf was history. But the decision to right old wrongs and induct a series of bands (the Crickets, the Comets, and the Famous Flames) that had been left behind when their leaders were inducted resulted in a show going until 1:30 a.m. If there was an after-party that year, I missed it.

In 2013, a failed experiment took the inductions to Los Angeles. At the time, there was thought of rotating the ceremony on a three-year basis among New York, Cleveland, and Los Angeles. I actually thought the concept of having every third year in a city other than New York or Cleveland sounded good, but I would have rotated among different cities in that third year. In fact, I would still do an induction in London some time, but Joel Peresman is reluctant because he doesn't have the infrastructure to support the production like he does in New York and Cleveland. Anyway, Los Angeles didn't turn out so well. It's a city with too many distractions and too much traffic. And the music industry on the West Coast didn't step up with financial support as promised.

Actually, the pre-party in Los Angeles the night before the show was fun, with a nice turnout of inductees and presenters, as well as some local glitterati. A highlight of the evening was spending an extended period of time with Tom Morello, the cofounder and lead guitarist for Rage Against the Machine as well as a fine solo artist. He had just returned from doing a tour of Australia as part of the E Street Band, subbing for Steve Van Zandt, who had a prior television commitment for his show *Lilyhammer*. Tom is an extraordinarily nice person. We talked about his kids (one of whom was having health issues at the time), and he told me his life story, including the fact that his father was the first Kenyan ambassador to the United Nations and had abandoned his mother when Tom was a toddler. She moved with her biracial child from New York to a small Illinois town, taught high school, and Tom ended up graduating from Harvard in 1986. Fascinating.

I also met Jackson Browne that night. Just a few months earlier, Kathy and I had attended a small fundraiser for U.S. Senator Sherrod Brown in Columbus at which Jackson had performed. When he finished, former Senator John Glenn took the microphone, told the gathering it was Jackson's birthday, and led us in singing "Happy Birthday" to him. Jackson appeared deeply moved. So that night in L.A., when I literally bumped into him at the party, it gave me a chance to introduce myself and tell him about being at the event in Columbus. He said, "That's nice," and moved on.

The inductions the next night were different, certainly in terms of seating. We were in the Nokia Theatre and there were very few tables, even compared to the Waldorf ballroom, let alone Public Auditorium. The tables were located on boards over the orchestra pit and were primarily occupied by inductees and presenters. My daughter Nora, living in Los Angeles at the time, was again my guest, and we sat in the second or third row of the theater. The ceremony itself was fine. John Mayer inducted Albert King and opened my eyes to his guitar-playing ability. Harry Belafonte and Spike Lee passionately inducted Public Enemy. A loud section of the audience went crazy over the induction of Rush, seen as a long-overdue honor by the record-buying public. I don't have a Rush song in my collection, but they were a popular selection and the first of a number of "populist" bands to receive the induction honor over the upcoming years. Oh, and the after-party in Los Angeles? It was pretty much a bust other than Nora getting her picture taken with Tommy Chong. *Really.*

YES, I HAVE ATTENDED EVERY Rock & Roll Hall of Fame induction ceremony since 2005. Each year has been fun. But 2014 takes the prize for me. It was the first time the New York induction was open to the public. A large contingent of friends attended, and we had a blast from start to finish.

The two-day series of events started with what has become an annual "Chairman's Dinner" the day before the ceremony. I suppose that's what that pre-party was in Los Angeles, but I don't remember one prior to 2013. The dinner was held at the Monkey Bar in the Hotel Elysée in Midtown Manhattan. When Kathy and I arrived, there was a line to get in the front door. The weekend got off to a good start when our immediate line mates turned out to be Nils Lofgren and his wife, with whom we had spent time at the Rock Hall's Annual Music Masters tribute to the Rolling Stones a few months earlier.

That was just the start. Although not all of the inductees were present, most of the E Street Band attended, all of whom graciously posed for pictures and chatted up the guests. By that point, I had been chair of the board for almost a year and had developed a good relationship with Jann Wenner, who spent an extended portion of the evening with me and a few of my friends. I actually turned the table on him, leading him through a fairly fascinating "interview" about his career, if I do say so.

The next day I hosted a lunch for my friends and members of the Cleveland board in New York for the inductions. Thirty or so of us gathered at the Landmark Tavern in the Hell's Kitchen area of Manhattan. Located at the corner of West 46th Street and Eleventh Avenue, it is one of the oldest continuously operating food-service establishments in New York. I've been going there since 1979, when it was so dangerous even the cabbies were uncomfortable driving in the area. This day, I hosted a wonderful mix and match group of people, and the buzz in the room was great. It was the start of a tradition that has continued with every New York induction ceremony since.

That evening, we all piled into buses for the long (especially in rush-hour traffic) drive to Barclays Center in Brooklyn. At a pre-ceremony buffet dinner at a large space in the interior of the building, lots of past inductees and other notables mingled with the folks who had purchased table seats on the floor or VIP packages upstairs, which is what many of my friends and I had done. After dinner, we made our way to our seats, where we found a swag bag that included the thick, glossy program for the evening. I opened it and was greeted by a one-paragraph introduction on the first page, in large font, written by Joel Peresman. It closed with:

> The past year has seen a new chapter for the Rock & Roll Hall of Fame: Greg Harris began his position in January as our president and CEO, and Alec Wightman is our new Cleveland board chairman. We have a strong team in place to lead us into the future.

That was pretty cool. Who would have ever thought?

The induction ceremony itself was memorable to the max. It opened with Peter Gabriel, inducted by Chris Martin from Coldplay. I must say, I never got into that whole Genesis/Phil Collins sound. But the rest of the night was one highlight after another. Art Garfunkel presented Cat Stevens (a.k.a. Yusuf Islam), who was stunning in a simple three-song performance that included his beautiful tearjerker "Father and Son." Art, by the way, didn't appear at either the Chairman's Dinner the night before or the after-party that night, so I didn't get a chance to speak with him.

That was not the case with Tom Morello, who presented Kiss. At the event the previous evening, he remembered me from Los Angeles, and I introduced him to Kathy. Tom has become a member of the Hall of Fame nominating committee, and although the deliberations are confidential, it is safe to say that his presence has been instrumental in changing the mix of nominees on the ballot to include more populist music, not to mention metal and hip-hop. Tom's introduction of Kiss was superb. Unfortunately, it wasn't equaled by the remarks of the band members themselves, some of whom apparently don't get along with each other nor, shall we say, value the Rock & Roll Hall of Fame.

The induction of Nirvana by Michael Stipe of R.E.M. was followed by acceptance speeches by the living band members or their representatives, including Dave Grohl (gracious as expected) and Kurt Cobain's widow, Courtney Love (you could hear an audible sigh of relief when she finished). Then there was a Nirvana performance that included four women rockers, Kim Gordon, Joan Jett, Lorde, and St. Vincent, who was particularly good. They brought down the house.

The highlight of the 2014 ceremony for me, and honestly the highlight of any induction ceremony I have attended, was the induction of Linda Ronstadt. Parkinson's Disease was taking its toll, and she said early on she likely wouldn't be present and, certainly, would not perform. But that gave Joel Peresman and his team the opportunity to put together an all-star lineup to do songs for which she is known. Glenn Frey of the Eagles, who had once been in Linda's backup band, gave the induction speech for the absent Linda. Then the curtains opened, the lights hit the stage, and standing there were, left to right, Emmylou Harris, Bonnie Raitt, Stevie Nicks, Sheryl Crow, and Carrie Underwood. Years later, I still smile just thinking about it. Carrie started, belting out the opening words to Michael Nesmith's "Different Drum," Linda's first hit from her days with the Stone Poneys. The ladies continued, exchanging leads and contributing harmonies to "Blue Bayou," "You're No Good," "It's So Easy," and "When Will I Be Loved," joined at times by Glenn. It was twenty minutes of some of the finest live music I have ever heard. Right in my sweet spot.

The night wasn't over. In fact, the ceremony ended with the induction of the E Street Band. When Bruce Springsteen was inducted in 1999, he and the band were just ending an extended hiatus from performing together. He entered the Hall of Fame as a solo artist, which is how his career started when he first signed with Columbia. This night, he personally presented his band for induction with a heartfelt explanation about what had gone down in 1999, conceding the disappointment felt by Steve Van Zandt, in particular. He talked about how much the band meant to him over the years and, certainly, still did in 2014. Unfortunately, that emotional moment was followed by a series of acceptance speeches that will live in infamy in the annals of the inductions. All eight living members of the E Street Band each stepped to the podium and spoke, even those who hadn't been in the band for more than forty years. In fact, those former members spoke the longest. They went on . . . and on . . . and on. When they finally finished, Bruce joined them for a raucous three-song set that ended with "Kitty's Back," showcasing their instrumental prowess. But the hour was late, and Jann, from his seat on the floor, pulled the plug on a planned finale featuring the inductees and presenters. I am sure it would have been fabulous, but he didn't want a repeat of 2012, and he knew he had a special after-party scheduled in the bowels of Barclays.

When the show was over, my friends and guests made their way to the buses that would take the Cleveland folks back to Midtown Manhattan. Unfortunately, "my" group got on a bus with a driver who had no idea where he was going. Talk about living in infamy in the annals of Rock Hall inductions. Instead of heading west, he went east, deeper into Brooklyn. At some point, he was persuaded to turn around and head to Manhattan, but even then, he was unsure about where to go. Once across the East River, two frustrated Columbusites asked to be let off to catch a cab, at which point one of them slipped and fell down the bus steps. Thankfully, although there were scrapes and bruises, no serious damage occurred.

The night ended better for Kathy and me. Jann had invited us to his private after-party in a room at Barclays—just inductees and presenters joined by Jann, Kathy and me, Greg Harris, and a handful of New York foundation board members. There couldn't have been more than thirty or forty people there. Everyone was on a high from the evening's performances. What a night! We talked to Nils and his wife for a while. I spent time with Garry W. Tallent, the E Street Band bassist who knew Tom Russell and was especially close to Greg Trooper. Another thrilling moment: Kathy, Greg, and I chatted with Bonnie Raitt, who graciously said Carrie Underwood hit notes on "Different Drum" that none of the others could have reached. That was also the night I walked up to Bruce (for the second time in my life), stuck out my hand, and this time introduced myself as "chair of the board of the Rock & Roll Hall of Fame."

That entire evening was a highlight of my life, musical or otherwise. But I have to say, the highlights didn't end when the limo drove us back to the hotel. Fast forward to 2015: Sheryl Crow agreed to come to Columbus to perform at a celebration for Pelotonia, a major bicycling event that supports the James Cancer Hospital at Ohio State. Sheryl is a breast cancer survivor herself and knows Doug Ulman, Pelotonia's CEO, from his days working at Livestrong and when she was with Lance Armstrong. The day of the celebration, I got a call from the James asking if I wanted to meet Sheryl following her tour of the hospital. Of course, I said yes.

So that afternoon, I was in a small conference room with a

handful of administrators and doctors when the door opened and my good friend Mike Caligiuri, then CEO of the James, led Sheryl into the room. I have witnesses: She walked across the room, right up to me, and said, "I know you from somewhere." I told her I'd been at that induction after-party at Barclays, and although I didn't think we had met, I'd stood in close proximity to her for a couple of hours. She smiled and said that must be it. I did get a great picture taken with her.

Speaking of great pictures, the 2015 induction ceremony generated some of those. Let's just say that year's event was filled with ups and downs, *literally*. The "ups" were many. In Cleveland, the "Captain's Dinner" the night before the Saturday inductions had now evolved into a major VIP bash at the Rock Hall with lots of food, drink, live music, and celebrities. I spent time that night with the great vocalist Darlene Love, and, yes, brother Jim did take a picture of us. There were more cool pictures before the weekend ended.

On the day of the inductions, Kathy and I were getting on the hotel elevator when who should jump in but Dave Grohl. It was just the three of us. I introduced myself (yes, I could still say, "I'm chair of the board of the Rock Hall" for another year), and he told us he was cutting it close for his 3:00 p.m. sound check at Public Auditorium. Dave explained he and the Foo Fighters had just come back from riding motorcycles to Niles, Ohio, where they had played a noon pop-up concert to celebrate national Record Store Day in a small shop on his grandmother's street. He was due next door because he would be playing that evening as part of the induction of Joan Jett and the Blackhearts. I told him where we would be sitting—that same favorite table—and we looked forward to seeing him onstage.

Ah, it was better than that . . . Dave swung by the table before the show to say hello. (It didn't hurt that Rock Hall CEO Greg Harris was standing with us.) I introduced him to the Moose, his wife, Lori, and their good friend Rosemary Downing; Eleanor Alvarez, our next-door neighbor in Columbus, and her friend Jerry Rosenberg; Jim and Lisa; and my daughter Emily and now-son-in-law Cameron. Dave's eyes got big and he said, "You brought the whole fucking family?!"

Dave was kind enough to pose for pictures with us, as did Darlene Love when she stopped by too. Celebrity sightings are a big part of the induction experience as the floor fills with inductees, past and present, and other personalities of stage and screen. On this night, we sat next to Jimmie Vaughan and his friends and family, and Moose struck up a "Texas conversation" with him before Jimmie inducted his late brother, Stevie Ray, and his band Double Trouble. Also that night, Kathy outdid Emily's performance from a few years ago, returning from the ladies' room, where she had run into Yoko Ono, in attendance for the induction of Ringo Starr.

Yes, the lineup of inductees and presenters that night was outstanding. Ringo was inducted by Paul McCartney and joined in performance by his brother-in-law, Joe Walsh. Stevie Wonder inducted Bill Withers, whose acceptance speech was very touching, and Stevie then performed Withers' music with John Legend. I was thrilled to see the induction of my longtime favorites the Paul Butterfield Blues Band, with the surviving members performing with country star Zac Brown and, once again, Tom Morello. Brown and Morello admirably filled the shoes of my guitar god, the late Mike Bloomfield. Morello had surprised me the day before by confessing he was unfamiliar with Bloomfield's music until he was asked to perform. And as promised, Dave Grohl took the stage to play with Joan Jett and the Blackhearts after a fairly "over the top" induction speech by Miley Cyrus.

There was one "down" to the evening and, at least at that moment, it was a big one. My brother Jim went down. Just as McCartney was finishing up his speech and Ringo was walking in front of us to the podium, Jim passed out. Facedown on the table. Scared the heck out of all of us. I thought he'd had the big one. Thankfully, all was okay, but not before some scary moments. On-site medics arrived quickly at the table and carried Jim out to the hallway, where he came to. Jim, not only a huge Beatles fan but also a drummer in his day, missed Ringo's acceptance speech and his subsequent performance. By that time, he and Lisa were in the back of an ambulance on their way to Cleveland Clinic. (I'm pleased to report that, even after a few days' stay, the doctors couldn't find anything wrong with him. A virus? Allergies? Dehydration? Who knows?)

The rest of the night is a blur for me. A giant finale featured all the presenters and inductees joining in on "With a Little Help From My Friends," but I really don't remember it. I am not sure what happened to the rest of our table when the show ended. We were all badly shaken by Jim's collapse and concerned about his condition. When we made it back to the hotel, Kathy went to the room and I ended up briefly sitting alone at the hotel bar, where the after-party was being held. I do know I spoke for a few minutes with Gary Clark Jr., who had played with Jimmie Vaughan. I have no idea what we discussed.

Fortunately, the inductions were less eventful through the balance of the decade. The ceremony returned to Barclays Center for 2016 and 2017; Cleveland played host in 2018; then it was back to Barclays in 2019. Thankfully, the official hotel in New York shifted to the Roxy in Tribeca starting in 2016, resulting in a much easier commute to Brooklyn. The hotel lobby bar and restaurant also made for a pleasant Captain's Dinner the evening before the ceremony, now featuring inductee interviews conducted by Rock Hall vice president of education, Jason Hanley. The New York after-parties switched to Tribeca and became more of an HBO event than a Rock Hall gathering. (HBO has contracted to televise the inductions the past few years, doing so on an edited basis starting a few weeks after the event itself.) One year, Kathy and I spent a good deal of time chatting with a friendly Bobby Cannavale and Juno Temple, then starring in HBO's *Vinyl*.

The inductions are always fun, even when the list of inductees doesn't exactly mirror my record collection. Sometimes the presenters are of more interest to me than those being honored. Other times I get exposed to music with which I wasn't otherwise familiar. There are always memorable moments, positive or not. The 2016 induction will be remembered for Steve Miller's obnoxious acceptance speech and his continuing rant backstage. Miller took the opportunity of being honored by the Rock Hall to criticize it for, among other things, a purported lack of focus on education, a patently false observation. The Black Keys—the Akron, Ohio, natives who presented him—said later they regretted doing so. And by the way, when Miller played Cleveland a few months later, his people asked if he could stop by the Hall, and while there, he participated in an on-site education program.

Joan Baez's induction by Jackson Browne in 2017 was especially meaningful after the 2016 election and the Trump administration's commitment to build a wall at the Mexican border. Joan, who I first heard sing at a Vietnam War protest on the Duke campus, did a powerful version of Woody Guthrie's "Deportee." She also told the crowd her granddaughter didn't even know who she was until they went backstage at a Taylor Swift concert and Swift fawned all over her.

In 2018, with the inductions in Cleveland, it provided an opportunity to show off the impact of the Rock Hall 2.0 Campaign. New inductees Bon Jovi and members of the Moody Blues joined Chris Connor and his family in christening the state-of-the-art Connor Theater, which features a film directed by the then-recently deceased Jonathan Demme highlighting the best moments from previous inductions.

The ceremony that year opened with the Killers paying tribute to the late Tom Petty by doing "American Girl," morphing into

"Free Falling." That may have been the highlight of the show for me. Bon Jovi proved why—as I always say—the eighties drove me to country music. And I had to chuckle when Ann Wilson from Heart, presenting the Moody Blues, described them as a "kick-ass band." Really? (Actually, they did do one of their early songs, "Ride My See-Saw," which I guess comes close.) The low point of the evening was the induction of Dire Straits. Apparently, Mark Knopfler, the leader of the band, waffled for weeks about even appearing at the ceremony, let alone reuniting with the band for a performance. In the end, he not only failed to support Joel and the team's efforts to arrange for a presenter (Keith Urban?), he also decided to not make the trip to Cleveland. His band mates were left to take the stage on their own for their acceptance speeches, with no personal induction. That was a first and it was really awkward.

The after-party in 2018 gave me a chance to say hello to Ric Ocasek from the Cars, who had just been inducted. Ric's son Adam was once our next-door neighbor in the German Village area of Columbus. In fact, I had met Ric and his wife, the supermodel Paulina Porizkova, a number of years earlier at an exhibit of Ric's art in a gallery run by Adam's former wife. A purchase from that evening continues to hang on our basement wall. Sadly, we lost Ric in 2019.

When the inductions returned to New York in 2019, I brought a contingent of friends and family that included the Mooses, Jim and Lisa, and my daughter Nora and her husband, Matt. (Of course the Mooses were there. Moose and Lori have become Rock Hall event regulars, causing him to once say, "I never knew how expensive it would be to be your friend.") As has been the case for every New York induction since 2014, I again hosted that traditional Landmark Tavern lunch the day of the event, now for a group of fifty or more that filled the private room in the back of the restaurant and expanded to a second floor I didn't even know existed. The ceremony itself was the usual mix and match of sounds, ranging from Def Leppard to Roxy Music to the Zombies. I have to say, the Cure stole the show.

Kathy and I stayed in New York a few extra nights to attend the grand opening of an exhibition at the Metropolitan Museum of Art, "Play It Loud: Instruments of Rock and Roll," co-curated by the Met and the Rock Hall. It was a fun evening as we brushed shoulders (literally) with the likes of Jimmy Page. It was also strange to see Jerry Lee Lewis' piano and Ringo's drum kit nestled among the Egyptian mummies. The night ended with performances by a number of folks celebrating the exhibit, including the Roots, Don Felder (of the Eagles), and . . . oh . . . Steve Miller.

TWELVE

A Family Affair

MUSIC HAS ALWAYS BEEN A BIG PART OF MY FAMILY LIFE. Certainly, the participation of my wife, mother, brother, and sister-in-law in the Zeppelin concerts made it special from the beginning. The Rock Hall involvement has given me an unbelievable opportunity to share lifetime experiences with family (and friends) that I never could have anticipated.

My kids have been along on some of those runs, but their memories focus more on events meaningful to their lives rather than mine. They both love music, but in their own ways, as it should be. Yes, I cherish our attendance at the Edmonton Folk Festival, but Nora still talks about the time I took her as a teenager to see the lesbian-icon singer-songwriter Melissa Ferrick. I was the only male in the entire room, not to mention that Nora and I were in a small heterosexual minority. Emily won't forget seeing me almost get into a fight at a Jason Isbell show after I told some obnoxious twenty-nine-year-old suit-and-tie MBA to shut up. (Hmm, I remember Kathy doing the same thing at a Crosby, Stills, Nash & Young show at Nationwide Arena a few years earlier.) There are dozens and dozens of those examples, but a few weeks in the fall of 2016 stand out as a wonderful family time.

First, Kathy and I took a driving vacation in the United States, our "Drive South/All Music" trip. Then, just a few days after our return, we headed to the Desert Trip concerts outside of Palm Springs, California, this time with our kids in tow.

I actually began the drive south in solo mode. Late in my career, I developed a niche practice of helping public-company boards with their self-evaluation process. They fly me around the country to interview the directors confidentially, I apply some judgment, and report back on what I've heard. It's a fabulous gig, if I do say so. In 2016, I'd been hired by Kimball Electronics, headquartered in Jasper, Indiana, and I agreed to stop by and meet the chair/CEO on my way to the first scheduled stop on our trip, the Americana Music Festival in Nashville. (Appropriate for the music theme of the trip, Kimball once made pianos and organs.)

After a long day of driving and a journey into deepest southern Indiana, I arrived in Nashville late on a Thursday afternoon. I checked into the hotel, picked up my festival credentials, and took the shuttle bus to the Union Station Hotel to see Billy Bragg and Joe Henry.

Billy and Joe had just released an album of railroad songs, recorded in different train stations all over America. They were now performing in what was once the ornate waiting room for the Nashville train station. Joe told the crowd it was the same room Bob Dylan walked through when he disembarked from New York to record *Nashville Skyline* almost fifty years earlier.

The duo was fascinating. I had never seen Billy before, but I'd known the music of Joe Henry since I saw him open for Uncle Tupelo at the old Agora in Columbus in 1993. (Uncle Tupelo is the legendary predecessor to the bands Son Volt and Wilco. Terry Lickona of *Austin City Limits* once told me he considers Wilco the quintessence of the music he strives to present on that long-lasting television show.) Billy and Joe performed classic railroad songs, naturally including "Waiting for a Train." They also played a powerful new song by singer-songwriter and playwright Anaïs Mitchell. (Four years later, Kathy and I saw her musical, *Hadestown*, on Broadway.)

The small world only gets smaller. I was taking notes in my Moleskine, as I am wont to do on vacation, when a gentleman asked if I was a "reviewer." It turned out he was the publicist for Billy and Joe. When I told him I promoted shows in Columbus, he got excited because his wife's uncle is a lawyer in town who I know. With that connection established, he summoned Joe, and we had a great conversation. Joe has produced a number of albums for Rodney Crowell, and I told Joe that Rodney always said I should bring him to Columbus. Just to complete the small world circle for the day, I ended the evening at Cannery Ballroom seeing Rodney do an up-tempo set with a full band.

Kathy flew to Nashville the next morning. We started the day sitting in on a panel discussion by Billy, Joe, and author/journalist Barry Mazor. Yes, the topic was "Those Great American Train Songs." Afterward, Joe came over to say hello and I introduced him to Kathy, telling Joe she's loved his music since she heard his song "Good Fortune" on NPR in the early nineties. Joe expressed enthusiasm about doing a Zeppelin show. He said all I had to do was call his agent. Uh oh, the same guy who represents Richard Thompson and Nick Lowe. Needless to say, Joe still hasn't made it to town.

Before the night was over, Kathy and I heard a lot of music. We saw Robbie Fulks, a favorite from SXSW, where the Mooses, Kathy, and I hosted Robbie and Rosie Flores for dinner one night. We also saw two Central Ohio natives who were breaking out nationally, Lydia Loveless (later a Zeppelin artist on a somewhat spontaneous opening slot just before the COVID-19 pandemic) and Aaron Lee Tasjan.

On Saturday morning, Kathy and I drove to Memphis, where we took the obligatory Stax and Sun Studio tours, both of which

I'd attended earlier when the city hosted our Rock Hall board re-treat. We also visited the powerful National Civil Rights Museum. And staying at the Peabody Hotel, we saw the ducks walk in and out of the lobby a couple of times. The highlight of our visit was Sunday morning, when Kathy and I went to the Full Gospel Tab-ernacle Church, hoping to catch a service with its pastor, the Reverend Al Green. I'd read that Reverend Green only preaches once a month, unannounced, so we had no idea if this would be his Sunday. It was. And oh, did he preach. And sing. Lots of call and response. Tremendous energy. The pews were filled with his usual parishioners, a busload of New Zealand tourists, and Kathy and me. This was the same Al Green we'd seen fall to his knees and sing Sam Cooke's "A Change Is Gonna Come" at the concert for the opening of the Rock Hall. Praise the Lord!

The next morning, on the way out of town, we toured Graceland—surprisingly small and enjoyable—and made our way down Highway 61 into Mississippi. The Blues Trail. Our first stop was the birthplace of James Cotton, that outstanding blues har-monica player who had been chased off the stage by the Dukies so many years ago. We visited the minuscule town of Friars Point, the birthplace of Conway Twitty and the spot where Muddy Wa-ters once saw Robert Johnson play and, according to writer Steve Cheseborough, was "intimidated by Johnson's fierceness and musicality."

Speaking of Robert Johnson, the "King of the Delta Blues," we also stopped at the intersection of Highways 61 and 49. That's the "Crossroads" where legend says Johnson sold his soul to the devil to learn to play guitar. Our visit to the Crossroads consisted of barbecue at Abe's, situated on one corner and billed as "Serving Swine Dining Since 1924."

Our day ended at the very spiffy Alluvian Hotel in Greenwood, Mississippi, built to accommodate visitors to the headquarters of Viking Range, located across the street. Imagine my surprise when I handed my Ohio driver's license to the young woman at the reception desk in this small Mississippi town and she asked, "Are you Emily's dad?" The hotel clerk was from the Columbus suburb of Bexley and had played field hockey against my daughter in high school.

The next morning Kathy and I stopped on a bridge over the Tallahatchie River with a plaque honoring Greenwood-native Bobbie Gentry. To make it clear, just as I didn't ask Jimmy Webb about the cake in the rain, I wouldn't ask Bobbie what the girl and Billie Joe threw off the bridge, even if I had the opportunity to do so. (And to be perfectly honest, the bridge referenced in the song "Ode to Billie Joe" is at Choctaw Ridge, located about ten miles north of Greenwood.)

Our final stop before leaving Greenwood was at the grave of Robert Johnson—at least what purports to be the "proven" grave of Johnson among the three that lay claim to his bones. I felt his spirit as I sang, *"When I leave this town, I'm going to bid you fare, farewell."* Cream's version of "Four Until Late" was the first Robert Johnson song I remember hearing, off that *Fresh Cream* album in 1967.

Kathy and I drove through the back-road hills of central and northern Mississippi, ending up in Muscle Shoals, Alabama. The next morning we toured both the iconic FAME Studios and Muscle Shoals Studios. The latter is now closed to the public, but an introductory phone call from Greg Harris to Rodney Hall, son of the late founder of FAME Rick Hall, gained us access. Both facilities were fascinating, and the list of recording artists who have graced their studios is mind-boggling. Everyone from the Rolling Stones to Paul Simon, from Aretha Franklin to Art Garfunkel. And of course, there's that first Boz Scaggs album. . . .

The rest of our trip kept with the music theme. We spent a night in Asheville, North Carolina, where we saw a plaque honoring Jimmie Rodgers, the "Father of Country Music" (and the composer of "Waiting for a Train"), who started his career there.

It was also in Asheville where I bought the Bruce Springsteen memoir on the day of its release and began to devour all 510 pages. Finally, we arrived at my old stomping grounds of Durham, North Carolina, for a meeting of the Duke Performances advisory board. After our board meeting, we saw a recital by a classical pianist, Simone Dinnerstein. The next day, and more to my taste, Kathy and I went to the Wide Open Bluegrass festival in Raleigh. And that night, the last evening of our trip, we had another small world experience as we saw "Three Women and the Truth," who just happened to be performing at Cat's Cradle in Carrboro (next to Chapel Hill). The "Women" are Mary Gauthier and two Zeppelin Artistes, Gretchen Peters and Eliza Gilkyson. We were home the next day, just in time to change suitcases and head for the desert.

I HAVE BEEN TO CONCERTS of all shapes and sizes, from intimate small clubs to giant arenas and stadiums. As executive partner of BakerHostetler, I once took an interviewee for our chief marketing officer position to a post-dinner Lynn Miles concert at Beachland Ballroom where, embarrassingly, there was only one other person in the "crowd." (He took the job, by the way.) At the other end of the spectrum, there was Desert Trip.

In the spring of 2016, the Coachella festival producers announced a series of concerts to be held over two weekends that October. The lineup: Bob Dylan and the Rolling Stones on the Friday evenings; Neil Young and Paul McCartney on the Saturdays; and the Who and Roger Waters (from Pink Floyd) on the Sundays. Planned for the Coachella property in the desert east of Los Angeles, the event was immediately dubbed "Old-chella," a reference to the age of both the performers and the anticipated crowd. Not surprisingly, tickets were expensive, ranging from $200 to $1,600, and in high demand. There were 400,000 ticket requests for an announced capacity of 75,000 each weekend, and they sold out in just a few hours.

Ah, but there are always advantages to being associated with the Rock Hall. Greg Harris put me in touch with the late Shelley Lazar, the founder of SLO Ticketing who was known in the music industry (and otherwise) as "the Ticket Queen." After working for Madison Square Garden and Bill Graham for many years, she struck out on her own in 2002 with a business exclusively devoted to managing premium tickets for folks like the Rolling Stones, the Who, Paul McCartney, and, when he "toured" the United States, the Pope. (I suppose those can all be religious experiences.)

Shelley arranged tickets for the first weekend for Kathy and me; Nora and her future husband, Matt; Emily and Cameron; and an honorary "family member" for the event, our next-door neighbor Eleanor Alvarez. Rather than sit on the field with the masses, I opted for very expensive box seats in temporary bleachers being constructed just for these shows. In uncharacteristic fashion, I arranged for those of us attending from Columbus to fly to Palm Springs on Friday, October 7, the first day of the show. (That violated the "Wightman rule" of not flying out of Columbus the day of an important event, like making an international connection or . . . going to Desert Trip.) I was surprised to learn that our tickets needed to be picked up at Shelley's temporary office by 3:00 p.m. that day and we wouldn't arrive in time to be there.

Not to worry, Nora lived in Los Angeles, and she and Matt could arrive in plenty of time to get the tickets. I was pleased to see a photo on my phone when we deplaned in Palm Springs showing Nora at Shelley's office, tickets in hand and nestled under the arm of six-foot-eleven Bill Walton, the other patron there to pick up tickets. (Nora, by the way, not a basketball aficionado, recognized Walton as a Grateful Dead fan.)

That evening, we convened at our rental SUV in the parking lot of the resort where I'd been lucky enough to book rooms (I think Shelley did that, too), and we began to make our way to the show. Uh-oh—the promoters hadn't effectively planned for the traffic. Although better the next two nights, it was a disaster on Friday. We crawled . . . and crawled . . . and crawled. At one point, while closing in on the grounds, but with the GPS telling us it would still take a while to get there, Nora and Matt jumped out and walked. When the rest of us finally arrived at our VIP parking lot, we still had a trek to our seats, a walk made even longer by my hobbling. (I was just three weeks away from total knee replacement surgery.)

Bob Dylan was already onstage and playing as we made it through the turnstiles. Comparing the notes from my ever-present pocket Moleskine to the set list posted online, we only missed "Rainy Day Women #12 and 35." However, we did hear what followed, including the next three: "Don't Think Twice, It's All Right," "Highway 61 Revisited," and "It's All Over Now, Baby Blue." I've seen Dylan many times over the past twenty years, and I'd rate those other shows between a three and a seven on a ten-point scale. My notes from Desert Trip, certainly influenced by the excitement of the moment, gave him a ten. He did his songs in a more recognizable style than is often the case, and they ranged from "Simple Twist of Fate" to "Make You Feel My Love." He did classics like "Desolation Row," finished his main set with "Ballad of a Thin Man," and encored with "Masters of War," the first time he had performed the latter since 2010.

As the sun went down, the scene really was magical. Tens of thousands of people spread out in front of us. Our box seats, located on the side of the field, were farther from the stage than I expected, but the magnificent sound system and giant screens made us feel like we were fifty feet away.

After a break and a set change, it was "Start Me Up"—the Rolling Stones. An eighteen-song set list plus two encores. After a few lesser-known tunes, they settled into all the classics. Just straight up rock & roll. My notes say, "No fancy staging," at least until the fireworks after the set closer, "Jumpin' Jack Flash," and again after the final encore, "Satisfaction." There's a reason why they are often called the greatest rock & roll band in the world.

How could that evening be topped? When Neil Young kicked off the festivities the next night. He opened at the piano, hushing close to 100,000 people with "After the Goldrush." Neil then moved to acoustic guitar for a solo "Heart of Gold." My notes say, "No sounds from the crowd. Fabulous." Next up, "Comes a Time." It is stunning what Neil, Bob Dylan, and Mick Jagger can do with a harmonica, and we'd heard all three in twenty-four hours.

Lukas Nelson & Promise of the Real—Neil's backup band for a while—joined him for "Out on the Weekend," another *Harvest* favorite. His "quiet" mode lasted through a couple of newer songs; at one point he struggled to tune his guitar and remarked, "Now, you all know I can't tune. It kind of got in my way for a few years." (Remember my favorite album, *Tonight's the Night*?) Once in tune, he played "Harvest Moon" and a couple of others, including his "tribute" to CSN, "Walk On." But Neil was just getting started.

Out came his iconic electric guitar, "Old Black," which I now know to be a 1953 Gibson Les Paul Goldtop painted black. He launched into that favorite of mine, "Powderfinger," followed by a version of "Down by the River" to end all versions. Electric Neil at his best. He did a couple more songs, grumbled about the time limits, and said he would play a "forty-second" portion of "Rockin' in the Free World." Instead, he did the whole rousing song. I am biased, but Neil was the highlight of a transcendent weekend for me.

Paul McCartney was up next on Saturday. Kathy and I had just seen him for the first time a couple months earlier in Cleveland. Honestly, I'd been disappointed that evening, especially given the rave reviews I always heard about his live shows. For me, the Beatles songs are mostly classics, but there is little McCartney output of the last forty years that made it to my record collection. Maybe it was just the scene, but I enjoyed him much more at Desert Trip. He opened with "A Hard Day's Night," and before the night was over, he did twenty-three other Beatles songs. A highlight for me, not surprising, was Neil joining him on "A Day in the Life," morphing into "Give Peace a Chance." Paul obviously wasn't under the same time constraints as Neil had been, not wrapping up until he'd played thirty-six songs.

Sunday night at Desert Trip opened with the Who. Just six songs into their set, they had already captured much of my Who 45 rpm collection from 1966 through 1968 with "I Can't Explain," "The Kids Are Alright," and "I Can See for Miles." As with McCartney, I'd been underwhelmed when I recently saw the Who in Columbus in May, and now they excelled. Roger Daltrey's voice sounded stronger, though I could have lived without the songs from *Quadrophenia*, an album I simply never "got."

Roger Waters closed out the weekend. Speaking of never "got," Pink Floyd never did it for me. A friend brought me *A Saucerful of Secrets* from England in 1968, and that's the only Pink Floyd record in my collection. I am probably the only rock & roll fan who doesn't own their 1979 classic, *The Wall*, not to mention *Dark Side of the Moon*. I will concede, however, I was surprised how many songs I recognized that evening.

Waters had by far the largest stage production of Desert Trip, taking full advantage of the available technology. At times, the sounds of trains and planes moved through speakers spread throughout the crowd—feeling like they were coming right through us. I read somewhere that Waters spent millions on his stage production, which he used on a subsequent tour.

Waters was also far and away the most political of the weekend's performers. Throughout his set, a giant inflatable pig floated above the crowd with messages bashing then-candidate Trump. On October 9, the eve of the 2016 election, he was prescient in his warning, "*If you aren't angry, you aren't paying attention.*"

THIRTEEN

Annual Music Masters

Y EAR IN, YEAR OUT, MY FAVORITE ROCK & ROLL HALL OF Fame event was the Annual Music Masters (AMM). The induction ceremonies are always memorable, and the special events, such as the 25th Anniversary Concerts, can be truly unique experiences. That said, I always thought AMM consistently did the best job of fulfilling the Rock Hall's mission: to engage, teach, and inspire through the power of rock & roll. Each AMM was well done, but two particularly rocked my world—the tributes in 2012 to Chuck Berry and in 2014 to the Everly Brothers.

Debuting in 1996 and continuing annually through 2016, Music Masters celebrated, in the words of Greg Harris, "artists who changed the shape and sound of our world." As Greg said in an AMM program, "Each year, the program explores the legacy of a Rock & Roll Hall of Fame inductee in a range of events that include exhibits, lectures, films, artist interviews, a celebration day at the Rock Hall, and a tribute concert benefiting our education program."

The inaugural Music Masters paid homage to Woody Guthrie, culminating in a Saturday night concert at Severance Hall. Headlined by Bruce Springsteen, the tribute included a lineup ranging

273

from future Zeppelin Artistes Joe Ely, Jimmie Dale Gilmore, and Ramblin' Jack Elliott to such contemporary voices as the Indigo Girls and Ani DiFranco (the same Ani whom my daughter Nora played every morning as I drove her to school, Ani's lyrics clearly saying things Nora wanted her dad to hear). Kathy, Jim, and I enjoyed the performance, seated in the same row as Pete Seeger, who also participated when he wasn't sitting among the people. It may have been the first "popular music" concert ever held in the hallowed home of the Cleveland Orchestra. (For sure, it was the only time AMM took place there, the show subsequently moving to the theaters at Playhouse Square.)

I didn't attend another Music Masters concert until I was on the Rock Hall board—the 2005 tribute to Sam Cooke. That concert featured Aretha Franklin and Solomon Burke (who did an amazing duet on "A Change Is Gonna Come"), Elvis Costello, the Blind Boys of Alabama, and many more. Former NAACP chairman Julian Bond and actor Morgan Freeman, two guys with great voices, served as emcees.

EVERY AMM WAS MEMORABLE, WITH a few having particularly personal connections or moments for me. For example, in 2008, Lauren Onkey, then–Rock Hall vice president of education and public programs, was producing a tribute to Les Paul. She had trouble finding a female vocalist to sing "How High the Moon," a hit for Les and Mary Ford, until I came to the rescue with Katy Moffatt.

By 2009's Janis Joplin tribute, Kathy, Jim, Lisa, and I had established what became a Music Masters tradition. The VIP after-party celebration was held at the now-closed Hard Rock Cafe in Cleveland's Tower City. Arriving immediately after the show, we established our position at the podium inside the door. That gave us the opportunity to greet friends, welcome performers who we might know, or, on occasion, introduce ourselves and create something of a safe haven for those we didn't. (Another Music Masters tradition: Jim would snag the directional poster for the after-party when we left, posters that now grace my basement wall.)

That very podium position set the stage for my 2009 discussion with Susan Tedeschi about doing a show in Columbus—"with Eric." Also memorable: Kathy spent ten or fifteen minutes in quiet conversation with one of her musical heroes, Lucinda Williams. Lucinda, by the way, closed the tribute show in 2009 with "Port Arthur," a song about Janis she had written for the occasion. An AMM first, it was also the first time the house band had played the song outside of a brief rehearsal, and it didn't start well. Lucinda stopped shortly after they began, sternly told the band what they'd done wrong, and started over. The look on her face reminded me why I'd never reached out to her for a Zeppelin show, notwithstanding how much I liked her music.

The 2011 Music Masters honored Aretha Franklin. My personal contribution that year was facilitating the attendance of Attorney General Eric Holder at the request of my friend and law partner, Steve Dettelbach, then the United States attorney for the Northern District of Ohio.

Aretha had insisted all week she would not perform, but Lauren was prepared just in case. When Aretha ascended the stage to accept her Music Masters award, she suddenly asked, "Is there a piano?" Of course, there was. It was rolled out, Aretha sat down, and, accompanied by Ronald Isley and her one-time romantic partner Dennis Edwards of the Temptations, she sang Leon Russell's "A Song for You." One of those heartfelt moments.

THE 2013 TRIBUTE TO THE Rolling Stones was something of a disappointment. Wonderful performances resulted from an excellent all-star house band led by renowned drummer Steve Jordan (who's worked closely with Keith Richards, among many others) and including Nils Lofgren and Bobby Keys. I enjoyed terrific performers like Patterson Hood from Drive-By Truckers, with whom I spoke at some length at the after-party. But in contrast to other Music Masters devoted to living performers, none of the Stones made an appearance. I will say that night (or early morning) did end on a high note for Kathy and me, however. As we sat in the dark concierge lounge of the Ritz-Carlton Hotel, doing our postmortem of the evening, the elevator door opened and out stepped Steve Jordan. He sat down and talked with us for an hour or more—we all need to decompress from time to time. A truly nice man.

For what it's worth, 2013 was the first year the honoree did not hail from the United States, causing a name change of the series from "American Music Masters," as it had been dubbed since inception, to "Annual Music Masters." That way, the event could still be "AMM" in Rock Hall parlance.

The Smokey Robinson tribute in 2015 was sensational. This time, the honoree fully participated. One of the highlights was when Berry Gordy Jr., the founder of Motown Records, made a rare public appearance to honor his friend and business partner. All of the music was superb. I met Smokey early in the weekend festivities and was introduced to him as the chair of the Rock Hall board. He immediately threw his arms around me and gave me a tight, extended hug. I was a little taken aback, being something of a non-hugger myself, but I thought that was a pretty special way of thanking me for my chairmanship. That is, until I noticed Smokey greeted everyone that way. He is definitely a hugger.

This was also the weekend I met Mary Wilson of the Supremes, who sat with my family and friends at the after-party (now held at the Westin Hotel). A few months later, I received a telephone call from Rock Hall board member Michael Drake, president of Ohio State. He was teaching a class that spring on "Rock & Roll and the Civil Rights Movement" and he was hoping Mary would be a guest speaker for one of his classes. He asked if I could help. A phone call to the Rock Hall was all it took. Mary came to Columbus to speak to his class. That evening, Kathy and I were guests for dinner with Mary at the Drakes' home. There were only ten of us. During dinner, a young Ohio State music student was playing background guitar in another room. When we finished eating, Mary called him into the dining room, and while we sat around the table, she proceeded to sing a number of classics, either accompanied by his tentative strumming or a cappella. Wow!

Digressing from Music Masters for a moment: Two years later, in the spring of 2018, Kathy and I were again beneficiaries of an invitation from President Drake to join him with one of his classroom speakers. This time it was Paul Simon. Michael has a longtime friend who serves on the board of a New York City charity that is important to Paul. The connection was made, and Paul agreed to come to Columbus. After Paul met with the class, Michael interviewed him on the stage of Weigel Hall on the OSU campus before several hundred music students and professors. Kathy and I sat in the front row for the fascinating interview, which Paul—playing acoustic guitar—brought to a close singing his "American Tune."

After the crowd exited, Paul returned onstage and a handful of us met with him. Michael introduced me as the "immediate past chair of the board of the Rock & Roll Hall of Fame," and that caught Paul's attention. Paul and I turned a planned five-to-ten-minute photo op into a half-hour discussion about the Rock Hall, where he had recently been the subject of a major exhibition. Paul was particularly assertive in his advocacy for the induction of more producers and engineers, including Tom Wilson, who produced the first Simon and Garfunkel album (not to mention the Dion and Bob Dylan records of the mid-sixties), and especially Roy Halee, who produced many more for the duo and Paul himself. Oh, and for obvious reasons, I didn't bring up my relationship with Art Garfunkel. I'd learned my lesson over the years.

AMM ran its course with a 2016 tribute to Johnny Cash. That year's concert was put in the hands of Cash's son, John Carter Cash, who served as executive bandleader. Unfortunately, he arranged a roster of performers who didn't seem quite worthy of his father's stature. My favorite part of the tribute occurred at the Rock Hall's Foster Theater two nights before the concert, when VP of Education Jason Hanley interviewed Rosanne Cash about her father. Afterward, Kathy and I hosted Rosanne, her manager Danny Kahn, and Shelby Morrison, the Rock Hall's director of artist and VIP relations, for dinner at the Hilton Hotel. Could it have been three decades since I first saw Rosanne perform at Bogart's?

I am sorry to report that the following year a decision was made to bring Music Masters to an end. The program was resurrected in a different format in 2019 with a fine tribute to Mavis Staples, the event now called "Rock Hall Honors." But those heritage Music Masters—particularly in 2012 and 2014—will always hold a very special place in my Hall of Fame memory bank.

CHUCK BERRY'S RELATIONSHIP WITH THE Rock Hall is long and deep. He was the first inductee into the Rock & Roll Hall of Fame, introduced at that 1986 ceremony by Keith Richards. Chuck played at Cleveland's Tower City for a party celebrating the kick-off of the city's efforts to bring the Hall of Fame to Cleveland. He was there with a shovel for the 1993 groundbreaking. And he was the final act at the concert on September 2, 1995, when the museum doors were opened. Now, on October 27, 2012, he was the honoree of the Seventeenth Annual Music Masters.

Chuck has been called the "father of rock & roll"—its "inventor." He made the electric guitar the featured instrument of the genre. He married country & western music with rhythm & blues—a major influence on the British Invasion bands. And true to my passion, Chuck was one of the great rock & roll songwriters—among the first to both write and perform. By reputation, Chuck was also difficult. A challenge. A little bit out there. But his peers and the generations that followed revered his music.

A friend in Columbus, Parker MacDonell, once played in Chuck's "touring" band in Southern California. (Chuck hired local sidemen in each location rather than pay for a traveling band.) Parker tells a great story about taking the stage without rehearsal and holding on for dear life. Chuck was also the king of the "get paid first, in cash" school, of which Aretha Franklin was apparently the queen.

By October 2012, I was the designee as the next chair of the Rock Hall board. I was on the executive committee, and I had now chaired the development committee for a number of years. More important, I had developed close friendships with the Rock Hall leadership team.

In that context I had an understanding with Lauren Onkey that I could toss out ideas for tribute-concert performers and she could ignore or pursue them. There really was no pressure at all. But my promoter instincts were in gear, especially for this one, and I had a ball batting names back and forth with her.

The lineup for the October 27 show turned out to be inspired. It included fellow inductees Ernie Isley and Run-DMC's Darryl McDaniels. There were guitar slingers like Joe Bonamassa, Lemmy Kilmister from Motörhead, and Earl Slick; such veterans as Ronnie Hawkins; and more contemporary artists like Vernon Reid from Living Colour. There was a breathtaking spectrum of musical styles, from David Johansen of the New York Dolls to Merle Haggard. But I have to say with some pride, the Chuck Berry tribute show had a certain Zeppelin Productions feel.

Dave Alvin opened the evening, a late addition to the roster as he'd waited to see if he would be excused from jury duty. Chuck Prophet performed, and he still talks about the thrill of being photographed backstage with Chuck Berry and Merle Haggard.

A very young and unknown John Fullbright, who had captured Lauren's attention when he played for our board retreat in Austin earlier that year, was the only person to play a Chuck Berry song on keyboard. (John received positive shout-outs in the next day's reviews.) And finally, Rosie Flores almost stole the show by being the only performer to pull off Chuck's trademark duck walk.

As great as the show was on Saturday, I really cherish a memory from Friday night. I reserved one of the private rooms upstairs at Johnny's Bar & Grille (one of my favorite restaurants) and hosted friends, family, and the Zeppelin Artistes for dinner. I can picture the table now. I was seated between Dave Alvin, on my left, and his (and Chuck Prophet's) agent, Brad Madison from Mongrel Music, on my right. Next to Dave was Greg Johnson, John Fullbright's manager and owner of the Blue Door music club in Oklahoma City. John's then girlfriend was seated between Greg and John. Chuck Prophet and his manager, Dan Kennedy, sat at the other end of the table with Cindy Barber, owner of Beachland Ballroom, and Brad's Mongrel partner, Chris Faville. Emily and Cameron were next to them, and then Lisa and Jim. Our end of the table had Rosie Flores and her manager, Kimiko Tokita, Kathy's book club compadre Lucinda Kirk and her husband, Bob, and Kathy, seated next to Brad. Greg Harris joined in time for dinner, replacing the Kirks, who had to leave early. We mixed and mingled over drinks and appetizers and then were seated for a long, wonderful meal. My worlds had collided in the best possible way. I still smile thinking about it.

One final highlight of the weekend occurred on Sunday morning. Kathy and I were having breakfast in the concierge lounge at the Ritz when Chuck Berry and his wife entered and sat down at the table next to us. By the way, the very presence of Chuck's wife for the weekend was buzzworthy among those in the know. Apparently, it was a very rare occasion to see her.

Kathy and I introduced ourselves and expressed appreciation and admiration for his music and, especially, his engagement and support of the weekend. At eighty-six, he had taken the stage the night before and, with some help, made it through "Johnny B. Goode," "Reelin' and Rockin'," and a finale of "Rock and Roll Music." When Chuck died five years later, Joel Peresman, CEO of the Rock & Roll Hall of Fame Foundation, was asked to be one of the speakers at his funeral. Chuck really did like the Rock Hall.

My worlds collided again with the 2014 Music Masters: a tribute to the Everly Brothers. I was well into my second year as chair of the board of the Rock & Roll Hall of Fame, and Kathy and I financially supported and attended the event—as did forty or so friends from Columbus, many of whom purchased "VIP" packages.

Musically, this was my absolute sweet spot: The Everly Brothers had not only been personal favorites since I was a kid, they were also key influences on the music of my life, ranging from the British Invasion bands to the singer-songwriters of the Americana genre. And let's just say that, through my Zeppelin Productions promotion efforts, I had something to do with putting the 2014 concert together, a show that was as fine an evening of music as I have ever experienced.

I advocated on behalf of the Everlys as Music Masters honorees for a number of years. However, every time I raised the subject, Lauren would nicely point out that it wouldn't work. We couldn't even get the brothers in the same room. Their renowned acrimony dated back to a show at Knott's Berry Farm in 1973, when Phil famously smashed his guitar and walked off the stage. The brothers eventually played a couple of reunion tours; in 1983, they ended their ten-year hiatus with a concert at the Royal Albert Hall, followed by a new studio album and a tour (which I saw in Columbus). Their last reunion tour was the badly misnamed "Old Friends" tour with Simon and Garfunkel in 2003–2004, the relationships within both acts having deteriorated to the point where the members of each duo avoided each other except on center stage. Don and Phil basically weren't speaking, nor were Paul and Art. Art Garfunkel told me the members of each act entered and exited the stage from opposite sides.

Phil Everly died of lung disease on January 3, 2014. I was perhaps a touch premature when I called Lauren shortly thereafter and asked if we could now do an Everly Brothers Music Masters. Lauren says she wouldn't have spoken quite so harshly to her board chair, but the gist of her response, as I recall, was that my suggestion was a bit "unseemly" within days of Phil's passing.

I persisted. A few weeks later, I read a newspaper story about the Americana Music Association's tribute to Phil the night before the Grammy Awards in Los Angeles. Near the close of the evening, with Phil's widow, Patti, in attendance, Rodney Crowell read a letter from Don Everly saying, among other things, that Don was "too brokenhearted" to attend. Light bulb moment: Don Everly trusted Rodney to read his letter at Phil's tribute. Had I identified a link between the estranged brothers that might open the door to a Music Masters program honoring them? I called Lauren, raised the possibility of working through Rodney, and received her blessing to gently tiptoe forward. But she made it clear this wasn't going anywhere unless we could get Don Everly on board, including a commitment to appear.

I then reached out to Joanne Gardner, Rodney's very good friend who accompanied him to Columbus for his last show at Valley Dale. She confirmed what I suspected, that Rodney was one of the few people who had remained close to both Don and Phil. She coached me on how to proceed, and I called Rodney. With his counsel, it was determined the best way to get to Don was through Jed Hilly, executive director of the Americana Music Association. In some combination, we reached out to Jed and he "brokered" a meeting in Nashville between Don, on the one hand, and Lauren and Greg Harris, on the other.

Lauren did her homework in advance of the meeting, sketching out what an Everly Brothers tribute might look like. As she says, she had the "narrative." She focused on interesting spins for the show that would appeal to Don, featuring his unique guitar style. I wasn't at the meeting, but Greg remembers that, at one point, he asked Don where in Kentucky he and Phil were born. Without saying a word, Don, who hadn't performed publicly in many years, broke into song. Sitting at a conference table in Nashville, he sang, "*And daddy, won't you take me back to Muhlenberg County, down by the green river where paradise lay*"—a verse from John Prine's classic "Paradise," a song the Everly Brothers recorded on a 1972 album.

Obviously, the chemistry worked. The narrative resounded with Don. He agreed on the spot. He would be supportive. And he would appear. Greg and Lauren walked out of the meeting stunned by their success, and the fact that they'd just heard that distinctive Don Everly voice in a conference room.

With Don committed, I then turned to Rodney. Over a phone call or two, I surfaced the concept of a Music Masters tribute . . . with Rodney as the musical director. Intrigued, he didn't swat me away. On May 14, Rodney played Valley Dale, that memorable show ending with his performance of "Pancho and Lefty." After he'd paid tribute to guitarist Steuart Smith in the greenroom, I brought him down to the floor to sign CDs and take photos with adoring fans.

When the place cleared out, I introduced him to Lauren and Jason Hanley (then her number two), who traveled from Cleveland for the show. I had prepared Rodney. He knew what was coming. Lauren asked him if he would serve as the musical director for an Everly Brothers tribute show that fall. Rodney agreed. He began to verbalize what the show might look like. "I'll get Emmylou," he said. "And Vince." My eyes got big. "You'll get Vince Gill?" I asked incredulously. Rodney said, "I'll break his leg if he says no."

There was one more piece to the puzzle. We needed the support of Patti Everly, Phil's widow. Once again, Jed Hilly was the "broker." He arranged a meeting with Patti at his offices for Greg, Lauren, and me. Sometimes things just come together. We had scheduled our board retreat in Nashville for June of that year, and so the three of us arrived a day early for the meeting. We met with Patti, accompanied by Don's eldest daughter, with whom I think he was estranged. By that time, we had Don locked in and Rodney had committed as musical director. We made our pitch. Patti was emotional, but amenable. Her only request was that the tribute would help spread the awareness of COPD, the illness that claimed her husband's life. That was an easy request to accommodate.

With Patti's support in hand, Greg, Lauren, and I went back to our hotel in ecstasy. That was the same week we shut down the Bluebird Cafe one night doing a sing-along with Gretchen Peters, Suzy Bogguss, Matraca Berg, and Jeff Hanna. Not a bad life I've led.

Having helped secure Rodney as musical director, I kept my promoter instincts in check as the roster of performers developed. At one point, I e-mailed Rodney, saying I'd just had "my (almost) daily update from Lauren Onkey and she described you as being 'on fire' when it comes to the Music Masters show." I added, "This is going to be fabulous and a blast. Thank you very, very, very much." Rodney replied, in words only a songwriter can muster: "I'm keen to equal your faith in me, make it the best show possible. I'm tempted to say it's all shaping up nicely." Master of the understatement.

Rodney did enlist Vince Gill for the show. And Emmylou. That was just a start. Other performers included Graham Nash; Peter Asher; Keb' Mo'; Alison Krauss; Shelby Lynne and her sister, Allison Moorer; and J.D. Souther. Rodney put together an all-star band of Nashville musicians, many of whom had played with the

Everlys along the way, not to mention the guitarist Albert Lee. Albert had served as musical director for the Everlys' Albert Hall reunion in 1983.

Those few days in October 2014 really are a highlight of my life, musical or otherwise. On Wednesday evening, Rodney, Peter Asher, and Albert Lee participated in a "Songwriters to Soundmen" panel in the Rock Hall's Foster Theater. Afterward, I joined the three of them for a casual dinner on the lower level of the Hall. I was in my glory.

It only got better. On Friday afternoon, we held a Cleveland Rock & Roll Inc. board meeting in the Foster Theater. I knew what was coming, but none of the other board members did. At 4:00 p.m., the appointed hour, Lauren led the reclusive Don Everly into the room. I introduced him to the board. Lauren says she has never seen me so happy. I was, in her words, "beaming." She then took the stage with Don, they settled into easy chairs, and she interviewed a Rock Hall inductee who had not appeared much in public for many years.

The night was young. First, we held a VIP reception in that same lower level of the Hall. Some of the performers were otherwise occupied with rehearsals in the State Theatre at Playhouse Square, but not all. In particular, Graham Nash mingled warmly with our board, spending a lot of time with Jim and me. Second, I had planned ahead. Once again, I'd reserved a private room at Johnny's. With the encouragement of Graham, and the assistance of Joanne, we rounded up a crew to join a handful of friends and family for dinner. I can still picture my table that evening too. Kathy was at one end, on my left. Peter Asher was next to her, across from me, with Rodney's wife, Claudia Church, next to him. (Rodney was running rehearsals all evening.) J.D. Souther sat at the other end of the table and Joanne was next to me.

By the way, I had sat next to J.D. at dinner in Nashville when we'd been there earlier in the year for our retreat. (He is a close friend of one of our board members, H. Leonards, owner of the Mansion on O Street hotel, in Washington, D.C.) That prior night, as was the case at Johnny's, J.D. was confident and charming. It's no wonder he was always a ladies' favorite, whether on the television show *Nashville* or with his songwriting and albums. At one point, Joanne leaned over to me, smiled, and whispered, "I wouldn't trust him with my daughter." J.D. was no more confident and charming that evening than Graham Nash, who also joined us for dinner. Graham sat next to my friend Eleanor Alvarez at another table, regaling her with stories of Joni Mitchell, including about the day they went to the market together and, upon return, he wrote "Our House."

The sold-out show the next night was simply extraordinary. It opened with Keb' Mo' and Rodney doing "Wake Up Little Susie." Before the night was over, Peter Asher and Albert Lee had harmonized on "Walk Right Back"; Emmylou Harris and Alison Krauss had done the same on "All I Have to Do Is Dream"; and Vince Gill and Graham Nash nailed "So Sad." That's just a sampler. Imagine.

Don took the stage to accept his Music Masters award. He had insisted he would not perform. He had not sung in public for many years. But when the entourage broke into "Bye Bye Love" for the finale, Don took the microphone and sang a verse. Vince Gill literally jumped up and down, tears streaming down his cheeks.

Then the after-party back at the Hard Rock: The family and I established post-position by the podium. I was in heaven. Dozens of friends streamed by, on a high from the show. As were the performers. Vince Gill was still emotional about hearing Don Everly sing. Talk about the realization that I had helped bring enormous joy to all those people. I had the feeling that night to the max.

There was a memorable moment at the end of the evening. Through much of the after-party, Rodney sat in a booth with Don Everly and Vince. Yes, the reclusive Don had come to the party, obviously basking in the glow of the evening. But no one was basking more than Rodney. The night was winding down. Rodney and I stood quietly in the thinning crowd. Just the two of us. He was getting ready to head to the bus for the late-night drive back to Nashville. I thanked him for what he'd done. He thanked me for the confidence I'd placed in him. He was a little emotional. Almost teary. He said he was extraordinarily proud of the evening. Me too.

FOURTEEN

The Wanderer

N MARCH 2019, I SAW A POST ON DION'S FACEBOOK PAGE REFER-
encing a musical about his life that was in the works. I called
Mindy Rich, a member of the Rock Hall board who has been
involved in many Broadway productions, and asked if she knew
anything about it. She didn't, at least not that day. Mindy called
me twenty-four hours later. The very day after my call, she got an
e-mail from Jill Menza, the producer of *The Wanderer*, asking if
she wanted to invest. Mindy said her plate was full and she had to
pass, but she would forward the e-mail to me.

I called Jill and we immediately clicked. During our lively conversation, she told me about the history of the production, the
background of the writer, and Dion's support for the project. I described my passion for Dion and his music, including the fact that
I was working on this book and that "he" was the first chapter. I
took her from my being a ten-year-old with a transistor radio to
seeing Dion at SXSW. I also told her about Zeppelin Productions
and my involvement with the Rock & Roll Hall of Fame. Jill said
she had sent the e-mail to Mindy after randomly picking her name
out of a directory of Broadway producers. There was no particular
method to her madness. It was *fate*.

A week later, I was in New York for some board interviews, staying at the Beekman in the Financial District. Jill met me at the hotel at 10:30 a.m. on the morning of April 9, bringing along Charles Messina, the writer and coproducer, and Chris Aniello, one of the general managers. They expounded on what Jill had told me over the phone, and she encouraged me to tell them about my passion for Dion. No surprise. On the spot, I agreed to invest. So, in addition to investing in a couple of restaurants, I was now investing in a musical. Those were things I spent forty years advising clients not to do. But to be clear, both investments were for "fun," not with expectations of financial return.

Actually, that point was brought home within hours. After we shook hands and parted ways at the Beekman, I headed to Midtown, where I had lunch with an old friend and client at Gabriel's near Columbus Circle (a restaurant where I once spotted Wynton Marsalis and Eric Clapton sitting at the table behind mine). My head was still spinning from the morning meeting. I told my friend what I had agreed to do. I was surprised to learn he had invested in more than thirty Broadway productions. An original investor in *The Book of Mormon*, he was too embarrassed to tell me how much money he had made on that investment. He also smiled and added that, with that particular success, he'd broken even with the others.

Regardless, I was all in. Over the balance of 2019 and early 2020, Jill kept me informed of the musical's progress. They refined the story line. I saw the proposed song list. Substantial money was being raised. They finalized the cast with a number of experienced Broadway performers. They added "staff and creatives," including a Tony Award–winning scenic designer. Most important, they secured a six-week run at Paper Mill Playhouse in New Jersey, a principal stepping-stone to Broadway, with a "press night" and cast party scheduled for June 2020 (sad to say, now pushed back to 2022 thanks to COVID-19).

In early 2020, Jill asked if Kathy and I wanted to attend a reading of the play set for February 28 in New York City. Of course we did. That's why we invested. For fun. I just didn't know how much fun it would be.

We flew to New York that morning, took a car from LaGuardia, checked in to the hotel, and meandered around Manhattan awaiting the appointed 2:00 p.m. hour. The reading was held in a combination warehouse/office building at the corner of West 55th Street and Eleventh Avenue. As we approached the building, there were numerous luxury travel buses and equipment trailers on the street. When we exited the elevator on the sixth floor, we saw multiple rehearsal spaces with lots of musician types wandering around. I didn't even know places like this existed.

As usual when I am involved, we were early. We checked in with a guy who seemed to be in charge. He found our name on the guest list and asked us to wait a few minutes. Right behind him, having lunch in a glass-enclosed conference room, sat Little Steven Van Zandt. The one-sheet "program" we were given said Steve serves as musical consultant.

When the door to our space opened, we entered with another forty or fifty people. It was a long, narrow room with three rows of folding chairs set up along a wall. Kathy and I made our way to the center aisle and took seats in the third row, with me on the aisle and Kathy on my left. The band was sitting in front and to the right, and the cast of the play was sitting in chairs directly ahead. There were a few music stands from which the actors would "read."

The room filled up. Little Steven went down to the far end and sat in front of the band. A few minutes before 2:00, in came Dion. Many of the folks knew him and greeted him warmly. Hands shaken. Hugs. He looked around, picked up one of the few available folding chairs, and sat it down in the aisle right next to me. *Really!*

The milling around continued, with the reading not starting for a few more minutes. So I turned and said to Dion, "There may be folks here who have invested more than I have, but there is no one who has more enthusiasm than me." He said thanks and asked my name. I said, "Alec Wightman." His eyes got big and he exclaimed, *"You're Alec Wightman?"*

Dion jumped to his feet, shook my hand, and beckoned to a man in the front row, saying to him, "This is Alec Wightman." The gentleman was Avery Friedman, a lawyer from Cleveland and a longtime friend of Dion. I didn't know Avery, but he sure knew me. He talked about what a great job I had done as chair of the Rock Hall board and said I'd been a "healer" with the New York foundation. So Dion clearly had a running start at me from Avery and, I'm sure, from Jill.

For the next three hours, I sat next to my childhood hero as we watched a musical about his life unfold. It opened with the coin flip at the Mason City airport in 1959. It explored his dysfunctional family and difficult relationship with his father; his career ups and downs; his heroin addiction; and his recovery and redemption. The actor playing Dion was tremendous, as was the actor cast as his teenage heartthrob and now wife of fifty-seven years, Susan.

And of course there was the music, all of which was played and sung in its entirety, and effectively used to advance the plot. The doo-wop sounds of the Bronx streets; the great early rock & roll hits, many of which Dion wrote; the nightclub sounds foisted on him by his new label; and, finally, the emotional comeback with "Abraham, Martin and John." Though just a reading in a rehearsal space, by the end, people in the audience were crying. It really is a powerful story.

During the extended intermission and after the reading, Dion, Kathy, and I conversed a lot. For me, it was like talking to an old friend. It had been nearly sixty years since I heard "The Wanderer" on my transistor radio in Euclid, Ohio. I was now in his hometown, New York City, chatting with Dion as if I'd known him all my life.

Maybe I had.

THE BACKSTORY AND ACKNOWLEDGMENTS

THIS BOOK HAS BEEN A LIFETIME PROJECT; IT'S JUST THAT FOR most of my life I didn't know I was working on it.

Describing this project to others as it neared completion, I heard myself saying there are three components to the story: my passion for music, twenty-six years of Zeppelin Productions concert promotions, and my involvement with the Rock & Roll Hall of Fame. Sometimes those worlds have collided.

My passion really did begin as a ten-year-old. For the following six decades, I have bought recorded music and foisted it on willing—and, I'm sure, sometimes unwilling—listeners. I've chased live music from small clubs to large arenas and every sized venue in between, dragging others along with me. Although music can be a meaningful solitary experience, it is at its best as a vehicle for making "connections" among people. I really want to thank those of you who have indulged my enthusiasm by letting me play "just one more song," all while I explained the music or the musicians, which interfered with actually listening to it. You know who you are.

Tom Russell gets the credit for talking me into promoting my first concert in 1995, keeping me in the business, and teaching me the early ropes. But Zeppelin Productions wouldn't be around twenty-six years later if I hadn't consistently presented great musicians who are nice people: the Artistes, many of whom I am proud to call friends. So thanks go not only to Tom, but also to Katy Moffatt, Rosie Flores, Dave Alvin, Andrew Hardin, Michael Fracasso, the late Greg Trooper, Lynn Miles, Kieran Kane, Kevin Welch, Fats Kaplin, Gretchen Peters, Barry Walsh, Bruce Robison, Kelly Willis, Chuck Prophet, Sarah Borges, Jimmie Dale Gilmore, Joe Ely, Butch Hancock, Suzy Bogguss, Matraca Berg, John Fullbright, Rodney Crowell, Eilen Jewell, Jorma Kaukonen, and all the others who have graced the Zeppelin stages with their artistry.

Those Zeppelin stages were housed in some welcoming venues: the original Columbus Music Hall, the Columbus Maennerchor, the Grand Valley Dale Ballroom, and now, two Natalie's—one in Worthington and one in Grandview. Thanks to the proprietors of each and, especially, Charlie Jackson of Natalie's, who has become a great friend, well beyond the business relationship.

None of the Zeppelin shows would be possible without Mitch Hyde, "Mitch the Soundman," who has made the music come to life over those two-and-a-half decades. I don't know what I would have done without him.

I am grateful to Ryan Humbert, a fine singer-songwriter from Northeast Ohio, who has designed and maintained the Zeppelin Productions website (zeppcolumbus.com) for many years.

Finally, the biggest Zeppelin thanks of all goes to the Music Fans, those thousand-plus people on my mailing list who have supported live music in Central Ohio for these many years. Some of them attend regularly, some sporadically, but their support is the only way these shows work.

My involvement with the Rock & Roll Hall of Fame has been more fun than you could ever imagine. And the three years I spent as chair of the board of Cleveland Rock & Roll Inc. were as rewarding as anything I have done in my life. I will be forever grateful to Greg Harris, the Rock Hall CEO since 2013, not only for making my job as chair easy by doing such a fabulous job himself, but also for the genuine friendship we developed right from the start.

I'd also like to express appreciation to the entire Rock Hall team, with a special thanks to Lauren Onkey, the former vice president of education and public programming, and now senior director of music for NPR, who was instrumental in producing the Annual Music Masters shows that meant so much to me, and to Caprice Bragg, the former vice president of development and external affairs. Caprice helped immensely with board relations during my term as chair and with the very successful Phase I to the "Rock Hall 2.0 Remixed and Remastered" capital campaign, of which I remain a proud co-chair.

Speaking of the Rock Hall board, my three-year run as chair would not have been successful without an engaged group of board members who are willing to contribute by rolling up their sleeves as well as writing checks. I am grateful to the board, generally, but especially to the committee chairs who contributed mightily to the success of the organization. Special thanks are due to Bill Rowley, my predecessor board chair, and the others who had the confidence to advance my candidacy for that role; my successors, Chris Connor and Paul Clark, who have led the organization to new heights (and kept me engaged, which I appreciate); and Joel Peresman, the executive director of the Rock & Roll Hall of Fame Foundation, who has contributed to a positive, harmonious relationship between "Cleveland" and "New York."

Yes, I have spent a lifetime foisting music, and the associated stories, on just about everyone in my life. Some said, "You should write a book," perhaps just to get me to stop talking! In 2016, I began to assemble thoughts on three-by-five note cards: names, places, concerts, songs, albums, stories. I organized them, reorganized them, and organized them some more. Then I began to write, tracking somewhat chronologically with "fast forwards." Over the next few years, I stopped and started multiple times, thinking I was really just writing for myself. Only a couple of people saw the work in process.

Then the pandemic hit. From mid-March to early May 2020, I wrote with intensity. By May 10, I had reduced all my thoughts—my notes—to writing. I had fifty-six "snippets." Maybe some would be suitable for blog posts or some such thing? But as I was wrapping up, I let a few more people see the work product, including Kathy; my brother, Jim (who actually had been reading it all along), and his wife, Lisa; Linda Kass, owner of Gramercy Books in the Columbus suburb of Bexley and an author in her own right, who has been encouraging from the beginning; Mark Sutter, a Music Fan extraordinaire; my cousin Ann Wightman, a retired professor of Latin American history at Wesleyan University; Thom Kren, a friend since junior high who retired in 2015 as associate director for collections at the J. Paul Getty Museum; Greg Harris; and John Collins, the Moose. I was surprised at the reaction—not only positive, but with strong suggestions that I should restructure those fifty-six snippets into a book. I really, really want to thank all those folks for their time, encouragement, and the very substantive suggestions I received as I "collapsed" the snippets into the fourteen chapters you've just read.

I now had a "book"—or, as I learned, a "manuscript"—and if I was to do anything else with it, a professional editor was in order. I received recommendations, telephonically interviewed a few candidates, and engaged Holly George-Warren to help me out. You can do your own research to see her impressive credentials, but she not only worked at *Rolling Stone* for nine years *and* has edited every Rock Hall inductions book since 1996, we also share very similar tastes in music. Her assistance as an editor and coach has been invaluable—and fun. Holly pointed me to Small Batch Books in Amherst, Massachusetts, for publishing services, and it has been a pleasure working with Trisha Thompson and Fred Levine, as well as with book designer Susan Turner, who surrounded me with some of my talented friends and made it into a cool cover.

A book needs photographs, and I appreciate the many Music Fans who responded to my call for pictures from the Zeppelin concerts (especially the early shows when, sadly, I didn't take any), including Roberta Garber, Paul Graham, Wayne Harvey, Betsy and George Hudak, Nancy Lahmers and Pete Sanderson, Scott Lavelle, Christopher Limle, Brenda and Kevin Scott, and Kathy and Ed Summers. A special acknowledgment goes to the Rock & Roll Hall of Fame and Andy Leach, senior director of Museum and Archival Collections, for the photos they permitted me to use. Also thanks to Michelle Drobik, reference archivist with the OSU Libraries University Archives, for help securing the photo of Neil Young at Mershon Auditorium in November 1973. And I need to confess that many of the pictures from "my" personal collection were actually taken by my brother, Jim.

The "backstory" of the music in my life wouldn't be complete without acknowledging the Moose, who has been part of it since we met at Duke in September 1968. For the next five decades (four of them with Lori, "Mrs. Moose"), we have shared a love of music—recorded and live—that formed the bond for a lasting friendship. Actually, it is just one of many bonds, because if I ever write a book about our international travels, the streets of New York City, or any number of other topics, the Mooses will be front and center there too.

The biggest thanks—as it should be—are to my family. Or maybe it's the other way around. I should thank the music in my life for bringing so much to my family.

I probably underestimate the extent to which my father's beloved Kenneth McKellar or his singing of show tunes like "Bali Hai" (the genetic roots of my terrible vocal abilities are clear) had a subliminal impact on me. But it was always clear my mother shared my love for music, and late in her life she threw herself into the Zeppelin Productions shows with an enthusiasm legendary among the Artistes and Music Fans alike.

So, too, has music provided a bond with my brother, from the moment as a twelve-year-old when he came downstairs and asked what I was playing (it was Neil Young's *Everybody Knows This Is Nowhere*) to today. Jim married Lisa about the time I started Zeppelin Productions, and we have all shared memorable experiences promoting shows, attending Rock Hall events, and simply enjoying the music wherever it is found.

Finally, music has been a constant in the lives of the "nuclear family"—Kathy, the girls, and me. We certainly have had our own shared music experiences, from the Beach Boys mix cassette we played driving a convertible up the California coast in 1994 to the Desert Trip in 2016. But truth be known, Nora and Emily have their own lives, found their own musical paths, and, thankfully, married guys (Matt and Cameron, respectively) who are on those paths with them. (I must say, I don't think the kids realized their dad did cool things until they were older!)

When music is as important as it is to me, it's imperative your spouse is on the same "path." For Kathy and me, it was obvious on our first dates, as we played E-7 on the jukebox at the Scioto Trail and saw Neil Young for the first of dozens of times. Stumbling into Jerry Jeff Walker (and Katy Moffatt) on our honeymoon was a sign. "Celebrating" the end of a pretty awful fourteen months of health issues by seeing *Springsteen on Broadway* was perfect. And the importance of music in our lives continues in the pandemic when we've been pretty much hunkered down, under the same roof, for months. I can't tell you how many times we've said how lucky we are that, after forty-four years of marriage, we still love each other and, maybe more important, *like* each other.

And, I might add . . . we still share those same musical tastes!

ZEPPELIN PRODUCTIONS VENUES

COLUMBUS MUSIC HALL

March 1995 - June 17, 2005

COLUMBUS MAENNERCHOR

August 13, 2005 - July 30, 2011

GRAND VALLEY DALE BALLROOM

September 29, 2011 - June 22, 2018

NATALIE'S COAL FIRED PIZZA AND LIVE MUSIC
(Worthington)

September 14, 2012 - present

NATALIE'S MUSIC HALL AND KITCHEN
(Grandview)

December 10, 2019 - present

ZEPPELIN PRODUCTIONS CONCERTS

(as of November 2020)

COLUMBUS MUSIC HALL

Tom Russell w/ Andrew Hardin—*March 1995*
John Stewart—*Summer 1995*
Tom Russell w/ Andrew Hardin—*September 19, 1995*
Katy Moffatt—*April 19, 1996*
Tom Russell w/ Andrew Hardin/Katy Moffatt—*May 24, 1996*
Katy Moffatt—*November 8, 1996*
Michael Fracasso/Greg Trooper—*January 17, 1997*
Tom Russell w/ Andrew Hardin—*February 21, 1997*
Katy Moffatt/Rosie Flores—*June 4, 1997*
Tom Russell w/ Andrew Hardin/Katy Moffatt—*September 17, 1997*
Steve Young—*October 24, 1997*
David Olney—*January 23, 1998*
Tom Russell w/ Andrew Hardin—*March 6, 1998*
Ray Wylie Hubbard/Slaid Cleaves—*April 24, 1998*
Dave Alvin—*July 1, 1998*
Katy Moffatt w/ Andrew Hardin—*July 16, 1998*
Michael Fracasso—*August 28, 1998*
Steve Young/Katy Moffatt—*October 2, 1998*
Darden Smith—*March 12, 1999*
Tom Russell w/ Andrew Hardin—*April 23, 1999*
Katy Moffatt—*June 25, 1999*

Rosie Flores—*September 10, 1999*

David Olney/Michael Fracasso—*October 15, 1999*

Tom Russell w/ Andrew Hardin—*February 11, 2000*

Lynn Miles—*May 19, 2000*

Terri Hendrix w/ Lloyd Maines—*July 7, 2000*

Rosie Flores w/ Tammy Rogers—*September 8, 2000*

Dave Alvin—*October 15, 2000*

Katy Moffatt—*January 5, 2001*

Paul Burch—*February 2, 2001*

Tom Russell w/ Andrew Hardin—*April 20, 2001*

Eliza Gilkyson—*June 15, 2001*

Rosie Flores—*September 7, 2001*

Michael Fracasso—*November 30, 2001*

Katy Moffatt—*January 4, 2002*

Kieran Kane and Kevin Welch—*February 22, 2002*

Tom Russell w/ Andrew Hardin—*April 5, 2002*

Steve Young—*July 26, 2002*

Rosie Flores—*September 6, 2002*

Dave Alvin—*September 27, 2002*

Tom Russell w/ Andrew Hardin/Eliza Gilkyson—*October 18, 2002*

Katy Moffatt/Denice Franke—*January 10, 2003*

Kieran Kane and Kevin Welch—*February 7, 2003*

Lynn Miles—*March 7, 2003*

Tom Russell w/ Andrew Hardin—*April 25, 2003*

Joy Lynn White—*January 16, 2004*

Kieran Kane and Kevin Welch—*February 6, 2004*

Tom Russell w/ Andrew Hardin—*March 5, 2004*

Guy Clark—*April 1, 2004*

Lynn Miles—*June 18, 2004*

Katy Moffatt and Rosie Flores—*September 17, 2004*

Michael Fracasso—*November 5, 2004*

Kieran Kane and Kevin Welch—*February 11, 2005*

Tom Russell w/ Andrew Hardin—*March 4, 2005*

Gretchen Peters—*April 8, 2005*
Lynn Miles—*June 17, 2005*

COLUMBUS MAENNERCHOR

Tom Russell w/ Andrew Hardin/Gretchen Peters—*August 13, 2005*
Katy Moffatt/Pat McLaughlin—*January 7, 2006*
Kane Welch Kaplin—*February 4, 2006*
Dave Alvin—*March 11, 2006*
Tom Russell w/ Andrew Hardin—*April 1, 2006*
Gretchen Peters—*May 6, 2006*
Lynn Miles—*June 10, 2006*
Dan Penn—*January 6, 2007*
Kane Welch Kaplin—*February 3, 2007*
Bruce Robison—*March 3, 2007*
Tom Russell—*April 14, 2007*
Gretchen Peters—*May 5, 2007*
Katy Moffatt w/ Andrew Hardin—*January 12, 2008*
Kane Welch Kaplin—*February 9, 2008*
Tom Russell—*March 8, 2008*
Gretchen Peters—*April 19, 2008*
Lynn Miles—*June 7, 2008*
Jimmie Dale Gilmore—*October 15, 2008*
Chuck Prophet/Michael Fracasso—*January 17, 2009*
Katy Moffatt w/ Andrew Hardin—*February 14, 2009*
Gretchen Peters—*March 14, 2009*
Dave Alvin—*April 25, 2009*
Kane Welch Kaplin—*May 9, 2009*
Bruce Robison—*June 13, 2009*
Jimmy Webb—*July 11, 2009*
Sarah Borges and the Broken Singles—*September 19, 2009*
Tom Russell—*October 8, 2009*
The Flatlanders/Ryan Bingham—*November 22, 2009*

Sarah Borges and the Broken Singles—*January 16, 2010*
Wine, Women & Song (Gretchen Peters, Suzy Bogguss,
and Matraca Berg)—*February 6, 2010*
Kane Welch Kaplin—*April 10, 2010*
Eliza Gilkyson/Lynn Miles—*May 1, 2010*
Katy and Hugh Moffatt—*May 29, 2010*
Joe Ely—*June 19, 2010*
Chuck Prophet—*July 31, 2010*
Suzy Bogguss—*October 8, 2010*
The Flatlanders—*January 23, 2011*
Rodney Crowell—*February 26, 2011*
Kane Welch Kaplin—*April 9, 2011*
Matraca Berg/Ryan Humbert—*May 14, 2011*
Kelly Willis and Bruce Robison—*June 11, 2011*
Michael Fracasso/John Fullbright—*July 30, 2011*

GRAND VALLEY DALE BALLROOM

Tom Russell—*September 29, 2011*
Dave Alvin—*November 18, 2011*
John Fullbright—*January 7, 2012*
Kane Welch Kaplin—*March 11, 2012*
Gretchen Peters w/ Barry Walsh—*April 12, 2012*
Kim Richey—*May 6, 2012*
The Flatlanders—*June 17, 2012*
Rodney Crowell—*October 18, 2012*
John Fullbright—*January 11, 2013*
Kelly Willis and Bruce Robison—*April 7, 2013*
Jesse Winchester—*May 2, 2013*
Art Garfunkel—*December 12, 2013*
John Fullbright—*January 17, 2014*
Eilen Jewell—*February 7, 2014*
Rodney Crowell—*May 14, 2014*

Joe Ely—*June 8, 2014*
Chuck Prophet and the Mission Express—*November 13, 2014*
Dave Alvin and Phil Alvin—*March 11, 2015*
John Fullbright—*May 17, 2015*
Dave Alvin and Phil Alvin—*March 10, 2016*
Dave Alvin and Jimmie Dale Gilmore—*June 22, 2018*

NATALIE'S COAL FIRED PIZZA AND LIVE MUSIC (WORTHINGTON)

Eilen Jewell—*September 14, 2012*
Zoe Muth—*September 25, 2012*
Guy Forsyth—*October 5, 2012*
Eilen Jewell—*February 22, 2013*
Katy Moffatt—*April 2, 2013*
Chuck Prophet—*May 12, 2013*
Kieran Kane—*June 11, 2013*
Rosie Flores—*July 12, 2013*
Greg Trooper—*August 8, 2013*
Hardin Burns—*September 9, 2013*
Kevin Welch—*October 12, 2013*
Tom Russell—*November 10, 2013*
Michael Fracasso—*March 23, 2014*
Sarah Borges/Girls, Guns & Glory—*July 3, 2014*
The Iguanas—*August 5, 2014*
Gilmore, Whitmore & Weber—*August 16, 2014*
Parker Millsap—*September 10, 2014*
Dayna Kurtz—*October 14, 2014*
Eliza Gilkyson—*October 21, 2014*
Greg Trooper—*November 16, 2014*
Sarah Borges/Girls, Guns & Glory—*November 18, 2014*
Eilen Jewell—*April 21, 2015*
Tom Russell—*May 5 and 6, 2015*

Amy Black/Sarah Borges—*July 7, 2015*

Fats Kaplin and Kristi Rose—*July 14, 2015*

Rosie Flores—*July 19, 2015*

Kevin Welch—*August 4, 2015*

Nell Robinson with Ramblin' Jack Elliott—*August 13, 2015*

Chuck Prophet—*September 13, 2015*

Kieran Kane—*September 17, 2015*

Gretchen Peters—*February 28, 2016*

Sarah Borges—*April 19, 2016*

Amy Black—*June 14, 2016*

John Fullbright—*July 3, 2016*

Kieran Kane—*September 11, 2016*

Tom Russell—*December 6, 2016*

Sarah Borges—*March 5, 2017*

Chuck Prophet and the Mission Express—*March 23, 2017*

Eilen Jewell—*April 24, 2017*

Amy Black—*June 6, 2017*

Chuck Prophet and the Mission Express—*August 3, 2017*

Tom Russell—*September 12, 2017*

Jorma Kaukonen—*October 3, 2017*

The Backroad Boys (John Fullbright, Kevin Welch, Michael Fracasso, and Dustin Welch)—*October 16 and 17, 2017*

Dave Alvin and Jimmie Dale Gilmore—*October 29, 2017*

Sarah Borges and the Broken Singles—*November 14, 2017*

Rosie Flores—*April 29, 2018*

Jorma Kaukonen—*June 12, 2018*

Kelly Willis—*June 29, 2018*

Sarah Borges and the Broken Singles—*June 30, 2018*

Chuck Prophet and the Mission Express—*July 22, 2018*

Richie Furay—*August 12, 2018*

Kieran Kane and Rayna Gellert—*September 9, 2018*

Chuck Prophet—*February 19, 2019*

Sarah Borges and the Broken Singles—*March 7, 2019*

Hot Tuna—*March 26, 2019*

Matraca Berg, Marshall Chapman,
and Tommy Womack—*May 19, 2019*

Tom Russell—*June 11, 2019*

John Fullbright—*June 23 and 24, 2019*

Eilen Jewell—*July 9, 2019*

Gretchen Peters—*July 11, 2019*

Dave Alvin—*July 14, 2019*

Richie Furay—*August 11, 2019*

Kieran Kane and Rayna Gellert—*October 20, 2019*

Kelly Willis and Bruce Robison—*November 1, 2019*

Hot Tuna—*November 5, 2019*

Bill Kirchen—*November 23, 2019*

Jeff Plankenhorn—*March 5, 2020*

Ward Hayden & the Outliers/Lydia Loveless—*March 13, 2020*

NATALIE'S MUSIC HALL AND KITCHEN
(GRANDVIEW)

Sarah Borges and the Broken Singles—*December 10, 2019*

Chuck Prophet—*January 28, 2020*

Hot Tuna—*November 10, 2020*

INDEX

E Street Band, 12, 124, 251, 256
  Rock Hall inductions and, 71,
    84, 252, 255–256
  Springsteen and, 80, 81, 82, 84,
    246, 255
Eagles, 77, 78, 106, 196, 241, 254,
  262
Earle, Steve, 106–107, 122, 124,
  138, 154, 192
East West (Paul Butterfield Blues
  Band), 27
Ed Sullivan Show, The (television
  show), 11
Edmonton Folk Festival, 98, 263
Edwards, Dennis, 23, 275
Electric Flag, 27
Electric Music for the Mind and Body
  (Country Joe and the Fish), 17
Elliott, Ramblin' Jack, 37–38, 99,
  171, 274
Ely, Joe, 57, 95, 142–147, *166*, 185,
  230, 244, 274
Emanuel, Rahm, 14–15
"Embryonic Journey" (Kaukonen), 19
Emmons, Bobby, 136–137
Ertegun, Ahmet, 231
Escovedo, Alejandro, 148
Evangeline Hotel, The (Moffatt),
  101, *157*
Everly, Don, *173*, *174*, 282, 283,
  285, 286–287
Everly, Patti, *174*, 282, 284
Everly, Phil, *174*, 281, 282–283, 284
Everly Brothers, 12, 100, 131, 231
  childhood fascination with, 8, 281
  Music Masters tribute to, *172*,
    174, *175*, 196, 273, 281–287
Every Picture Tells a Story (Rod
  Stewart), 45
Everybody Knows This Is Nowhere
  (Young), 68
Everywhere (Trooper), 124
Exile on Main Street (Rolling
  Stones), 191

Fabares, Shelley, 8
Faces, 45
Fagen, Donald, 50
FAME Studios, 267
Family Band, 60
Famous Flames, 250
"Father and Son" (Stevens), 254
Faville, Chris, *167*, 280
Felder, Don, 262
Fergie, 246
Ferrick, Melissa, 263
Fewer Things (Moffatt), 103–104
"Fight Test" (Flaming Lips), 230
"Fightin' for My Life" (Ely), 230
"Fightin' Side of Me, The"
  (Haggard), 57
Finch, Stephanie, 50, 148, 149, 151
"Fire and Rain" (Taylor), 37, 43
"First Love" (Furay), 39
Flaming Lips, 230
Flatiron, Columbus, 94
  jukebox at, 91, 102, 218–219
  post-show meals at, 91, 95, 97,
    102, 103, 105, 106, 108, 128,
    129, 136, 138, 140, *161*, 195,
    215–216, 218
Flatlanders, 95, 142–147, *165*, 185,
  199, 210
Flores, Rosie, 107–108, 130, 143,
  167, *168*, 280
  friendship with, 105–106, *161*,
    245, 265
  Zeppelin shows with, 57, 103,
    104–106, 108, 120–121, *161*,
    185, 222
Flying Burrito Brothers, 135, 190–
  191
"Flying on the Ground" (Young), 75
Fogerty, John, 246
folk blues, 13, 48
folk music, 9, 13, 20, 36–37, 38, 53,
  54, 60–61, 79, 144, 190, 191,
  221
folk opera, 99

ALEC WIGHTMAN is a senior partner in the national law firm of BakerHostetler, with a long career as a corporate lawyer and a member of the firm's management. Born and raised in the Cleveland area, Alec graduated from Duke University in 1972 and the Moritz College of Law at Ohio State University in 1975. With a lifelong passion for music, he formed Zeppelin Productions, Inc., in 1995, beginning twenty-six years of promoting national act singer-songwriter concerts in Columbus, Ohio. Alec has been a member of the board of the Rock & Roll Hall of Fame since 2004, serving as chair from 2013 to 2016. He remains active with the Rock Hall, including as a co-chair of its current capital campaign, and as a member of the board of the Rock & Roll Hall of Fame Foundation. He is also a director of the Ohio State University Foundation, a member of the Duke Performances advisory board, and a director of the Columbus Music Commission. Alec and his wife, Kathy, live in the German Village area of Columbus and have two grown daughters, Nora and Emily. This is his first book.